Women's Plac

Architecture and Desi

What was different about the environments that women created as architects, designers and clients at a time when they were gaining increasing political and social status in a male world? Through a series of case studies, *Women's Places: Architecture and Design 1860–1960*, examines in detail the professional and domestic spaces created by women who had money and the opportunity to achieve their ideal. Set against a background of accepted notions of modernity relating to design and architecture of the late 19th and early 20th centuries, this book provides a fascinating insight into women's social aspirations and identities.

The variety of case studies looking at women as producers, clients, consumers and theorists examines: Princess Louise, Kate Greenaway, the Hall sisters, Josephine Baker, Elsie de Wolfe, Eileen Gray, Elizabeth Denby, Dora Gordine and Marie Dormoy.

With 57 illustrations and drawing on original and pioneering research, this book provides new information and new interpretations in the study of gender, material culture and the built environment in the period 1860–1960.

Employed initially as the research assistant during the restoration of Dorich House, the former home and studio of the sculptor Dora Gordine and her husband, the Hon. Richard Hare, **Brenda Martin** is now its Curator, and continues her work as a design historian. Her research interests include 1930s' interiors and design and artists' studios.

Penny Sparke is a design historian who has written many books and researched widely in the field of design and modern interiors, both in the UK and the USA. She was responsible for setting up the V&A Museum/Royal College of Art Postgraduate History of Design Programme. She is currently the Dean of the Faculty of Art, Design & Music and a Professor of Design History at Kingston University. Her current research interests include gender and American interiors in the early 20th century.

Contributors: Louise Campbell, Elizabeth Darling, Alice T. Friedman, Tanis Hinchcliffe, Trevor Keeble, Lynne Walker

Women's Places:

Architecture and Design 1860–1960

Edited by Brenda Martin and Penny Sparke

Routledge
Taylor & Francis Group

LONDON AND NEW YORK

First published 2003 by Routledge
11 New Fetter Lane, London EC4P 4EE

Simultaneously published in the USA and Canada by Routledge
29 West 35th Street, New York, NY 10001

Routledge is an imprint of the Taylor & Francis Group

© 2003 Selection and editorial, Brenda Martin and Penny Sparke; individual
chapters, the authors

Typeset in ITC Charter by Ninety Seven Plus
Printed and bound in Great Britain by St Edmundsbury Press, Suffolk

British Library Cataloguing in Publication Data
A catalogue record for this book is available from the British Library

Library of Congress Cataloging in Publication Data
Women's places : architecture and design 1860-1960 / edited by Brenda Martin
    and Penny Sparke.
        p. cm.
    Includes bibliographical references and index.
    ISBN 0-415-28448-1 (hardcover : alk. paper) – ISBN 0-415-28449-X
    (paperback : alk. paper)
    1. Women architects. 2. Women designers. 3. Aesthetic movement (Art)
I. Martin, Brenda. II. Sparke, Penny.

NA1997 .W67 2003
720'.82–dc21

                                                            2002152015
ISBN 0-415-28449-X (pb)
ISBN 0-415-28448-1 (hb)

Contents

Illustration credits

The authors and the publishers would like to thank the following individuals and institutions for giving permission to reproduce illustrations. We have made every effort to contact copyright holders, but if any errors have been made we would be happy to correct them at a later printing.

Aaron, P./Esto
Adam, P.
Architectural Press
Beinecke Library, Yale University
British Architect
Bromley Borough Council
Canadian Center for Architecture, Montreal
Carlu, J. *et al.*
Centraal Museum, Utrecht
de Wolfe, E. *The House in Good Taste*, New York: The Century Company, 1913
de Wolfe, E. *After All*, New York: Harper & Brothers, 1935
English Heritage
Frank den Oudsten
Friedman, A.T.
Ginain, L.
Greenaway, K. *Under the Window*, 1879
Irvine, A.
Larkin Brothers
Library of Congress, Washington DC
Murry, J.S.
National Monuments Record Centre
National Portrait Gallery, London
Perret, A.
RIBA
Royal School of Art Needlework
Spielman, M. and Layard, G., *Kate Greenaway* (London: Adam and Charles Black, 1905)
Victoria and Albert Museum

Contributors

Louise Campbell is a Senior Lecturer in the History of Art Department at the University of Warwick. She is the author of *Coventry Cathedral: Art and Architecture in Post-war Britain* (Clarendon Studies in the History of Art, OUP, 1996), a chapter in *Frederic Leighton: Antiquity, Renaissance, Modernity* (Yale University Press, 1998), and of articles in *Architectural Review*, *Architectural History*, *RIBA Journal*, *Apollo*, *Twentieth-century Architecture* and *British Art Journal*. She is the editor of the millennial volume published by the Society of Architectural Historians of Great Britain, *Twentieth-Century Architecture and its Histories* (2000). She is currently working on a study of artists' habitats in France and Britain.

Elizabeth Darling is an architectural historian and runs the undergraduate programme in history and theory in the School of Architecture and Design at the University of Brighton. Her doctoral thesis considered the work of the housing consultant Elizabeth Denby while her other research interests include design reform in the 1930s and the relationship between health reform and the built environment in inter-war Britain. She has published articles on architecture and its users; on the ideology of the voluntary housing sector in inter-war Britain and on housing exhibitions in the 1930s. Her most recent project is the production of a module about post-war British exhibition design for the JISC-funded Distributed National Electronic Resource project, hosted by the University of Brighton, to develop electronic learning packages on British design culture.

Alice T. Friedman is Professor of Art and Director of the Architecture Program at Wellesley College Massachusetts, USA, where she has taught since 1979. From 1999–2002 she held the Luella LaMer Professorship in Women's Studies. Professor Friedman is the author of two books: *House and Household in Elizabethan England: Wollaton Hall and the Willoughby Family* (University of Chicago Press, 1989) and *Women and the Making of the Modern House: A Social and Architectural History* (Harry Abrams, New York, 1998), as well as numerous articles on architecture, gender and social history. She is currently completing a book about American and European architecture in the period following the Second World War.

Tanis Hinchcliffe is Senior Lecturer in the Department of Architecture at the University of Westminster where she teaches history. Her research interests are the culture and theory of architecture in eighteenth-century France; modes of domesticity in the nineteenth century; and the modernist project in France and England during the twentith century. She is the author of *North Oxford* (Yale University Press, 1992), and articles on Peter Collins, eighteenth-century French architects and their women clients, and on Quatremère de Quincy.

Trevor Keeble is a Senior Lecturer in the School of Art and Design History at Kingston University, London. He is currently working on a PhD entitled 'The domestic moment: design, taste and identity in the late Victorian English domestic interior'.

Brenda Martin is the Curator of Dorich House, the former home and studio of the sculptor Dora Gordine and her husband, the Hon. Richard Hare, and now part of the Faculty of Art, Design & Music at Kingston University, London. Her research interests include 1930s' interiors and design and artists' studios. She is currently preparing a catalogue of the collection of sculpture of Dora Gordine in Dorich House for publication in 2003.

Penny Sparke is Dean of the Faculty of Art, Design & Music and a Professor of Design History at Kingston University, London. Until 1999 she was the Course Director of the joint V&A Museum/Royal College of Art Postgraduate History of Design Programme. She has published widely in the field of Design History and latterly on the subject of gender and design. Her recent publications include *A Century of Design* (Mitchell Beazley, 1999) and *As Long as It's Pink: The Sexual Politics of Taste* (Pandora, 1995). Her current research interests include gender and American interiors in the early twentieth century.

Lynne Walker was formerly Senior Lecturer in the History of Architecture and Design at the University of Northumbria, and is currently Senior Research Fellow at the Institute of Historical Research, University of London. She has published widely on gender, space and architecture and has curated two major exhibitions on related issues, most recently, 'Drawing on diversity: women, architecture and practice' (RIBA Heinz Gallery, 1997). She is writing a history of British women and architecture.

Introduction

Penny Sparke

Appearing as it does after thirty years of writings about women's relationships with architecture and design *Women's Places: Architecture and Design 1860–1960* belongs to an academic tradition that is well established. However, it brings to that tradition a new perspective and offers fresh insights. That it can do this is dependent upon its awareness of existing work and its focus on case studies and the personal biographies of a number of specific women who have interacted with architecture and design over the hundred-year period, 1860–1960. This approach has provided the subject both with new material and with new interpretations. Straddling the usually distinct worlds of architecture and interior design, *Women's Places* is also able to suggest new ways of thinking about the relationships between women and these two disciplines which cross the boundaries between them. In addition, it seeks to embrace a wider range of relationships than have traditionally been covered, showing that women have interfaced with architecture and design not only as producers and consumers and clients but also as collaborators and commentators. As this collection of case studies will clearly demonstrate, women have brought a number of ways of working and a range of approaches and attitudes to these subtle and shifting relationships. Above all, *Women's Places* offers a pluralistic reading of some of the ways in which women living in the Western industrialised world have worked with, and related to, architecture and design.

  The tradition which this publication recognises, respects and extends has dealt with the relationships of women to the material and spatial environment they have inhabited over the last century and a half. It began in earnest in the early 1970s and has gone through a number of methodological transformations. Not until the women's movement of the late 1960s and early 1970s had raised the consciousness of large numbers of women who sought to assert their rights in a wide range of fields did a rigorous approach to the subject emerge. In the early years interest lay, as it did in many other fields of enquiry into women's roles in history, in the names of women who had been excluded from the accounts that had been written about the creative arts which had come to form the accepted canon. This 'hidden from history' approach, which involved a great deal of primary research and new analysis, was an important part of the feminist project of the 1970s and 1980s which aimed to capture women's contributions to the cultural past and demonstrate that, within patriarchy, the fact that women had been edited out of the picture, was just another example of male domination. Back in 1973 Doris Cole wrote her influential book *From Tipi to Skyscraper* in which she clearly demonstrated that women had played, and continued to play, a central role within the male-dominated world of architecture.[1] It established an important tradition which others were to follow. Four years later Susan Torre picked up the baton and edited a book of essays entitled *Women in American Architecture: A Historic and Contemporary Perspective*.[2] In the same year Gwendolyn Wright published her essay entitled 'On the Fringe of the Profession: Women in American Architecture' in an edited volume.[3] Dorothy M. Anderson's *Women, Design and the Cambridge School* followed in 1980, focusing attention on a group of female architects working in a particular context while Ellen Perry Berkeley and Mathilda McQuaid's edited book of essays entitled *Architecture: A Place for Women* appeared at the end of the decade.[4] Lynne Walker moved the emphasis to the other side of the Atlantic in her essay, also published in 1989, 'Women Architects' which dealt with female British architects working in the late nineteenth and early twentieth centuries.[5] Some years later another British publication – edited by K. Ruedi, S. Wigglesworth and D. McCorquodale *Desiring Practices: Architecture, Gender and the Interdisciplinary* – developed these ideas in their discussions of some of the ways in which women contributed to the practice of architecture.[6] Gradually studies of individual women working in architecture began to surface, especially in the USA, and monographs appeared on individuals, such as Julia Morgan, the architect of Hearst Castle in California, who had made significant contributions to the built environment. Texts such as these sought to raise women's achievements to the level of their male counterparts and to show how a number of women – albeit inevitably a smaller number than men – had been effective and influential architects. The list gradually expanded and the work of women in areas such as garden design – Ellen Shipman among them – began to be documented thereby broadening the narrow emphasis on the built structure. The 1990s saw a huge expansion of yet more studies which focused on the subject of women and architecture, many of them concerned to show that women had worked as architects but that their work had not been documented.

That architecture, rather than industrial design, craft or interior design, was the first area of material culture to track down its female protagonists was a result of the fact that it was an overridingly masculine, and even more importantly, professionalised, field in which women felt they had to prove themselves and show that they had participated and could continue to participate. Inside the domestic sphere – the physical arena of interior decoration and the hand-made and the industrially manufactured object – the traditional links with feminine culture were stronger and it took longer for women to want to celebrate their involvements with these activities. It was believed, in the early years of the women's movement, less was to be achieved by claiming creative achievements in a sphere in which women were already accepted. Gradually, however, these arenas too came to be retrieved from their 'hidden from history' status. Isabelle Anscombe's *A Woman's Touch: Women in Design from 1860 to the Present Day* was published in 1984 ensuring that women's achievements inside the house, as well as outside it, were recognised.[7] Later, in 1991, Jill Seddon and Suzette Worden provided documentation relating to women designers working in Britain in the inter-war years which added a whole new list of names to those already reclaimed by Anscombe.[8]

It is significant that the period covered by Anscombe's book was that recognised as the modernist era. It was becoming apparent that the majority of women who were being reclaimed, both in architecture and design, could, for the most part, be inserted into the modernist paradigm, or at least added to the edges of it. What this meant was that while new names were emerging, their work was being analysed and judged by the same criteria that were used to describe and position the work of those contributors to the modernist canon. Thus, when the work of individuals such as Eileen Gray, Lilly Reich, Charlotte Perriand, and more recently Ray Eames, was reclaimed, it was clear that their contribution was recognised because it extended the modernist canon.[9] The same can be said, to some extent, of many of the female designers and craftswomen whose names began to be familiar – among them Marion Dorn and Susie Cooper – whose work can be seen as modernist, although at the decorative end of the spectrum.[10] Interestingly, the addition of women interior decorators to the list of female achievers, along with a number of other female practitioners in a range of other design fields, had to wait until 2000 for publication in Pat Kirkham's *Women Designers in the USA, 1900–2000*, so far removed are the ethos and the aesthetic of their work from the modernist ideal.[11]

While the 'hidden from history' approach represented a crucial stage in the addition of a number of named women to the context of architecture and design, it was, however, only a first step. The tendency was to add them to the 'great and the good' and their work to the modernist canon, rather than let it pose new, more difficult questions which demanded new answers. Gradually, however, a number of key texts took scholarship in this area into a number of new directions. All of them have provided important foundations for *Women's Places*.

Within architectural history Dolores Hayden's *The Grand Domestic Revolution: A History of Feminist Designs for American Homes, Neighborhoods and Cities* of 1981 and Gwendolyn Wright's *Moralism and the Modern Home* took the emphasis away from architectural modernism and placed it on women and their relationship with domesticity.[12] Stemming from their feminist beliefs, both historians sought to consider women's interventions in architecture less as contributions to the canon than as activities undertaken on their own terms. A new approach was instigated which was aligned to contemporary female historians' growing interest in the concept of the 'separate spheres'. Their motivation was to find a level of women's contribution which took place within the private, non-paid arena of the home rather than in the masculine sphere of the professionalised workplace. Hayden's female architects were simultaneously both producers and consumers and, as a result, crossed the public/private divide. Wright's interests repositioned women's interventions in architecture in the private sphere and established new meanings for them.

The impact of these texts was to move the emphasis away from the 'hidden from history' approach and to open the door for women to interact with architecture as non-professionals and non-modernists. It was a shift which, in many ways, found more fertile ground in design history than in architectural history as, in the former, the consumer, the amateur, the everyday, and the anti-modernist were more fully developed. This was helped by design's 'newcomer' status when viewed alongside architecture, as well as by its clear alliance with popular culture. The close liaison that developed between cultural studies and design history in the first half of the 1980s moved the latter discipline away from the modernist paradigm and encouraged historians to think of designed artefacts in new ways. Books such as Rozsika Parker's *The Subversive Stitch: Embroidery and the Making of the Feminine* provided innovative accounts of the relationship between women and material culture, in this instance with goods embroidered at home for the domestic sphere, taking a diametrically opposed approach to the 'hidden from history' texts.[13] It opened the field for other accounts of feminine material culture which was not modernist in emphasis. Other studies to have extended this tradition include the area of sewing as well as studies such as Cheryl Buckley's *Potters and Paintresses: Women Designers in the Pottery Industry 1870–1990* which takes as its object of study the women in the

English pottery industry who were lowly paid workers involved in adding decoration to pre-existing ceramic forms, the antipathy of modernist practice. [14]

By the mid-1980s it was clear that women's relationships with architecture and design were both complex and varied and that a deep analysis of the design process and the resulting work could lead to a paradigm shift in the way in which those material forms had hitherto been studied. Not only was it deemed necessary to let alternative aesthetic preferences emerge, it was also considered important to focus on the role of amateur producers and consumers. The contribution of cultural studies was particularly influential in the power it bestowed on the consumer/user. This was especially visible in design historical work in which women who were defined as housewives, shoppers, hostesses and a number of other domestic, unpaid roles, came to the fore. A number of essays in Judy Attfield and Pat Kirkham's edited book *A View from the Interior* – among them Attfield's 'Inside Pram Town: A case study of Harlow house interiors, 1951–1961 – bore witness to this new direction providing evidence of female consumers' responses to the environments they inhabited. [15]

This approach influenced work on the interior in which the notion of 'identity' came to be uppermost. The shift from an interest in the agency of the producer to that of the consumer took longer to influence architectural history but was fundamental to Alice T. Friedman's 1998 study of the influence of female clients on a number of iconic modernist buildings. Her book, *Women and the Making of the Modern House*, was tellingly subtitled, *A Social and Architectural History*. [16] The book employed the categories of gender and consumption to show that the selected women were not passive clients, that their preferences were not necessarily in accord with those of the modernist architects with which they worked, and that the client-consumer was as much as producer as the architect. Friedman's problematis-ation of stereotypical views of gender, taste and consumption was an important breakthrough for architectural history in this context and has inspired work in this present volume.

The 1990s saw many books published in the fields of both architectural and design history and theory which took all these themes forward and built upon them. In the former the emphasis moved from the built structure to the concepts of space and place which provided rich offerings and new perspectives. Beatriz Colomina's readings of space led the way and she added the concept of sexuality to that of gender. [17] The shift from architecture to space opened the door for a much broader definition which included the effects of the media. Thus, a continuum was created in architectural discourse which moved from the city to the interior to the window to the represented image and the world created by the mass media. The analyses that emerged positioned the concept of 'meaning' rather than production as the prime focus under the influence, once again, of cultural studies. The concept of gender, defined in terms of the complex meanings generated by the separation of, and ambiguities between, the separate spheres, remained central to these analyses although now in a more integrated way.

Within architectural theory the notion of 'place' became as pre-eminent as space in the 1990s, the city in particular taking on a key significance in discussions about modernity and postmodernity. Inspired by the masculine concept of the 'flâneur' in early modernism, architectural and social historians sought to locate the 'feminine' in the modern cityscape. In her study of 1991 – *The Sphinx in the City: Urban Life, the Control of Disorder, and Women* – Elizabeth Wilson equated women with the concept of 'disorder' showing how notions of gender and sexuality have played a role in the formation of the spaces of modern city life.[18]

A plethora of other approaches took the debate about gender, architecture and design into new incarnations in the years leading up to 2000. Penny Sparke's text of 1995, for example, *As Long as It's Pink: The Sexual Politics of Taste* set out to show how modernism had displaced women who became linked with the 'bad taste' that was believed, by modernist protagonists, to reside within the world of consumption and commerce and how 'feminine culture' provided, throughout the twentieth century, an alternative set of taste values which, in spite of their centrality to everyday life, were constantly being marginalised by 'high culture'.[19] A number of other publications, among them *Not at Home: The Suppression of Domesticity in Modern Art and Culture*, edited by Christopher Reed, followed a similar line of argument showing how fundamental the ideology of the separate spheres had been to twentieth-century cultural life.[20] Victoria de Grazia and Ellen Furlough's *The Sex of Things: Gender and Consumption in Historical Perspective* and Pat Kirkham's edited volume *The Gendered Object* pursued a similar path, seeing the notion of gender as being culturally embedded in objects which become its key communicators.[21]

Women's Places can only exist because it recognises the importance of, and extends, the vast body of work that has been sketchily outlined above. In summary, the effort to reclaim forgotten female architects and designers was supplemented by the attempt to find new methodologies arising from what was found. In that attempt the authority of the producer and of the modernist project was questioned and concepts and propositions such as the 'separate spheres', the relativity of taste values, the authority of the consumer, and a postmodern reading of spatiality, were focused upon as starting points for a deeper investigation of the relationship between women and the material and spatial environment they inhabit. This volume is also dependent on these concepts and propositions although it seeks, through case studies, both to test and to question them. The chapters have all maintained an open-endedness in the face of the material they have unearthed, anxious to let it speak for itself and suggest new questions. At the same time, certain methodological conventions have been maintained. Some of the work presented here, for example, reinvestigates well-known 'hidden from history' women, Eileen Gray, for example. The aim here is to look again with lessons learnt from other, less conventional studies. The work of a number of key modernist architects, Gerrit Rietveld among them, is also examined. Here the challenge is to look at it from another point of view, from that of the female client, for example.

None of the women highlighted in these chapters are 'ordinary'. They are all – from Josephine Baker to Princess Louise to Elsie de Wolfe to Dora Gordine to Elizabeth Denby to Marie Dormoy – 'extraordinary' in a number of different ways, whether because they were wealthy, unmarried, homosexual or unusually independent for a number of other reasons. The aim is not, however, to elevate them to the status of 'heroines' but rather to use them as examples of women who actively engaged with architecture and/or design in the period in question and who, in so doing, highlighted themes which increase our understanding of the relationships of women with the built and designed environment more generally. From these case studies, it is suggested, certain themes arise which can inform the way in which we can approach this subject in the future. They include the relationship of women to modernism; the importance of the interior as a theatrical setting for women's lives; the ways in which the idea of the 'separate spheres' is continually negotiated and challenged; the relationship of 'taste' to class and economic status; the links between amateurism and professionalism; the role of sexuality; the relationship between identity, material culture, space and place; the link, in women's culture, between fashion, the decorative arts and the interior; and many others besides.

The structure of the book

The structure of the book is dictated by chronology. The first two chapters, Louise Campbell's 'Questions of identity: women, architecture and the Aesthetic Movement' and Trevor Keeble's 'Creating "The New Room": the Hall sisters of West Wickham and Richard Norman Shaw', are both situated in the late nineteenth century. They both feature British women acting as clients for architectural and design projects, the first focusing on the sculpture studio of the daughter of Queen Victoria, Princess Louise, Marchioness of Lorne, created by E. W. Godwin in 1878 and the studio-house of a well-known illustrator, Kate Greenaway, designed by Richard Norman Shaw, seven years later, while Keeble provides an account, based on documentation presented in personal diaries, of the Hall sisters' commission to Richard Norman Shaw to create a room for them in their middle-class house in West Wickham. Both chapters have a 'hidden from history' element to them, not because new women professional architects have been discovered, but rather that four female architectural clients have been found who had a considerable input into the projects they commissioned. They also make possible a modified reading of the Aesthetic Movement. All four women had a strong sense of what they wanted and provided the architect with a high level of guidance. Whether or not this was respected varies. Although separated from each other by their different levels of wealth and reputation the three commissions under discussion share some operational similarities. In all cases women are working with male architects in the context of the private sphere of the home. Both chapters point out the complex negotiations that were entered into and the power struggles that ensued when everybody's preferences were not fully respected. In the case of Princess Louise, however, herself an artist, social status guaranteed the level of her authority while Greenaway also held a position of some status as a tastemaker in the context of Victorian society. Although both women had a level of artistic control in the context of architectural commissions they could not, Campbell tells us, be considered to be fully-fledged 'artists' by the society they inhabited. The Hall sisters were unusual women, independent, widely travelled and 'collectors' of artistic items. They were, nonetheless, clearly not treated with the same level of respect by Shaw as Greenaway. He imposed his taste upon the sisters, and, according to them, tried to overcharge them. In their eyes he was not a gentleman, however highly he has been regarded by architectural historians. Both chapters inform us about the significance of class, wealth and social status for women who acted as commissioners of architecture and design in the second half of the nineteenth century and the way in which the professional male architect negotiated his level of authority accordingly. They also provide a level of entry into the process of making architecture which is frequently overlooked by historians, a perspective which comes to the fore through the emphasis upon the female clients.

Chapter 3, written by Penny Sparke – 'Elsie de Wolfe and her female clients, 1905–1915: gender, class and the professional interior decorator' – takes us into the twentieth century and across the Atlantic to the USA. The focus stays with wealthy female clients but replaces the 'gentleman' architect with the newly-professionalised, although untrained, female interior decorator in the person of Elsie de Wolfe. Her personal background offers a link between fashionable dress, theatre sets and the interior which remains in place for some decades. The chapter's main contribution to the volume lies in its documentation of an aesthetic arena in which women worked with other women in a creative collaboration (although the authority of the professional remains uppermost); its demonstration of the way in which the birth of the professional, female decorator working in the domestic arena served to blur the edges between the private and the public spheres; its emphasis on the growing importance at that time between women's class and gender identities and their domestic interiors; and its indication of the way in which, what Alison Light later calls a concept of 'feminine modernity', was beginning to emerge in the context of the domestic interior.[22] The chapter acts as a bridge between the pre-modern, Victorian taste and social values of the late nineteenth century and the more fluid situation of the inter-war years.

The architectural projects selected by Alice Friedman in Chapter 4, 'Your place or mine? The client's contribution to domestic architecture' to elucidate her ideas about exceptional women (and men) in terms of their level of independence, race and sexuality, span a chronological period from the 1920s to the 1950s. Her analyses of the projects undertaken by Gerritt Rietveld and Truus Schröder; the unrealised scheme created by Adolf Loos for Josephine Baker (followed by Baker's own choices of residences which included a medieval château); and Paul Rudolph's design for his own New York apartment are offered to demonstrate the way in which these unconventional clients, or more importantly the cultural categories which defined them, played a key role in the architectural process. Developing ideas elucidated in her 1998 book, Friedman demonstrates that architecture is not a result of a single creative figure working in isolation but rather of negotiations rooted in the cultural context of gender, race and sexuality.

The second half of the book focuses on the years between the two world wars. Chapters 5 and 6 – Lynne Walker's, entitled 'Eileen Gray, gender and modernism', and Tanis Hinchcliffe's, 'Marie Dormoy and the architectural conversation' – concentrate on French case studies while Brenda Martin's 'A house of her own: Dora Gordine and Dorich House (1936); and Elizabeth Darling's 'Elizabeth Denby or Maxwell Fry?: A matter of attribution' – focus on subjects which are located in inter-war Britain.

Lynne Walker's chapter takes a new look at that 'modernist heroine', Eileen Gray, revisiting the way in which that designer's work was added to the 'canon' from the early 1970s onwards. Walker demonstrates that, although Gray was recognised by historians, Reyner Banham among them, as a significant modern architect/designer, she was both ignored in her own lifetime and has not yet been adequately appraised subsequently. As

Walker explains, 'Eileen Gray's strong and systematic mind ... has been overlooked and recast.' Instead, she has been 'feminised', i.e., considered, primarily, as an architect of 'instinct and emotion' rather than one of logic and order. Thus, while her work has been added to the modernist canon, its intrinsic worth has not been fully recognised. Walker goes on to explain that, while we have moved beyond the use of exclusively modernist interpretations of her work and can now provide a more nuanced account of it which considers gender and sexuality, we have to acknowledge that, in the inter-war years, modernism provided an important platform on which women such as Gray could express themselves.

Chapter 6 on the subject of Marie Dormoy introduces a new role for a woman in this context, i.e., that of an 'architectural witness'. Dormoy is an enigmatic figure but her role as a writer and critic on architecture undoubtedly played a role in the larger picture of Parisian architecture of the 1920s and 1930s. Her strong links with Auguste Perret were especially significant. Hinchcliffe emphasises the important role that social contacts played in her personal and professional life and the fact that her life and work 'provide insights into the social practice of architecture in the early twentieth century', i.e., activities which are further away from the actual practice of architectural design itself but which nonetheless impinge upon it. This contextualisation of architectural design is a key theme of the work, demonstrating that while women may not have always been centre-stage, they were very frequently in the wings, playing a role which influenced the final outcome.

Returning to Britain, the last two chapters in the volume both pose questions on which discussion is possible but for which no answers can be reached. Martin's question is whether or not the Russian emigrée sculptor, Dora Gordine, designed Dorich House on Kingston Hill, which was built in 1936. The chapter's significance lies less in an answer to the question than in the way it discusses architectural design as a process in which several people, in addition to abstract contextual forces, play a part. As was the case with Princess Louise and Kate Greenaway, Gordine's artistic self-definition demanded that she participated in the design of the environment in which she lived and worked and evidence is supplied here to show what aesthetic decisions she probably made. Martin focuses on the biography of Gordine in order to show the derivations of many of her artistic ideas which found their way into architectural solutions. She also provides a telling contrast between the architectural design for Gordine's planned studio in Hampstead, where the sculptor's ideas came into conflict with those of the modernist architect, Godfrey Samuel, who was commissioned to undertake the project, and that of Dorich House where no architect was employed and Gordine had a much freer hand.

The debate as to whether Maxwell Fry, the architect, or Elizabeth Denby the self-styled 'housing consultant' should have been credited for, and given 'ownership' of, the design of a number of British housing projects of the 1930s, Kensal House among them, is the question raised by Elizabeth Darling in the final chapter. Once again the author demonstrates that architecture is the result of a process which involves many inputs from many individuals, not just the named architect. That many of those who are left out of the picture are women is no coincidence. The dispute is rendered even more complex by the personal relationship between the two protagonists. This case study focused on the architectural process – 'the act of design' – shows, with important evidence from primary sources to support it, that architecture has been a key arena of gender dispute and negotiation in the twentieth century and argues that our understanding of this 'act' should be significantly broadened to include other agencies. Darling positions her case study within the tradition of literature which provides its foundations and which makes the message of the Denby/Fry debate significant for women's relationship with architecture in general. As with all the case studies presented here, the details of the particular historical events apply to many other comparable situations, past, present and, without doubt, in the future as well.

The strength of this volume lies not just in its pluralistic approach, in its coverage not only of many of the varied themes which have arisen over thirty years of the subject being debated, but more importantly in the new historical evidence that it offers to demonstrate the detailed ways in which particular women's relationships with architecture and design were actually expressed and negotiated. It offers a very strong message about the importance of crediting women for their interventions and giving them recognition for their creative work; it recognises the importance of the separate spheres, however much men and women have moved across them and blurred the boundary between them; it suggests that work produced within the context of feminine culture may have different aesthetic values and priorities attached to it than its masculine equivalent; it reminds us that architectural and design historians have a responsibility to understand the ideological roots of their disciplines and to ensure that they constantly challenge them; and, most importantly, it tells us that there is not a single 'woman's place' where she sits imprisoned, but rather many 'women's places' which are the result of positive interventions and where we can all feel at home.

Notes

1 D. Cole *From Tipi to Skyscraper*, Boston: i Press, 1973.

2 S. Torre (ed.) *Women in American Architecture*, New York: Whitney Library of Design, 1977.

3 G. Wright 'On the Fringe of the Profession: Women in American Architecture,' in S. Kostof (ed.) *The Architect: Chapters in the History of the Profession*, Oxford Oxford University Press, 1977, pp. 280–309.

4 D. M. Anderson, *Women, Design and the Cambridge School*, Indiana: PDA Publishers Corp., 1980, and E. P. Berkeley and M. McQuaid, *Architecture: A Place for Women*, Washington, DC: Smithsonian Institution Press, 1989.

5 L. Walker 'Women Architects,' in J. Attfield and P. Kirkham, *A View from the Interior*, London: The Women's Press, 1989.

6 K. Ruedi, S. Wigglesworth and D. McCorquodale, *Desiring Practices: Architecture, Gender and the Interdisciplinary*, London: Black Dog Pub., 1991.

7 I. Anscombe, *A Woman's Touch: Women in Design from 1860 to the Present Day*, London: Virago, 1984.

8 J. Seddon and S. Worden, *Women Designing: Redefining Design in Britain between the Wars*, Brighton: University of Brighton Press, 1994.

9 See P. Adam, *Eileen Gray, Architect/Designer,* London: Thames and Hudson, 1987, and P. Kirkham, *Charles and Ray Eames: Designers of the Twentieth Century*, Cambridge, MA: MIT Press, 1995.

10 See Anscombe, op. cit.

11 P. Kirkham and P. Sparke, ' "A Woman's Place ...?": Women Designers in the Twentieth Century', in P. Kirkham (ed.) *Women Designers in the USA, 1900–2000: Diversity and Difference*, New Haven, CT, and London: Yale University Press, 2000.

12 D. Hayden, *The Grand Domestic Revolution*, Cambridge, MA: MIT Press, 1981, and G. Wright, *Moralism and the Modern Home*, Chicago Chicago University Press, 1980.

13 R. Parker, *The Subversive Stitch: Embroidery and the Making of the Feminine*, London: Women's Press, 1984.

14 C. Buckley, *Potters and Paintresses: Women Designers in the Pottery Industry 1870–1955*, London: Women's Press, 1990.

15 J. Attfield, 'Inside Pram Town: A Case study of Harlow House Interiors, 1951–1961,' in J. Attfield and P. Kirkham, op. cit.

16 A. T. Friedman, *Women and the Making of the Modern House: A Social and Architectural History*, New York: Harry N. Abrams, Inc., 1998.

17 B. Colomina, *Privacy and Privacy: Modern Architecture as Mass Media*, Cambridge, MA: MIT Press, 1994.

18 E. Wilson, *The Sphinx in the City*, London: Virago, 1991.

19 P. Sparke, *As Long as It's Pink: The Sexual Politics of Taste*, London: Pandora, 1995.

20 C. Reed (ed.), *Not At Home: The Suppression of Domesticity in Modern Art and Architecture*, London: Thames and Hudson, 1996.

21 V. de Grazia and E. Furlough (eds), *The Sex of Things: Gender and Consumption in Historical Perspective*, Berkeley: University of California Press, 1996 and P. Kirkham (ed.), *The Gendered Object*, Manchester: Manchester University Press, 1996.

22 A. Light, *Forever England: Femininity, Literature and Conservatism between the Wars*, London and New York: Routledge, 1991.

Chapter 1

Questions of identity
Women, architecture and the
Aesthetic Movement

Louise Campbell

Roger Stein, writing of the Aesthetic Movement in America, has shrewdly observed that, 'in many respects the Aesthetic movement was a women's movement. Women were among the leading producers of aesthetic goods, and insofar as the movement was primarily directed toward the domestic realm, they were also its chief consumers.'[1] Although few women on the other side of the Atlantic attained the celebrity of the interior decorator and textile designer Candace Wheeler or her daughter Dora, designer and painter, who was portrayed by William Merritt Chase surrounded by the evidence of her artistry (the sumptuous décor and superb blue pot),[2] women in Britain were also commissioning, producing and consuming aesthetic artefacts across a wide economic spectrum. They included Frances Leyland, who posed for Whistler in 1873 in a dress inspired by one in a painting by Watteau, and made especially for this occasion,[3] and Carrie Pooter, wife of the eponymous hero of George and Weedon Grossmith's *The Diary of a Nobody* of 1892, who bought a piece of silk from Liberty's with which to drape the photographs on the parlour mantelpiece of their home at 'The Laurels', Brickfield Terrace, Holloway.[4] However, most of the authors who have written about the Aesthetic Movement in Britain have a different emphasis. For art historians like Robin Spencer and Lionel Lambourne, the chief protagonists of the Aesthetic Movement were the painters James

McNeill Whistler and Albert Moore, the architects Edward William Godwin and Richard Norman Shaw, and the designers Walter Crane and Christopher Dresser.[5] By contrast, historians of architecture and design have done considerably more to chart the networks underpinning the endeavours of artists, designers and architects, and have helped to ground this movement for design reform more securely in the specific historical and cultural context from which it sprang.[6] Their work has revealed that what Mark Girouard characterised in 1977 as a generation in revolt against the tastes of their parents was also a generation which was involved in much broader areas of social change.[7] One of these areas was the expansion of the activities of women beyond the domestic sphere and the negotiation of new roles for them in the years between the second Reform Bill of 1867 and the Married Women's Property Act of 1882.[8]

This chapter considers two women who made use of architecture to devise for themselves a distinctive artistic and personal identity, and for whom architecture was to represent a significant aspect of their influence upon their contemporaries. Their careers indicate the diversity of the Aesthetic Movement, suggesting the existence of not one but several movements: on the one hand, elitist, hyper-refined, concerned with the cultivation of individual sensation and sensibility and signalling allegiance to an artistic avant-garde, and on the other, democratising, concerned with art education, with improving standards of design and manufacture, and with broadening access to contemporary art.[9]

My first example, Queen Victoria's fourth daughter Louise (1848–1939) (Figure 1.1) demonstrates the powerful fascination which the arts exerted for wealthy Britons during the late nineteenth century; in her case, they helped to fashion a new kind of persona for a royal princess. Like all her siblings, Princess Louise had been taught how to draw and paint from a young age.[10] More unusually, she also received instruction in sculpture. In the 1860s the sculptor Mary Thornycroft was commissioned to execute portraits of the Queen's children, and, following the example of her father John Thornycroft, who had helped Prince Albert to execute a bust of his father twenty years before, she gave lessons to Louise.[11] A studio was subsequently established at Osborne House on the Isle of Wight for the Princess's use.[12]

In 1868 Princess Louise enrolled at the National Art Training School at South Kensington, where she was taught by the sculptor Joseph Edgar Boehm, but regular attendance there was made impossible by the demands on her time made by the Queen, to whom she had acted as social secretary following the marriage of her elder sister Helena. Louise's own marriage in 1871 to the Marquess of Lorne represented an escape from this

1.1
Princess Louise:
Self bust,
terracotta, c. 1870s
National Portrait
Gallery

role and allowed her to pursue her interest in art and also in women's rights.[13] Lorne was well educated, cultivated and progressive, deeply interested in poetry and in art, and introduced her to a social and artistic circle much broader than that which she had previously known.[14] His relatives included George and Rosalind Howard (amateur painters and patrons of the architect Philip Webb), Lord Ronald Leveson-Gower (the sculptor upon whom Oscar Wilde based the character of the dissolute Lord Henry Wotton in his novel of 1891 *The Picture of Dorian Gray*), the architect Eustace Balfour and his wife Frances, and Archibald and Janey Campbell, passionately interested in the theatre, and loyal patrons of Whistler.[15] It was through this unconventional couple that Louise began to meet artists socially.[16] The rigidity of the social distinctions which had been observed in the early Victorian period between professional people, those whose wealth derived from commerce and industry, and the upper classes and landed gentry, was beginning to break down by the 1860s. A remarkable degree of social fluidity appears to have operated in venues like the Grosvenor Gallery, opened in 1877, where the guest list for receptions and private views comprised a carefully calculated mixture of bankers and painters, actors and aristocrats, entrepreneurs and aesthetes. At the gallery, which showed work by invited artists only, an attempt was made to offer an alternative to the incoherent hanging and display conditions of the contemporary Royal Academy. The Grosvenor Gallery managed to convey the impression of both artistic and social exclusivity. Works by a given artist were grouped together, and spaced more generously than the cramped frame-to-frame hang for which the Royal Academy was notorious.[17] The décor contrived to suggest not a commercial art gallery but somewhere far more select: 'This is no public picture exhibition, but rather a patrician's private gallery, shown by courtesy of its owner.'[18] Financial backing for the Gallery came from Blanche Lindsay, a Rothschild heiress married to the owner, Sir Coutts Lindsay.[19] As well as showing her sculpture at the Royal Academy in 1868, 1869 and 1874 (the first member of her family to exhibit there), and at the Old Water Colour Society, Louise exhibited both sculptures and paintings at the Grosvenor Gallery from 1878 to 1889, including an accomplished portrait of the sculptress Henrietta Montalba, a fellow student at South Kensington.[20]

As a Grosvenor Gallery exhibitor, Louise was introduced to the painters associated with the Aesthetic Movement and to avant-garde design. Through Janey Campbell she had met Whistler, and was one of the many visitors to the Peacock Room, the celebrated dining-room which he decorated at the Leylands' London house at 49 Princes Gate between the summer of 1876 and the spring of 1877.[21] Obliterating a pre-existing scheme featuring antique leather wall-coverings, Whistler painted the ceiling, walls and window shutters with a striking gold pattern derived from peacock plumage, painted on a ground of deep blue-green to serve as a setting for Leyland's large collection of Nankin pottery. As he worked, Whistler held a series of receptions and press views to which journalists, friends and fellow-artists were invited. It may have been in this extraordinary setting that the Princess met Whistler's friend and architect Edward Godwin. Such connections helped her to articulate the difference between her own tastes and way of life and that of her parents, who had warned of the folly of mixing socially with artists, or of believing that people in their own position could be professional artists.[22] But for Louise, as for her contemporaries, the world of art represented an antidote to the prevalent materialism of the period and suggested the possibility of a different sort of hierarchy, in which talent and taste would be valued more highly than title or wealth.[23]

For their part, Whistler and Godwin cultivated their new acquaintance keenly in order to defend their work from philistine criticism and to help generate commissions among wealthy and influential patrons. In 1877 Godwin dedicated an illustrated catalogue of his designs for art furniture manufactured by the firm of William Watt to the Princess, with her permission.[24] In 1878 Whistler enlisted her help over his difficulty in getting permission to build The White House, the studio-house which Godwin had designed for him in Tite Street, Chelsea, and which the ground landlord, the Metropolitan Board of Works, and its commissioner Sir James Hogg were insisting should be modified in order to fit in with the style of the fashionable Queen Anne Movement houses being constructed on nearby plots.[25] Racing against time in order to complete the house, to move in and begin to take in the pupils whose fees he hoped would defray his own considerable living expenses, Whistler dreaded the prospect of further delay. He described to Godwin what happened when he told the Princess of his predicament.

> She greatly sympathized – and I made a grand stroke! I said that if her Royal Highness would only drive past and say how beautiful she thought the house that of course this would put an end to the whole trouble. She laughed saying that she didn't believe her influence was as strong as that! but afterwards said in a reflective way that "Lorne knows Sir James I think ..."[26]

It is generally claimed that the house was approved as a result of the strategic changes made by Godwin to the façade design.[27] However, the Princess's support may well have expedited matters, for Whistler presented her with a painting of the River Thames that autumn 'as a tribute of devotion and gratitude'.[28] Of more lasting significance was the gesture of endorsement which the Princess provided for Godwin as designer of tasteful and practical studio-houses, something which was further cemented by the commission which she gave Godwin in 1878 to design her a new studio in London.[29]

Louise's commission to Godwin consisted of a studio without living accommodation, because she and her husband occupied an apartment in Kensington Palace. The apartment, which was decorated in 1874 by George Aitchison, Lord Leighton's architect, provided the setting for more conventional kinds of social occasions. The colour scheme consisted of:

> green woodwork and green and red walls in the ante-room; brown woodwork and dull pink walls in the small dining-room; green woodwork and gold walls in the drawing-room; red woodwork and gold walls in the large dining-room.[30]

Furnishings apparently included green-stained armchairs designed by Richard Norman Shaw.[31] The studio, by contrast, was the place for work and for informal socialising, for 'laughter and skylarking'.[32] Godwin provided the following account of the design process:

> a builder had volunteered to put up a studio for about £800. The Princess Louise thought this was rather too much for a simple building at the bottom of the garden, and a friend advised her to "go to Mr. Godwin." I built a studio 17ft. high and put over it a kind of Mansard roof, with windows looking into the garden. It is about 25 ft. square and has an ante-room attached for the Marquess of Lorne, a little hall, and three entrances. The walls are of red brick, there are green slates on the roof to match the old house, and few would notice that anything had been added to the old building. It is quite as pretty as the builder's would have been. It is admirably suited for a studio, and we managed to put it up for between £600 and £700, including architect's fees. All the light is reflected so as to reduce the horizontal ceiling as much as possible. This studio seems perfectly satisfactory to the Princess, to Mr. Boehm, the sculptor (for it is a sculptor's studio), and also to myself. [33]

In designing it, Godwin made use of the existing perimeter wall of the Palace garden, against which the new studio building abutted to the south and west. To the north, a three-light window was set into an enormous roof (Figure 1.2). With its red brick walls and a picturesque shaped gable surmounting the east wall to echo the seventeenth-century palace architecture, this building responds sensitively to its context in a very different manner from the wilful iconoclasm displayed in the designs for Whistler's house.

Correspondence between Godwin and members of Louise's staff

1.2
E.W. Godwin:
*Studio at
Kensington for
HRH the Princess
Louise*, 1880.
**Drawing by Raffles
Davison**
British Architect,
1880

STUDIO AT KENSINGTON
FOR H·R·H THE PRINCESS LOUISE

discusses the character of the internal finishing and furnishing. Godwin produced sketches showing a panelled fireplace surround in the studio, with a coved chimey breast supporting a broad mantel-shelf, upon which oriental ceramics were displayed.[34] He proposed to base the design of the surround on a combination of simple square motifs and naturalistic ones inspired by 'one of the treasures of the Royal Irish Academy', conferring on it a more traditional character than the angular, Japanese-inspired joinery which he had designed for Whistler and for the artist Frank Miles in Tite Street.[35] Intriguingly, however, Godwin's design for the mantelpiece in the ante-room has a daintier, Orientalising quality (Figure 1.3, bottom left). In a rather fascinating reversal of the roles conventionally assigned to artist and spouse, it conjures up the image of Lorne reading poetry in the inglenook while Louise engaged in the physical labour of sculpture. Given Lorne's association with Miles and with Leveson-Gower – both homosexual artists – Godwin's pretty interiors suggest a place where new kinds of artistic, social and sexual identity could be developed.[36]

In fact, however, the interior may never actually have looked like this. Photographs taken in 1940 show a studio with a very different appearance, with no sign of the dainty woodwork around windows and fireplaces shown in Godwin's drawings.[37] Susan Weber Soros, citing a letter from Godwin which proposed using deal instead of oak panels for window shutters and for the fireplace surround, suggests that the Princess was concerned with practicality, economy and speed, preferring to spend money on a well-insulated roof and ceiling, and durable studio windows with teak sills, rather than elaborate, expensive joinery.[38] It appears to have been a typical sculptor's workshop: a dirty place where clay, stone chippings and dust were everywhere in evidence. Perhaps there was a difference between the architect's conception of the setting appropriate for a sculptor-princess and her own ideas, for the drawing of a romantic pavilion in a park which was published in the *British Architect* in 1880 made a striking contrast with Louise's pragmatic approach to her work place.[39]

In 1878 Lorne was appointed Governor General of Canada, the kind of far away job which the British establishment tends to reserve for members of the royal family whose behaviour departs from convention, and Louise spent much of the period from 1878 to 1883 in Canada with him. In an attempt to 'recreate their cultural life' in a new environment, they took with them the painter Sydney Prior Hall.[40] Louise continued to sculpt and to paint. She decorated the doorway to her studio at Rideau Hall, their official residence in Ottawa, with a delightful design of foliage scrolling across the panels, forming the interface between living space and work-space.[41] She also designed a sketching box on wheels, with a glass side, in which she could work outdoors in bad weather.[42]

On her return to England, Louise maintained her interest in architecture and design, albeit in a new direction. She had a new studio constructed alongside the old one but without the help of Godwin, who died

1.3
E.W. Godwin: sketch designs from a letter to Princess Louise for windows, alcove and fireplace at her proposed studio at Kensington, 31 August 1878
Victoria & Albert Museum, Archive of Architecture and Design

1.4
Princess Louise (attrib.): curtains for Manchester Town Hall with appliqué and embroidery in crewel wools, made by the Royal School of Art Needlework, 1877
Aslin, 1981

in 1886.[43] Experiencing increasing difficulties in her marriage, Louise distanced herself from the inner circle of the Aesthetic Movement (still dominated by her husband's first cousins Archie and Janey Campbell), and she threw herself into other activities.[44] As a counterpart to her own practice as artist and as patron of architecture, Louise lent her support to bodies like the Royal Drawing Society, which awarded prizes to encourage children to produce original drawings rather than copying works of art, was a patron of the Kyrle Society, dedicated to improving public access to art, and founded the Ladies' Work Society, dedicated to obtaining needlework commissions 'for ladies who are dependent on their own exertions'.[45] She thus combined the cultural aims of the Aesthetic Movement with the philanthropic activities typical of women of her position.

Through the Royal School of Art Needlework, which in the 1870s had executed work to her designs including curtains with a motif of sunflowers for Alfred Waterhouse's new Manchester Town Hall (Figure 1.4), Louise met the embroideress and gardener Gertrude Jekyll. Jekyll may have been responsible for introducing her to a younger generation of architects, and also to garden design. The Princess designed the garden layout at Macharioch, the house near Inverary which had been enlarged and modernised for Louise and Lorne after their marriage by George Devey, an architect popular with aristocrats and liberal politicians.[46] The improvements which were subsequently initiated on their Scottish estate in the years before Lorne succeeded his father as Duke of Argyll provide an index to their changing tastes.[47] Louise's patronage of Godwin, as we have seen, corresponded with the height of her involvement with the Aesthetic Movement and with avant-garde artistic activity in London. However, it was an architect of a very different kind, Edwin Lutyens (a young protégé of Gertrude Jekyll) whom Louise asked in 1895 to advise on alterations to Kilkatrine House, Inverary, and to rebuild the Ferry Inn at Rosneath, Dunbartonshire in 1896.[48] Lutyens apparently had high hopes of this royal connection, to the extent of fantasising about being recommended to do work at Windsor Castle; he was therefore mortified subsequently to discover that the Princess had dropped him in favour of his former assistant E. Baynes Badcock to do some work for her at Cowes.[49]

Nevertheless, the Princess's employment of Lutyens in the 1890s was, however brief, to be of considerable help in advancing the architect's career, providing him with a network of further clients via her Campbell relations, and publicizing the picturesque vernacular idiom in which he was then working. Speaking during the 1890s at a meeting of the Old Guildford Society, something which Gertrude Jekyll, with her passion for rural traditions, had helped to establish, Louise recommended Lutyens to the Society 'as a person who is likely to make his mark'.[50] Lutyens's successful architectural practice was founded upon the commissions for large country houses which then followed in abundance.[51]

The second artist whom I wish to consider, Kate Greenaway (1846–1901), represents a different aspect of the Aesthetic Movement: the involvement of artists in producing work for a mass market, the market for illustrated books for children, which had expanded rapidly after the 1870 Education Act. Greenaway achieved great celebrity in this field in the 1880s. As Pamela Gerrish Nunn has shrewdly observed, Greenaway represented 'the acceptable mode of women's creativity as far as the art world was concerned'.[52] Much of Greenaway's work was executed in a delicate medium – watercolour – on an intimate scale, and was largely domestic in theme. The image of Greenaway as an unworldly, retiring and ladylike individual, conveyed by her biographers, was an image which she seems actively to have endorsed. It has proved to be both enduring and difficult to penetrate.[53] The house which Richard Norman Shaw designed for her in Hampstead in 1883–4, illustrated in the *British Architect* in 1885 (Figure 1.5), was a key element in the creation of Greenaway's artistic and professional identity. It also provides clues to the presence of the more complex and interesting individual behind it. The house, prettily detailed, with a great bargeboarded gable and a canted bay, the upper half hung with red tiles of a fishscale pattern, had a studied simplicity compared with Shaw's other houses for artists nearby in Fitzjohn's Avenue or in Melbury Road, Kensington.[54] Greenaway's studio occupied the top floor of the house; its great window

1.5
**Richard Norman
Shaw: house for
Kate Greenaway,
Frognal,
Hampstead,
1884–1885**
British Architect,
1885

was set slant-wise to take advantage of the north-east light and giving views over what was then open countryside towards Hampstead village and the Heath. The plan, which contained a narrow flight of stairs to the studio instead of a grand ceremonial approach, and with no separate staircase to allow servants and models to circulate out of sight of the family and their visitors, has been described by Andrew Saint as corresponding to 'the wants of a maiden lady who does her own housekeeping'.[55] But arrangements were not quite like this, nor was the house as straightforward as it first appeared.

It housed Greenaway, her father, mother and brother – something like a family business, with each member contributing in some way to the economic improvement which made possible the trajectory from the slums of

Hoxton to Islington, to Holloway and then to Hampstead.[56] Trained at the Finsbury School of Art, at the National Art Training School at South Kensington from 1865 and then at the Slade, Greenaway began her career making illustrations for magazines and greetings cards, a field related to those in which other members of her family worked.[57] Her father was a draughtsman and wood-engraver for the *Illustrated London News* and for *Punch* magazine, and he was thus in a position to advise her when she entered into partnership with the expert printer Edmund Evans in 1877. Their first book, *Under the Window* sold 70,000 copies in two years, and Greenaway astutely negotiated a half share of royalties on their subsequent publications. Her income from card design in 1871 had been £70. In 1879 she was earning eight times that amount and she and her father together bought the lease of a house off the Archway Road with enough space for her to work there.[58] It was on the basis of three best-sellers, *Under the Window* (1879), *Kate Greenaway's Birthday Book for Children* (1880), and the slightly less successful *Mother Goose* (1881) that she decided to purchase for £2,000 a site in Hampstead for a new house.[59]

Greenaway dealt firmly with architect, builder and rate assessor.[60] In response to the plans which Shaw sent her, Greenaway requested changes to the bedroom floor, and also to the position of the drawing-room. This, she specified, should run from the front to the back of the house, an arrangement which she considered to be: 'so much more cheerful. I don't mind how long it is – how wonky (?) – how it turns about or if it looks like three little rooms – I see the tea room does loop (?) in and out which is what I like so much.' She continued reproachfully: 'You have not put us in the little morning room which we should want ...'.[61] Her wish for this additional sitting room was satisfied by the re-designed double drawing-room, in which Shaw provided several alcoves for privacy.[62]

The 40-foot-long studio was designed very carefully so as to enable Greenaway to produce the intricately detailed art-work which her books required. Although considered by her friends to be 'less charming' than the previous one,[63] the new studio was more functional, providing more space and more light and allowing Greenaway to paint landscape views in all weathers.[64] Detailed work was done here in the mornings, with a further hour or two after lunch. The adjoining tea-room provided space for entertaining her child models and their chaperones (Figures 1.6 and 1.7). In the afternoon she took a walk with a sketchbook on the Heath. The evenings were spent letter-writing, making costumes for her sitters and in working on page layouts, and in the summer, tending her flower garden. The house appears to have been a hive of highly focused activity. Greenaway's mother ran the house, and as a former milliner, provided expert help with dress and bonnet-

1.6
Interior of Kate Greenaway's studio, Frognal
Spielmann and Layard, 1905

1.7
Tea-room, Kate Greenaway house, Frognal
Spielmann and Layard, 1905

making. Her brother, a chemist and keen amateur photographer, may have made himself useful with his camera. Freed from domestic chores by her mother and at least one living-in servant, Greenaway protected herself from the time-consuming, tiring and expensive rituals of bourgeois society by declining invitations to dine out.[65] Sociability was confined as far as possible to tea parties.[66]

One gets a certain sense of masquerade.[67] The house, although then set in a meadow, with a great avenue of elms behind it, was no longer quite in the country but was one of the first buildings in a newly created road, Frognal. The exterior details of the house – the carved and bracketed door-case, the small-paned windows, the use of wood (rather than modern-looking cast-iron) for railings, balcony balustrade and gate – are insistently pre-industrial in character. Greenaway seems to have deliberately emulated the gentle rhythms of country (or perhaps village) life, with its walks, its restricted visiting and social life revolving around the home. These rhythms provide a marked contrast to the patterns of late nineteenth-century urban sociability, and the increased mobility brought by the expansion of the metropolitan transport system, which allowed the residents of outer London to spend the evening in the West End.[68] Similarly, Greenaway's house served to endow with old-fashioned charm and to render individual, feminine and domestic what was in practice a highly disciplined routine in which the entire family was to some degree involved.

The studio was dominated by a great window. One end of the room was functionally equipped with a model's throne, a fireplace, storage cupboards and a five-light window overlooking the road; the other end, with doors opening onto the balcony, into the tea-room and the staircase landing, was more formally furnished. The tea-room, lit by a small window over-looking the garden, was very carefully arranged and furnished. An elegant Shaw-designed fireplace, surrounded by blue-and-white patterned tiles, was surmounted by a collection of porcelain and portrait miniatures. Japanese fans, framed Old Master prints, drawings, plates by William de Morgan, wicker chairs and lengths of pretty fabric, provided a setting which was both intimate and fashionable.[69]

During this period, many artists devised interiors which would function as a frame or stage, and which helped to accentuate particular aspects of their endeavours.[70] But there are some significant differences. The artists' houses in Melbury Road, Kensington served as showcases for their owners' achievements, well appointed, spatially complex and opulently furnished. The house designed by Norman Shaw for Marcus Stone, for example, contained two well-lit studios, one for winter and one for summer use, as well as two large reception rooms; three staircases – one for family and visitors, one for servants, and one for models – discreetly provided separate circulation systems.[71] Greenaway, who already had a mass market, had no need to use her studio for displaying her work to prospective buyers or dealers, as painters did, or as a venue for the studio receptions which they habitually held every May on 'Show Sunday', allowing the public a privileged preview of works before they were sent off to the annual Royal Academy exhibition.[72] However, Greenaway's house was no less important to her career, because it conferred upon her work an ostensibly unworldly and uncommercial air. For many of her London artist contemporaries, the studio-house was the centre of a well-organised enterprise whose economic *raison d'être* was masked by a variety of exotic trappings. A carefully designed living and working environment suggested an artist's distinctive taste and vision, evidence of travel and a cultivated eye, and of an existence unfettered by bourgeois convention.[73] Deborah Cherry has indicated the difficulties which women encountered in an art world which was dominated by such flamboyant public displays of creativity. Women artists in the 1870s and 1880s, she suggests, responded by fashioning 'themselves as aesthetic objects', devising their appearance, their surroundings and their social personae with the utmost care.[74] Greenaway's demeanour indicates someone who, although sharing this concern with personal style, declined to conform to current conceptions of how an artist looked, lived and worked. In pointed contrast to her contemporaries' theatrical style of self-presentation, she instead created for herself the persona of a modest English gentlewoman.[75]

The apparently easy fit between the artist and the house created for her by Shaw begs the question of whether at Hampstead Greenaway embraced an identity which had been fabricated for her by an artist who had a reputation for being good with clients.[76] As we have seen, she had firm views on what she liked and required, with which Shaw complied. Evidence suggests that Greenaway's prim style was something which she herself had cultivated, as an ingenious alternative to the ostentation of the 'show studios' of the period. Interestingly, we know that Greenaway made forays with the painter Helen Allingham to rural Surrey and Hampshire in order to paint cottages and farm-buildings. Allingham's account of these painting expeditions suggests patterns of behaviour which contrast markedly with Greenaway's public image of propriety, fragility and reticence, and conjures up an unexpectedly unconventional and adventurous practice.[77] There is also a striking mismatch between the squalid living conditions which Greenaway probably encountered in Surrey (then notoriously primitive and inaccessible) and the anaemic and generalised representation of architecture and village life contained in the book illustrations which Greenaway derived from the sketches which she made there (Figure 1.8). Greenaway's own house possesses a comparably fantastic quality, providing a quasi-pastoral setting for an artist who was born and bred in the grimiest of London suburbs.[78]

For Greenaway, as for the more privileged Princess Louise, conventions associated with their gender and their class affected their attempt to gain acceptance and recognition as artists. Louise never had to earn her own living and was unable to benefit financially from the sale of her work, but instead donated the proceeds to charity.[79] For Greenaway, increasing prosperity brought particular problems and social pressures; she felt obliged to present her hard-working and profitable artisanal practice in terms of a lady-like occupation, or genteel pastime.[80] For both women, architecture perhaps represented an alternative arena of (surrogate) creativity, a sphere in which their taste and powers of discrimination might be more freely exercised, and influence exerted.[81] During the 1870s and 1880s, Louise's ostentatiously aesthetic tastes served to stimulate an interest in contemporary design among her wealthy and aristocratic contemporaries. Her significance for architecture lies less in the extent of her personal commissions than in the public support which she gave first to Godwin and then to Lutyens at critical moments in each of their careers. Greenaway, whose books were bought for huge numbers of children, shaped the visual imagination of their readers at a formative age, and fostered a taste for the small-scale, the intimate and the old-fashioned. One of these small readers was W.B. Yeats, who was taken by his parents to live in the aesthetic suburb of Bedford Park in west London, designed by Godwin and Norman Shaw in 1876–80. Yeats described the shock of recognition which he experienced at seeing the buildings and the quaintness of the environment which had been created there by means of careful landscaping and layout and a restricted range of building materials and motifs. He recalled the strange sensation that he had entered the pages of a picture-book when he and his family moved into a house 'like those we had seen in story-books …[we felt] that we were living among toys'.[82] By such means Greenaway helped to encourage a new appreciative perception of rural architecture as picturesque, and thus shape the anti-urban and anti-industrial attitudes which were to be fundamental to the Arts and Crafts Movement in the 1890s.

During that decade, a new concept of architecture as the product of craft skills, and an appreciation of buildings as organically related to locality, community and to landscape began to gain a wider currency. To these concepts Princess Louise, with her interest in the traditions of rural Surrey, her support of the crafts and her patronage of the National Trust made a significant contribution.[83] Although today such attitudes are regarded as essentially romantic, tending to encourage an appreciation of the old at the

1.8
**Kate Greenaway:
'Two little girls at
tea' from** *Under
the Window*, **1879**

expense of innovation, at the turn of the century they appeared rather as an extension of the more radical aspects of the Aesthetic Movement. By 1900, nature, community and craft represented an attractive alternative to contemporary modes of living and building, and enjoyed that special place in the imagination which for the generation active during the 1870s had been dominated by the idea of the artist, and of the 'artistic' interior as a place in which alternatives to prevailing artistic and social conventions might be explored and enjoyed.

Notes

1 R. Stein, 'Artifact as Ideology: The Aesthetic Movement in its American Cultural Context', in D. Bulger Burke *et al.* (eds) *In Pursuit of Beauty: Americans and the Aesthetic Movement*, New York: Metropolitan Museum of Art/Rizzoli, 1987, p. 24. Stein provides a stimulating and wide-ranging analysis, to which the following chapter is much indebted.

2 *Portrait of Miss Dora Wheeler*, 1883, Cleveland Museum of Art, illustrated Stein, 'Artifact as Ideology', p. 325.

3 *Symphony in Flesh Colour and Pink: Portrait of Mrs. Frances Leyland*, 1871–4, Frick Collection, New York.

4 G. Grossmith and W. Grossmith, *The Diary of a Nobody*, London: Bradbury and Agnew, 1892.

5 R. Spencer, *The Aesthetic Movement: Theory and Practice*, London: Studio Vista, 1972; L. Lambourne, *The Aesthetic Movement*, London: Phaidon, 1996.

6 For example, E. Aslin, *The Aesthetic Movement: Prelude to Art Nouveau*, London: Ferndale Editions, 1981; E. Aslin, *E. W. Godwin: Furniture and Interior Decoration*, London: John Murray, 1986; M. Girouard, *Sweetness and Light: The 'Queen Anne' Movement 1860–1900,* Oxford: Oxford University Press, 1977; A. Callen, *Women in the Arts and Crafts Movement 1870–1914*, London: Astragal, 1977; S. Weber Soros (ed.), *E.W. Godwin: Aesthetic Movement Architect and Designer*, New Haven, CT: Yale University Press, 2000.

7 Girouard, *Sweetness and and Light*, pp. 4–5.

8 The Act, by giving married women the right to retain their own property after marriage 'gave married women the same rights as spinsters and widows', according to D. Cherry, *Painting Women: Victorian Women Artists*, London: Routledge, 1993, p. 97.

9 Other key women in the Aesthetic Movement were Madeline Wyndham, Janey Campbell, and the painters Marie Spartali and Louise Jopling.

10 On Princess Louise's instruction in painting under Edward Henry Corbould and William Leighton Leitch, see J. Roberts, *Royal Artists*, London: Grafton Books, 1987, pp. 146–49; E. Longford, *Darling Loosy: Letters to Princess Louise 1856–1939*, London: Weidenfeld and Nicolson, 1991, pp. 6–14; H. Hunt-Lewis, 'The Art of Princess Louise' in D. Duff, *The Life Story of HRH Princess Louise*, London: Stanley Paul and Co., 1940, pp. 337–9.

11 On her training in sculpture with first Theed, then Mary Thornycroft and subsequently Boehm, see Roberts, *Royal Artists*, pp. 148–58. Mary Thornycroft initially executed her pupil's work, at first producing marble busts after Louise's carvings, and then acting as her collabor-

ator. Roberts, *op.cit.*, provides an overview of Louise's work over five decades.

12 Longford, *Darling Loosy*, p. 13.

13 Louise met Elizabeth Garrett and Josephine Butler in the 1860s, writing to the latter in 1869: 'I do take great interest in the happiness, and wellbeing of women, and long to do everything that I can to promote all efforts in that direction.' However, she was forced by her family to send back Mrs Butler's present of *Women's Work and Women's culture* and encouraged to re-direct her energies towards charitable activities (see Longford, *Darling Loosy*, pp. 17, 36). Her new husband had the reputation of being a feminist. He and Louise convened an Educational Parliament at their London house in 1872, and founded a trust for girls' education (see R. Stamp, *Royal Rebels: Louise and the Marquess of Lorne*, Toronto and Oxford: Dundurn Press, 1988, p. 101).

14 John Douglas Sutherland Campbell, Marquess of Lorne (1845-1914) was considered to be an unsuitable match for the Princess, according to *J. Wake, Princess Louise: Queen Victoria's Unconventional Daughter*, London: Collins, 1988, pp. 204–5 and Stamp, *Royal Rebels*. By contrast, D. Cantelupe, entry for Princess Louise in L. Wickham Legg, *Dictionary of National Biography 1931–1940*, London: Oxford University Press, 1949, p. 544 wrote that Lorne's non-royal status, and the fact that he was a Scot 'had the strong approval of the Queen'. See Longford, *Darling Loosy*, pp. 27, 36 for a discussion of Lorne as poet and writer.

15 See C. Dakers, *The Holland Park Circle: Artists and Victorian Society*, London and New York: Yale University Press, 1999, pp. 124–7.

16 See Wake, *Princess Louise*, pp. 204–5.

17 See S. Casteras and C. Denney (eds), *The Grosvenor Gallery: A Palace of Art in Victorian England*, New Haven, CT: Yale University Press, 1996, pp. 9–58 for accounts of the Grosvenor Gallery.

18 Agnes Atkinson in *Portfolio,*1877, quoted

in Cherry, *Painting Women*, p.87.

19 Lady Lindsay's watercolour *Portrait of HRH the Princess Louise* (reproduced in Casteras and Denney, *Grosvenor Gallery*, plate 4) was exhibited at the Grosvenor Gallery in 1878.

20 Louise's *Portrait of Henrietta Skerrett Montalba* (National Gallery of Canada) is reproduced in Casteras and Denney, *Grosvenor Gallery*, p. 195. Montalba's portrait bust of Lorne is at Inverary Castle.

21 See Wake, *Princess Louise*, pp. 205–11. Longford, op. cit., p. 224 quotes a letter from Whistler to the Princess inviting her to come to see the room, but erroneously gives a date of 8 November 1882.

22 Roberts, *Royal Artists*, p. 34 quotes Prince Albert: 'I consider that persons in our position of life can never be distinguished artists ... Our business is not so much to create, as to learn to appreciate and understand the works of others, and we never do this until we have realised the difficulties to be overcome.' C. Gere, 'The Art of Dress, Victorian Artists and Aesthetic Style', in *Simply Stunning: The Pre-Raphaelite Art of Dressing*, Cheltenham: Museum and Art Gallery, 1996, p. 13 quotes Queen Victoria's warning to Louise: 'Beware of artists, they mix with all classes of society and are therefore most dangerous.'

23 R. Ellman, *Oscar Wilde*, London: Hamish Hamilton, 1988, p. 107, writes of Wilde's equation of his wit with Lillie Langtry's beauty, each serving as a passport enabling its possessor to infiltrate high society.

24 *Art Furniture Designed by Edward W. Godwin FSA, and Manufactured by William Watt, 21 Grafton Street, Gower Street, London* London: B.T. Batsford, 1877.

25 See Girouard, *Sweetness and Light*, pp. 179–81 for an analysis of the two successive designs.

26 D. Bendix, *Diabolical Designs: Paintings, Interiors and Exhibitions of James McNeill Whistler*, Washington and London: Smithsonian Institution Press, 1995, p. 149. Letter of 1878.

27 See Girouard, *Sweetness and Light*, p. 179.

28 A picture of the Thames at Battersea according to Wake, *Princess Louise*, p. 201. Longford, *Darling Loosy*, pp. 214–15, quotes a letter from Whistler to Princess Louise of 8 November 1878: 'May I venture to offer your Royal Highness as a tribute of devotion and gratitude, a favourite picture of my own ...'.

29 See Girouard, *Sweetness and Light* for details of the house for Frank Miles of 1878–9 and a block of studio-flats, the Tower House of 1884–5. The sequence of events is significant: Whistler's White House designed Aug.– Sept. 1877; submitted to MBoW late autumn. Amended design submitted Jan. 1878; approved March, but lease withheld pending the addition of sculpted reliefs to the façade. These were never added, but the lease was granted May 1878. Princess Louise's studio commissioned May 1878; contract dated July 1878.

30 Dakers, *Holland Park Circle*, p.127.

31 A. Saint, *Richard Norman Shaw*, London and New York: Yale University Press, 1976, p. 172, refers to 'green armchairs, as supplied to the Princess Louise' shown at the 1878 Paris Exhibition.

32 Longford, *Darling Loosy*, p.41

33 Plans are in the British Architectural Library, RAN 7/F/2, and are reproduced by A. Reid, 'The Architectural Career of E.W. Godwin', in Soros, *E.W. Godwin*, p. 170. Godwin's account comes from his 'Studios and Mouldings', *The Building News*, vol. 36. 1879, p. 251.

34 Aslin, *E.W.Godwin*, p. 20, refers to the Princess's collection of Oriental ceramics.

35 Draft of letter from Godwin to Princess Louise, Victoria & Albert Museum, Archive of Architecture & Design, 4/190–1988. A tiny attached pen sketch shows the arrangement. Miles's studio is illustrated in Girouard, *Sweetness and Light*, pp. 182–3.

36 For references to Lorne's possible homosexuality, see Dakers, op. cit., p.127.

37 Interior illustrated S.W. Soros, 'E.W. Godwin and Interior Design,' in Soros, *E.W.Godwin*, p. 214; the exterior is

illustrated on p. 170. The studio was used by the sculptor Alfred Gilbert in the early twentieth century, and demolished after the Second World War.

38 Soros, 'E.W. Godwin and Interior Design', p. 214; see also Aslin, *E.W. Godwin*, p. 20.

39 Figure 1.2, published in *British Architect*, vol. 14, 1880, p. 238.

40 R. Tovell, 'A Wonderful Talent for Art', in *The Rebel Princess: Watercolours by HRH The Princess Louise*, Bermuda: The Bermuda National Gallery, 1998, pp. 10–11. Hall illustrated Lorne's book *Canadian Pictures* of 1884.

41 Illustrated in Roberts, *Royal Artists*, plate 51.

42 Roberts, *Royal Artists*, p. 152.

43 According to Reid, 'The Architectural Career of E. W. Godwin', p. 182, n. 245, it was demolished in 1925.

44 Louise is reputed to have been conducting a love affair with Boehm. He died suddenly in 1890, alone with Louise in his studio in circumstances which were the subject of considerable gossip. See Wake, Princess Louise and Dakers, *Holland Park Circle*, p. 128.

45 Callen, *Women in the Arts and Crafts Movement*, p. 110.

46 Wake, *Princess Louise*, p. 318. Louise's work in and around Inverary Castle merits a through documentation. She designed the decorative wrought iron railings to the Gallery Library and executed wall-paintings there and at Ben More Lodge on the Island of Mull.

47 Lorne succeeded his father in 1900, and as a result of heavy death duties was afterwards unable to undertake ambitious building projects.

48 See C. Hussey *The Life of Sir Edwin Lutyens*, London: Country Life, 1950, pp. 72–3. Lutyens's proposed alterations to Kilkatrine were not executed. For Rosneath, see F. Walker, *Buildings of Scotland: Argyll and Bute,* London: Penguin, 2000, pp. 444–5. According to Longford, op. cit., Lutyens introduced Louise to Jekyll in 1897. According to Wake, op. cit., p. 318, Jekyll brought Louise and Lutyens together.

49 Hussey, *Lutyens*, p. 98.

50 Wake, *Princess Louise*, p. 318.

51 See Hussey, *Lutyens*.

52 P. G. Nunn, *Victorian Women Artists*, London: The Women's Press, 1987, p. 220.

53 The standard biographies are M. Spielmann and G. Layard, *Kate Greenaway*, London: Adam and Charles Black, 1905; R. Engen, *Kate Greenaway: A Biography*, London: Macdonald Futura, 1981.

54 See Saint, *Richard Norman Shaw*, pp. 153–62.

55 Ibid., p. 159.

56 See Engen, *Kate Greenaway*.

57 According to Callen, *Women in the Arts and Crafts Movement*, one of Greenaway's aunts was a bookbinder and another an engraver.

58 11 Pemberton Gardens, according to Engen, *Kate Greenaway*, pp. 55–6.

59 Callen, *Women in the Arts and Crafts Movement*, p. 203.

60 According to Engen, *Kate Greenaway*, p.119, she appealed against 'unfair property assessment early in 1884' and dealt directly with her builder. Engen's description of the interior arrangement of the house on p. 120 is unfortunately very inaccurate.

61 Letter from Kate Greenaway to Richard Norman Shaw, 25 September 1883, Victoria & Albert Museum Library, MSL.41–1982. Press-mark 86.WW.1.

62 Saint, *Richard Norman Shaw*, publishes the final plans on p. 160, re-drawn. The contract plans on which his drawings are based, together with elevations and sections (dated March 1884) and details (dated June and September 1884) are in the Royal Academy Library, RP 1/12 B. In G. Walkley, *Artists' Houses in London 1764–1914*, London: Scolar Press, pp. 114–15, the plans are illustrated in greater detail than Saint, and the front part of the drawing room is identified as a morning room.

63 Spielmann and Layard, *Kate Greenaway*, p. 144.

64 Greenaway's letter to Shaw implies that

some modification had already occurred here too: 'The studio floor is a triumph and I think it will make all the difference on the outside ...' V & A, MSL. 41–1982.

65 Spielmann and Layard, *Kate Greenaway*, p. 145.

66 Ibid., p. 44.

67 The phrase is Deborah Cherry's. See *Painting Women*, p. 197.

68 See R. Porter, *London: A Social History*, London: Penguin Books, 1994, Chapter 13.

69 The colour scheme is not recorded, but Shaw's drawings at the RA show panelling, skirting, doors and staircase painted or stained blue-green, echoing the porcelain on display in the tea-room.

70 See Walkley, *Artists' Houses in London*.

71 Illustrated in Saint, *Richard Norman Shaw*, pp. 154–5.

72 See P. Gillett, *The Victorian Painter's World*, Gloucester: Alan Sutton, 1990, pp. 193–8. Cherry, *Painting Women*, p. 87, discusses the artist-house as 'the sign and visible manifestation of artistic masculinity'. By contrast, there are very few recorded examples of women artists commissioning studio-houses from architects during the 1870s and 1880s. Beside Princess Louise and Kate Greenaway, Mary Thornycroft (together with her husband and artist-son and daughters) built a house in Melbury Road in 1876; the painters Louise Jopling and Anna Lea Merritt built studios in Chelsea around 1880.

73 See L. Campbell, 'Decoration, Display, Disguise: Leighton House Reconsidered', in T. Barringer and L. Prettejohn, *Frederic Leighton: Antiquity Renaissance Modernity*, New Haven, CT: Yale

University Press, 1999 for a discussion of these issues.

74 Cherry, *Painting Women*, pp. 87–90.

75 Some select pieces of antique furniture and a Georgian firegrate in the studio reinforced the allusion to eighteenth-century life which permeates accounts of Greenaway's Hampstead existence.

76 See Saint, *Richard Norman Shaw*, pp. 144–53. Interestingly, Greenaway's curious correspondence with Ruskin suggests her willingness to accept the elderly critic's view of her work and her personality. Extracts are given in Spielmann and Layard, op. cit., pp. 142–51.

77 See Cherry, *Painting Women*, p. 177.

78 Girouard, *Sweetness and Light*, p. 147, points out that Greenaway's books constitute 'a Londoner's vision of an ideal country childhood'.

79 Hunt-Lewis, 'The Art of Princess Louise,' in Duff, *Princess Louise*, p. 344.

80 As regards Greenaway's move from the working class to the middle class, see Cherry, *Painting Women*, Chapter 1, for an interesting discussion of the position of women in artist-families, and of the advantages which artisan status conferred.

81 As well as her support for organisations like the Kyrle Society, Louise wrote articles on art for magazines under the pseudonym of Myra Fontenoy. See Roberts, *Royal Artists*, p.155.

82 Quoted by W. Creese, *In Search of Environment: The Garden City: Before and After*, New Haven, CT: Yale University Press, 1976, p.106.

83 See Roberts, *Royal Rebels*, p. 155.

Chapter 2

Creating 'The New Room'
The Hall sisters of West Wickham and Richard Norman Shaw

Trevor Keeble

On Saturday 6 November 1869 Emily Hall recorded in her diary that while shopping about London, in pouring rain she had 'discussed the plans for altering the house & making a library with Mr. Shaw = his plans won't do – in some respects = but we have now fairly broken the ice – taken the first steps – & shall I hope go on successfully'.[1] Emily's hopes for a successful venture into what she termed 'bricks and mortar mania' would in the short term at least, prove somewhat in vain.

This chapter considers a very specific moment in the Hall sister's lives when over the period 1869–1872 they undertook to remodel their home. Through a close reading of the sisters' diaries the chapter aims to uncover the very specific conditions surrounding the commission, construction and payment of domestic building work during the late nineteenth century. The evidence of the diaries exposes a complex and dynamic relationship between the Hall sisters as middle-class clients and Richard Norman Shaw as an increasingly prolific 'gentleman' architect. This relationship, enacted at the juncture between public and private spheres, underwent considerable revision and negotiation in the processes of decision-making and choice. This revision centres upon the relative authority and status of the parties concerned.

In a broader sense, the material considered explores the relationship of the female client to the male architect more generally, and questions

the uncertain interface between what has been characterised as the feminine sphere of the home and the public realm of professional architecture in this period. The chapter uses the Hall sisters' diaries to uncover factors and evidence which challenge and complicate any 'assumed' position of the female householder in the second half of the nineteenth century, and which in turn indicate the increasing influence of the 'gentleman' architect over the sovereignty of the private sphere. Ultimately, this chapter suggests that this influence and authority are derived not simply through the gendered domination of a female householder by a male architect but also through the increasing subjugation of the domestic sphere to the expectation and regulation of the public realm, irrespective of the gender of the head of the household.

Emily Hall (1819–1901) lived with her younger sister Ellen (1822–1911) in the village of West Wickham near Bromley (Figures 2.1 and 2.2). The youngest of six surviving siblings, they lived unmarried at Ravenswood, the home left to them on the death of their father in 1853 (Figure 2.3). The lives which both sisters document in their diaries spanned the second half of the nineteenth century and reflect the increasingly genteel poverty which their decisions not to marry forced upon them. Throughout their lifelong partnership the sisters appear to have established personal

2.3
Front view of Ravenswood
Bromley Borough Council.
Ref: F8/136

identities which, though intrinsically interdependent, are quite different and in many ways complementary. Of the two, Emily was undoubtedly the more dominant and maintained a position of independence, a position which she clearly contrasted to her married friends. Although perhaps atypical as examples of Victorian lives, Emily and Ellen Hall lived extremely active and full lives as single women which seem in only the most limited of circumstances to have been circumscribed by their lack of husbands. They travelled widely in Europe, often in order to let their home, and from the 1870s they frequented Algeria almost annually on one occasion taking up residence for some three years. The diaries, which comprise a combined forty-five volumes, detail the everyday lives of the women and their society, and in this context shed light on the workings of Victorian domestic material culture.

The journals, as the sisters referred to them, were deposited along with those of their older married sister, Louisa Sherrard, in the Kent Archives Office in 1962, before being moved to the Bromley Borough Archives in 1984. Edited extracts and summaries of the diaries were published under the titles *Two Victorian Girls*, *The Halls of Ravenswood* and *Two Victorian Ladies*, however, these were constructed as linear narratives of what was considered at the time as the largely inconsequential lives of the sisters.[2] These publications are imbued with an anti-Victorianism redolent of the mid-twentieth century. In recent years the diaries have been used and cited within local history studies of West Wickham and the surrounding areas, most notably in Joyce Walker's *Vanished West Wickham*[3] but they have yet to be the subject of exhaustive analysis and criticism.

The diary has emerged as a very particular source for the writing of women's histories as is suggested by Anaïs Nin's account of her own diary writing which she characterises as providing a space and moment for her authentic self, a self not revealed in public, 'I did what I called my duty. But at the same time the diary kept my other self alive, it showed what I really wanted, what I really felt, what I really thought.'[4] The role of the diary as a personal and objective account of thoughts and feelings needs to be continually questioned. Certainly with regard to the diaries of Emily and Ellen Hall, it is possible to suggest that each may have had access to the journal of the other and that this would have undoubtedly affected the content. However, while it is clear that the diaries give form to what the sisters 'discussed and deplored, pronounced and praised, assessing everyone and everything',[5] they also convey a self-consciousness born, not simply from the possibility of the scrutiny of others but of a need to explain themselves and meditate upon their marginalised position within the world. Lynn Bloom has suggested that the truly private diary is in many ways largely perfunctory and gives little 'feeling'. This occurs because 'In such truly private diaries the diarist does not shape the evidence to reinforce a preconceived and therefore self-controlled authorial persona.'[6] This conclusion appears to deny any preconception or self-control which I would suggest was fundamental to the ascribed position of middle-class Victorian women, and which is highly evident in the writing of the Hall sisters, in particular Emily. What Bloom suggests as 'feeling' might be interpreted more broadly as 'character', and need not be construed as evidence of an 'audience hovering at the edge of the page' but an essential manifestation of an author's breeding, character and opinion, qualities which in the absence of employment, husband or children gave self-definition to a Victorian woman's everyday life. In their study of women's diary writing, Suzanne L. Bunkers and Cynthia A. Huff have suggested the diary is a 'logical' object for the interdisciplinary study of everyday life. By studying the diary they propose,

> a genre that challenges boundaries and enhances transdisciplinary thinking by indicating how the content and form of diaries disclose how we construct knowledge, and by helping us understand how we relate to ourselves, to others, and to our culture through the mediation of language.[7]

Drawing on the work of Mary Jane Moffat and Charlotte Painter, Bunkers and Huff went on to suggest the diary as a meaningful form to women, 'partly because it is an analogue to their lives: emotional, fragmentary, interrupted, modest, not to be taken seriously, private, restricted, daily, trivial, formless, concerned with self, as endless as their tasks'.[8] In many senses this analogy might be extended to the domestic space of the private sphere and in so doing, reveal the ways in which domestic culture, another manifestation of the feminine, has been subordinated by the public realm.

Griselda Pollock has articulated the ideological implications and practical manifestations of the separate spheres as a key and defining feature of modernity, and it is within the context of the gendered problematic which she identifies that the Hall sisters' writings about their domestic choices and interactions are considered.

> The public and private division functioned on many levels. As a metaphorical map in ideology, it structured the very meaning of the terms 'masculine' and 'feminine' within its mythic boundaries. In practice, as the ideology of domesticity became hegemonic, it regulated women's and men's behaviour in the respective public and private spaces. Presence in either of the domains determined one's social identity and therefore, in objective terms, the separation

of the spheres problematized women's relation to the very activities and experiences we typically accept as defining modernity.[9]

While much of the material discussed in this chapter questions the lived reality of the separated spheres, it nonetheless articulates the daily frustrations of women challenged by the authority of the public realm.

For the Hall sisters of West Wickham, Emily in particular, diary-keeping allowed a woman to make her case in such a way as to give meaning to her life. Such diligent and conscientious diary-keeping over such an extended period of time reveals the sister's belief in the importance of a Victorian woman's life and, possibly, that one day her words might even be read.

In his biography *Richard Norman Shaw*, Andrew Saint notes under 'miscellaneous jobs' that Shaw's account book recorded the sum of £48 12s 2d received in 1873 from Miss Hall of Ravenswood, West Wickham.[10] The reasoning behind the Hall sisters' choice of architect is never actually documented within their diaries, however, it is fair to say that their commissioning of Richard Norman Shaw to make alterations to their home is most likely due to works he had undertaken locally for Mr and Mrs Craik (née Dinah Mullock) at Shortlands, and Mr William McAndrew Steuart at West Wickham House.[11] In their discussion of their neighbours' alterations both sisters expressed an ambivalence about their architect's work as is clear from the account Emily made of a visit to the Steuarts in May 1870:

> Went over Mr Steuarts place – the same architect Mr. Shaw is doing his – & nearly all of it is coming down! – the timbers in many parts are rotten – & they have found the strangest arrangement – a set of bell wires actually going thro' a chimney! – & in another part a flue was giving way, cracked seriously, into a chimney which was stuffed with straw – so that the slightest accident in the world would have sufficed beset it all on fire – Mr. Shaw has persisted in the old site – which is the greatest mistake – seeing that he has more than 70 acres in front with a pretty outlook which the old place has not.[12]

The very next day Emily and Ellen visited Mrs Craik at Shortlands. Emily provided a description of Mrs Craik's dining room and its inglenook fireplace, which despite its subsequent centrality to Shaw's idiom and its fervent mythologising within the 'Old English' style, is a feature evidently somewhat new to her,

> We looked in at the Craik's house = the dining room has a most enchanting "ingle-nook"- that is a recess with a window at each

end – & the fireplace in the middle – divided from the room by an archway projecting where one can sit and read + big enough for huge armchairs = pictures = a rich colouring – most enchanting – & quite a piece for a picture = the mantel has for a motto " East or West Hame is Best". Mr Shaw has made some great mistakes to my thinking, but generally I approve his taste = but he should have projected the eaves & put Barge boards.[13]

Also finding the room 'quite charming' Ellen questioned the architect's taste in paint, 'the room is spoiled by vile dark greenish blue colour used round the skirting & the doors & the beams across the ceiling. I could not help looking at this heavy ugly colour with astonishment.'[14] Having initially engaged Shaw to simply put new windows into their drawing room, Emily met with him in June 1870 to discuss the possibility of more extensive building work,

Had an interview with Mr. Shaw & made arrangements about putting a room over the drawing rooms incited thereto by the charming room of that kind at Mr. Christies. He will permit me this time to have if pretty; it is to go high up in the roof & to have a level ceiling, something ornamented – I hope we shall manage at last to have something pretty.[15]

Evidently bitten by both the desire to expand, and the charms of their neighbour's property, the decision to build a new room seems to have preceded any discussion about its purpose or use. For the two sisters, and their live-in cook and maid, space was certainly not in any great shortage. This uncertainty of purpose is apparent when Emily described the new room as 'the library – or attic – or whatever it will be called'.[16] Having engaged Shaw to build them a new room, Emily found both he and Simpson, the builder, refusing to put up some old oak panelling which the sisters had acquired from the Bromley College Chapel for their Hall. Emily was quite outraged by their declaration that 'it will cost so much for the show of it! & recommend me to sell it!!!!!'[17] In rejecting their advice Emily identified a complicity in Shaw and Simpson, and noted that, 'They butter one another up incessantly – Mr Simpson praises Mr Shaw's designs & he Mr Simpson's work, & Stuarts the foreman as is duty bound administers mild doses of admiration to both!'[18]

A central concern of both sisters was that the wood used in their renovation would remain unpainted and it is on this point that they met with the objection of their architect. Showing their neighbour Mr Harrison around the ongoing works, Emily noted:

He inspected the work carefully & admired it generally, only thinking (of course) that I am wrong in not having it painted – & in not having larger panes of glass – The plain wood is my own doing – the glass I have left to Mr Shaw = on whose shoulders the praise or the shame must rest.[19]

Despite Emily's resolve against paint, a visit to the newly renovated Wimbledon home of Mrs Kingston Oliphant gave her momentary cause for reflection,

they have used deal unpainted throughout their house = & very nice indeed it looks = tho' I am obliged to confess that in some parts it has got sadly <u>dinted</u> as Mr. Shaw says it will = & for which he objects against it. The walls are done with Pompeian papers – & the effect is altogether very quiet and good.[20]

The relative position and expectation of the sisters as commissioning clients of Norman Shaw are suggested by a diary entry which details Mr Simpson's attempts to get the sisters to indulge their architect's wishes. Informing Emily that the wood used was always intended to be painted and was hence of inferior quality, Simpson urged her to reconsider 'if you could persuade yourself to paint and decorate it as Mr. Shaw designed it Ma'am it would be the most beautiful room in the country', to which Emily countered according to her own reasoning 'but quite unsuited to the rest of the house'.[21] It might be tempting to suggest that these attempts by architect and builder to assert their professional authority were simply an articulation of gendered domination, however, within the context of the domestic space such an understanding is complicated by evidence that these professional controlling impulses found less resistance from male clients such as William Steuart. Emily recorded that, while admiring her ornamented ceiling, Mr Steuart confided that he too had 'wanted to have geometrical ceilings in his own home but Mr Shaw would not let him on account of the expense'.[22] The use of the motto in the later nineteenth-century domestic interior represented one of the most explicit attempts to construct 'identity' for the domestic space. Referred to as 'sentimental texts', Saint notes that these domestic inscriptions, usually found above an inglenook fireplace as in the Craiks' home at Shortlands, were beloved by the picturesque architects such as W.E. Nesfield and Shaw to such an extent that he suggests they made them 'their own'.[23] Saint goes on to suggest that '"East or West Home's Best" wins hands down on number of appearances.'[24] The very choice of motto presented the opportunity for the householder to confirm the authority of their architect or decorator, or alternatively assign the room with a character of their own, as is suggested by the following diary entry concerning the new home of the Kingston Oliphants of Wimbledon:

> The hall is open to the top of the house, with a gallery running round it from which the bedrooms open. On the woodwork supporting this gallery he has printed in Latin "Except the Lord build the house their labour is but lost that build it." I suppose they had said something to the architect about having a legend, for he sent down to them two of his own choice, for their approval, "Oh, that this house may ever be the home of love and charity" which as Mr. Oliphant said laughing was very much like the tale of a Valentine or the motto from a Cracker – & the other "From envy hatred malice & all uncharitableness Good Lord deliver us" which they did not like very much better. There own selection is very good only that instead of being painted I think it has been carved in the wood.[25]

Unlike many of Shaw's clients, the Kingston-Oliphants chose to reject their architect's suggestions in favour of an inscription of their own, and in doing so make an explicit and personal mark on the interior of their home.[26]

By July 1870 Emily recorded that work on the 'attic' or 'sumptuous room' as 'Mr. Shaw calls it'[27] was under way and she looked forward to her forthcoming extended visit to Europe which would keep her away from the 'dust & discomfort' of the building work. On Monday 25 July Emily and Ellen left Ravenswood for the Continent.

Little mention was made of the alterations at home until late September when repeated reports from an unidentified correspondent suggested that there were only two men working on the project which would often be left alone completely for many days at a time. Emily was provoked to write, 'a regular scold to Mr. Shaw of the contractor = a most comfortable scapegoat, as I could not scold Mr. S!'[28] Shaw's response arrived a month later and was so unyielding in its tone Ellen felt she had to conceal it from Emily for a whole day. The letter which was found by Emily to be 'most discourteous'[29] complained that the sisters had failed to make financial provision for the work and expenses of the builder:

> both Simpson and I have fully redeemed our promises & I have no doubt that when you see the work you will regret having treated us so ... not having the money makes me very helpless as it is due twice over![30]

Emily vehemently contested the charges that she had in some way neglected her financial obligations by writing a letter to Shaw which reminded him of their discussion prior to her departure and his reassurances that no money would be required before her return at Christmas.

> The letter is enough to make any one angry: the whole tone is most discourteous: I may say ungentlemanly: he implies that we have neglected to pay Simpson's just demands for work done, "which is due & due twice over", the consequence of which is that S. has thrown up the contract! – & we shall have to pay more to get it no (*sic*) finished. The fact being that before we left England Mr Shaw told us, when we called to make arrangements about paying, that Simpson would wait until Xmas. We have written to Mr. Shaw six different times without receiving any answer: & we have received no certificate of any sort from either Mr. Shaw or Simpson – It seems to me an extraordinary thing, that not having made any demand for money the builder should be able to throw up a contract because he does not get it: when moreover he had arranged to wait two months longer for it! – But of course they can settle the matter as they choose, & we are utterly helpless – Mr Shaw has only written to us once before this very angry, impertinent & ungentlemanly letter & in that he made passing remark "I have had to give Simpson an order for money" – nothing more. The last time Simpson wanted money Mr Shaw wrote a certificate that "So far the work was done according to agreement" & we paid the sum required at once. But he seems to imagine that his slight observation was to be met by us, by our sending a cheque for an unmentioned sum! tho' he had told us no money would be wanted until Christmas! – I think he must have been irritated in some way & wrote under that feeling to us: having quite forgotten his own arrangements.[31]

The sisters set about concocting a reply which would eventually be written twice due to having been torn up initially. Ellen hoped it 'would make Mr. Shaw shake in his shoes'.[32] Nevertheless, having had their say in reply to Mr Shaw, Emily used the pages of her diary to reflect upon his 'odious' letter at some length and in doing so clearly ascribes a somewhat liminal social position to her architect:

> I am much disappointed, because I thought he was a gentleman, with whom we could be on pleasant relations – now we shall have to be as stiff as fire irons, & always on the merest business terms. There was a fire at Simpson's workshop some weeks ago, which delayed the work considerably & I can not help thinking that this

has put both builder & architect <u>out</u> – of their reckoning & their temper too! Unless he writes us a humble letter of excuse or apology, which being a Scotchman he <u>won't</u> do, there is an end of any like pleasure in our transactions. I felt tempted to send him a cheque for all of the money we could spare, without a word + but we decided it would be better to write & we concocted a letter between us, which will I hope make him feel a little ashamed of himself – if it is possible ever to penetrate the crocodile skin of self conceit which a Scotchman carries about with him! It has all vexed & annoyed me excessively because we took all precautions against such an event =& having appropriated the needful money in July, we placed it in a deposit bank = on finding that it would not be wanted until xmas. We could just as easily arranged to draw out £100 monthly, had Mr. S wished for it.[33]

Within the month a reply came from Shaw, 'declaring that in 5 weeks he had received as many letters complaining of the slowness of the work & soundly upbraiding him, for neglecting our interests which he had under-taken to protect'.[34] Emily's revised assessment of Shaw's character was con-firmed and reiterated upon receiving his response:

> Received – at last, a letter for Mr. Shaw = which so far sets mat-ters straight, that we shall be able to carry on our business; but no more = he is not a gentleman: & I had thought he was so from hence forward I must treat him as a tradesman = & put the pleas-anter notions quite aside. I said he was too much of a Scotchman to make an apology, & I was so far right, – he has made none & his letter is a curious mixture of self vindication, acknowledge-ment that he "was partly to blame" in that he had quite forgotten the conversation in July about the money, & thirdly throwing all of the fault of his angry impertinent & most ungentlemanly & indefensible letter on us! – But in one way he makes bad, worse in his self vindication.[35]

Despite this evident reclassification of Shaw's social standing and the revised manner in which she would now do business with him, Emily's dis-cussion of the matter ended with a concession which obviously recognised his talent and also his wider social standing as an increasingly eminent fig-ure within his field,

> I don't choose to take any notice of his letter or only the very slightest – as I don't wish to put it out of my power to employ him again at any future time + but this is an end of everything, every

word – but the simplest & hardest business –.[36]

To all intents, the matter of the rather fractious correspondence seems to have ended there, and within the fortnight Emily and Ellen returned home to Ravenswood in the early evening of Tuesday 6 December. Their joy at being once again home seems to have been only slightly marred by the unfinished state of the building 'thanks to the dawdling dilatoriness of the Builder'[37] and yet this state of relative calm was to be short-lived as Emily discovered the next day when she ventured to inspect the work:

> The new room has been <u>painted</u>! I am perfectly furious at Mr Shaw – I have no words to say how abominably I think he has acted, = if there was one point I insisted on more than another it was that there should be no paint anywhere – & now I find that just because we have been away all the woodwork has been daubed over with this detestable white paint = taking advantage of our being away to do what he must know I should never have allowed if I had been at home – it makes me dislike the whole addition – glaring ghastly odious chalky abomination – where I wanted only simple wood – I was very angry with Mr Shaw for his most impertinent I may say insolent letter about the money – but really this painting is beyond endurance =& I hardly know what to do or say – However it shall be taken off & let him say what he will it is perfectly intolerable that a man should take one's orders & make one pay for employing him and then free his own fancies upon one in this manner = I won't endure it – the inside is all unfinished – filled with scaffolding =& the windows with glass such as I hate all yellow & green, instead of being pure & colourless – in short I am disgusted & extremely angry – & regret very much that we trusted anything to him instead of having every single particular down in black and white =& then he talks of our not having any confidence in him! I treated him like a gentleman – & he isn't one – & I made a great mistake –.[38]

The work found slightly more moderate opinion from Ellen who thought that although 'the wood work has been painted though expressly against Emily's wishes – ...the outline is very picturesque & good'. However, 'The white paint outside & ugly glass inside (just what I hate yellow – thick & green all dotted about) make it very unlike what we expected or intended.'[39]

Evidently despite discussion of the design and provision of what Emily referred to as a sketch,[40] the scheme for the sisters 'sumptuous room' had gone somewhat awry in the their absence. Once again Emily was moved to contact her architect, and his response, much to her annoyance, articulated his envisaged distance between himself and his clients:

> Mr Shaw and I am likely to come to fisty cuffs – in words – I wrote a short note expressing my surprise at finding the wood work painted = against my distinctly expressed wishes = & he replies by a few words which really made my blood boil = for a while "that he must know best – & that the paint was right – & that if I would ask the opinion of any one capable of giving an opinion I should probably thinks so too". It is well I am compelled to write & not to speak or he would probably throw up the whole affair. However in writing I have endeavoured to do so calmly, tho positively refusing to have his or any ones views forced upon us against my clearly expressed wishes – when he first undertook the work – & requiring him to have it taken off – The man has a violent temper & a more than usual scotch determination to be always in the right tho' it is against the whole world ... I begin to wish I had never set eyes upon him = however good his taste as architect may be, it is rather too bad that he should undertake the work, knowing my wishes, & then force his own upon me regardless of what I wish – His manners are plausible – so long as he carried the thing entirely his own way.[41]

This diary entry clearly reflects the extent to which Emily's (and possibly Ellen's) sovereignty as a client was being imposed upon by the professional authority of her architect, and following a visit from him she attempts to explain and articulate her objections. In this explanation she clearly asserted her propriety of an individual taste, separate from any notion of a professional or architectural taste:

> Mr Shaw came – as he said:- I felt so angry & indignant that I could hardly bring myself to speak to him – He insists upon it, that he did not understand that I objected against paint outside!! -& thought it was only to the inside work my dislike applied & which only shows I was a fool not to have everything written down = to treat him as if he were a gentleman, he feels like a tradesman & I should have acted towards him as such = nothing could be plainer than my words: & I am perfectly certain that he did understand perfectly at the beginning, but being self-opinionated, & forgetful, he may have forgotten it. However he has given orders that it shall be scraped off inside = I have agreed to wait a few months to see if I can reconcile myself to the paint outside, if not he will have it

all taken off. – I am quite sure that I will not like then any better than now – He may talk as he will about colour but paint must always be abominable = it was only used to make cheap deal last, when houses were built with oak wood, no one ever dreamt of painting it & if cheap deal could be preserved from the effects of weather & retain even its pale colour, it would soon be felt to suit better with English Red brick, than any kind of dead chalky colour. But of course when Mr. Shaw truly enough but most discourteously says "I must know best" I can only reply = "unquestionably in your line – but this is a point of taste & of taste there is not limit in disputing -" acting on the Diplomatists principle of "treating your enemies as if they might one day be your friends," I put a huge complaint on myself – so we parted more amiably than we met, tho I managed to shake hands with him – which I don't think he expected & I did only to please Ellen.[42]

By asserting her right to her individual taste Emily Hall established a distance between herself and her architect, less in terms of degrees of profession and more along the definitions of class. Her repeated attempts to denigrate Shaw as merely a tradesman were symptomatic of a middle-class anxiety which would find fuller elaboration some years later in the work of Mrs H.R. Haweis. In her 1881 publication *The Art of Decoration*, Mary Eliza Haweis championed the role of individuality in the creation of the domestic space. Her book is perhaps less concerned with the practicalities and processes of decorating than with 'the cool power of choice'.[43] Having proposed an 'instinctual' character to art which 'properly applied would counteract the influence of books'. Mrs Haweis asserted the defining power of the consumer, 'Changes must emanate from the public, not from their servant, the producer: for it is they who pay for the work, not any elect body'.[44] Of the architect she suggested, 'He is so hampered by superstitions and opposition that he is often but an upper-class builder, when he *ought* to be a "phoenix for fine and curious masonrie."'[45] Interestingly, this is a position not too different from that articulated by Shaw himself when called upon, some years later, to defend the noble cause of architecture from the moves toward professionalisation. In his essay concerning 'The Fallacy that the Architect who Makes Design his first Consideration must be Impractical' of 1892, Shaw drew a number of divisions between the true architect as 'artist' and mere 'practical men'.[46] He suggested that public concerns regarding the regulation of architects arose from the public's desire to prioritise sound and economic building over 'imagination, power of design and refinement of taste'.[47] The resulting proposals to use the Institute's letters (RIBA) as a badge confirming the ability and standing of the architect were dismissed by Shaw as 'very tradesmanlike and in very poor taste'. This position stemmed from a belief, held by certain other of Shaw's contemporaries, that architecture as an 'art' was unexaminable and therefore unregulatable. A principal argument of the 'Memorialists', as those opposed to professionalisation became known, was that regulation would separate architecture from the other arts.[48] This, it has been suggested, characterised the approach of Shaw as 'the sympathetic sovereign-architect enabling the work of craftsmen',[49] a characterisation common to those architects such as W.R. Lethaby who in the late nineteenth century built within the 'arts & craft' tradition but perhaps less appropriate for Shaw, who drew repeatedly on the model of the master builder in his celebration of Brunelleschi, Michelangelo and Wren. The roots of Shaw's own conviction lay in his belief that, 'a man must, beyond all doubt, be endowed by nature with the special gift; that he cannot acquire any more than people unendowed with the necessary gifts can expect to become painters or sculptors'.[50]

Such an essentialist characterisation of the artist clearly mirrors Mrs Haweis' declaration that 'the artist, the true Phoenix, whether cultured or not, is born, not made'[51] and in many ways is consonant with Emily Hall's somewhat class-based belief that 'of taste there is not limit in disputing', and yet both Emily Hall and Richard Norman Shaw sought to distance themselves from one another, thus establishing themselves as the authority of this particular and contested domestic space. Even Emily's subsequent attempts to restore cordial feeling with her architect only reaffirmed her dissatisfaction and outright disdain for Shaw:

> A letter came from Mr. Shaw – in reply to mine, I felt it only due to myself in requiring that the wood work should be cleaned of the paint he has had put on, to show him that I have grounds, reasonable & well considered for my objections = I wrote formally – & only to the point: but it would have been better to leave well alone – for he has the impertinence to "compliment one on the altered tone of your letter – which is the pleasantest I have received since July last" – he puts himself completely on a level with me & plainly thinks he is rather gracious & condescending in wishing "you & your sister a happy new year & c, & c,." – He is a radically <u>vulgar</u> man, who piques himself upon being "quite a gentleman", & whose assumption is in consequence intolerable & being a Scotchman, & therefor incapable of making a mistake or an apology he absolutely tells falsehoods, in pursuance of his self

justification – as I am sure he did when saying he did not understand that I objected so much to paint – The more I think about the work the worse I feel he has acted & now acts. He has considered himself & the Builders, & has let us go to the wall entirely = & now is angry & impertinent because we feel & resent his so treating us –.'[52]

Emily and Ellen found another means of going against the opinion of their architect by finding someone to install the old oak panelling in their hall which he had so forcefully refused to do. In March 1871 Emily wrote:

Bagaley & his men have begun the work that I am now glad Mr. Shaw refused to undertake as he has been so disagreeable it is far better we should have as little to do with him as possible. The Hall is to be panelled with the oak which Mr. Shaw stigmatised as "a lot of old pews" – out of the Bromley College Chapel. So they began by stripping everything back to the brickwork ... Bagaley is to press the work forward so as if possible to give us a tidy home by Easter.[53]

Shortly after this work had commenced Ellen Hall recalled a visit from Lady Caroline Legge which may have led Emily to temporarily regret her decision to re-use the old oak. While viewing the preparations for the panelled hall Lady Caroline noticed the inscription in gold letter to the benevolent Miss Shepherd whose endowment to Bromley College had provided the oak for the college chapel from whence it came. 'It puzzled her so much that Em was forced to explain that the oak came from the Bromley College chapel. She did not appear to be at all shocked by it as Emily thought.'[54] Shaw's opinion of the refurbished hall is never alluded to, however, on its completion Emily recorded that:

the carpenters have only left the Hall on Saturday tho' it is our own & mostly by our own wits adorned. I must say it is <u>delightful</u> & so pretty – Bagaley – has done it very well – of course there are <u>blots</u> – I see some mistakes = made by his not taking in what I wished = but I <u>won't</u> mind them or let them spoil my enjoyment of the rest.[55]

Despite the various and ongoing recriminations concerning the design of the project, it would be another six months before the new room would be inhabitable and in the intervening time Emily and Ellen kept a close eye on the execution of the work, even at times calling upon the opinion of friends and neighbours which allowed for a certain pursuit of their grievance against architect and builder rather than simply a reliable judgement of the work:

> Mr Charles Hoare called & I took him to see the windows in the
> drawing room and he looked at it with the aim of a man who has
> built things himself & knows what they should be like – he
> examined the shutters & quite agreed that the work was not well
> done. – but it amused me to see how this man who seems to have
> no eye for anything but a horse put his finger instantly upon the
> bad pieces of work.[56]

Repeated questioning and complaints about knots in the wood and the
carelessness of the builders eventually led Shaw back to West Wickham
informing the sisters that they had had 'too much of his work already'. This
was because, Emily presumed, she had an opinion of her own and 'objected
to his having not made the hand rail to the new room to match the staircase'.[57]
This accusation was countered by the claim that Emily was being 'hypercritical'
and that the work was relative to the money. The ongoing bad feeling between
architect and clients was clearly felt by Emily to impair her ability to oversee
the construction work as is suggested by the following extract,

> We are abominably used by Shaw and Simpson – they will not
> put any sheeting up & so the rain and the thaw, drip water through
> the roof & into the conservatory, – destroying the plants, flooding
> the floor, & running all over into the drawing room – the work in
> the new room goes on but slowly. I believe Easter will be upon us
> before the place will be habitable – & now it is so disagreeable to
> see Mr. Shaw & even to write to him that I can't choose between
> the annoyances – the wet on the one side – Mr. S's impertinences
> on the other![58]

Unfortunately for the Hall sisters the completion of their renovations did not
see the end to their disagreements with builder and architect and in July
1871 Emily wrote with astonishment that:

> Simpson's Bill has arrived – we had need of a pretty room – & one
> to be admired by all beholders! for the sum total is frightful! When
> I saw the figures I laughed = otherwise I should have cried! we
> expected £650 – & the sum he demands is £996 –! & this when not
> one brick or plank has been altered from Shaw's design. If we
> <u>must</u> pay so much we had need go away & live on a few grains of
> rice daily – till we have saved the money! but it is a hard case for
> us! & comes of having no contract![59]

Having forwarded Simpson's demand to Shaw, who declared the charges
far too high and "simply absurd", Emily received a visit from the builder

which angered her enormously due to his never having managed 'to call when we wanted to see him on our own account'. This encounter did little to reconcile Emily and Ellen to either architect or builder and only served to heighten their suspicion of the men's motives and their complicit intent:

> E came in and put a stop to it; being very angry at his impertinence at going into the drawing room. She thinks, correctly I fancy, that Mr. Shaw being angry with us but also feeling the Bill to be unfair told Simpson to try what he could do himself, privately thinking if we were such geese as to pay the demand without his certification, why we could! However Mr Simpson has taken nothing of his motion at present & I am resolved not to give anything till Mr. Shaw says I must – It is no wonder Builders and Architects are always making their Bills higher than expected, if they always go on as Mr Shaw did – Getting estimates for part of the work & leaving the rest & doing it all in a loose unbusiness like fashion: having no contract & altering the work after it has been begun as S. says he did with our windows – making the agreements for ordinary glass & then putting in a plate glass at over £40! additional price! of which not one word was ever said to us![60]

It would be a whole year before Emily would be able to record that Mr Shaw had managed to get Simpson's bill reduced by £200 to £796 which even then was felt to be a good £200 in excess of what the sisters had expected. 'Such is the folly', Emily felt, 'of beginning a work without a contract because we are made to suppose the architect is a <u>gentleman</u>. I would not mind if the work was good but the joiner part is <u>abominable</u>!'[61] In spite of their very clear misgivings about the work of their architect, it wasn't long before his addition to their house began to attract welcome attention and it seems that this attention somewhat mitigated the anxieties of recent months.

> Mr Steuart walked home with me & manifested so great a desire to see the new room, that in spite of all the scaffolding being about I took him up – he expressed himself greatly delighted with it = specially with the ceiling & on seeing the outside laughingly declared that "we shall never be able to endure the old part with its box like squareness – he foresaw we shall soon be altering it." … "You are like the gentleman who in an evil hour received a present of a pair of embroidered slippers – it obliged him to refurbish his whole house!"[62]

Mr Steuart's prophesy was certainly acknowledged in part some weeks later when Emily confided to her diary that 'indeed it is plain that we shall have someday of necessity to alter the outside – the new & the old will else drive us out of our wits. The West bedroom box is unendurable beside the picturesque wing which Mr Shaw has given us',[63] (Figures 2.4, 2.5 and 2.6). Such talk of picturesque gifts does little, however, to lessen the animosity which the sisters felt for their architect. In February 1871 Emily attended a dinner party at the Craiks where she attempted to explain her ongoing dispute to Mr Craik whom she found rather unsympathetic,

> For he declared that it was "his business to study such questions, & he knew best & therefor if he (Mr. Shaw) said paint was best, he should let him paint," – So that I soon saw it was no more use talking to him on this matter than talking to a child – he assured us "he had no contract" – "he never saw a contract" – "He spent a great deal more than the contract" – "there never was any trouble about money between us – I gave him money whenever he wanted it" & so on, back & forwards, contradicting himself continually = from which I argued that he really knew nothing about the business & that it was all managed by his wife: who I suspects looks sharply after the financial matters – He assured me he has always found Mr Shaw "a perfect gentleman"![64]

Returning once again to the vexed issue of the 'absent contract' Emily asserted her grievance against the architect and the builder, but also more generally against a public world where dishonesty and avarice were the guiding principles and the binding legality of a contract was a person's only defence. Whereas once a person's class and status may have assured a degree of honesty and even-handedness, such certainties concerning the standing of a 'gentleman' or a 'tradesman' were clearly becoming undone.

In her essay, 'Women Architects', Lynne Walker has suggested that the ruminations concerning the practice and status of architecture as either profession or art, and the subsequent reclassification of 'architect' from the 'Industrial Class' of the 1881 census to that of 'artist' in the 'Professional Class' of the census ten years later made architecture "a potentially suitable activity for women"'.[65] Yet, in spite of this, even those male architects who supported the entry of women to their ranks were found to ascribe them a significantly lesser position.[66] In truth, it seems the only direct role for women within the practice of architecture during the late nineteenth century was as a client and, as this chapter has shown, even here the possibilities for participation in this capacity were often limited and circumscribed by the expectations and demands of the 'professional' sphere (whether it chose to identify itself as

2.4
West view of Ravenswood showing the exterior and balcony of the Shaw addition to the house. *c.* mid 1920s
Bromley Borough Council. Ref: L26.8

2.5
Exterior side view of the Shaw addition to the house. *c.* mid-1920s
Bromley Borough Council. Ref: L26.8

2.6
Photograph of the interior of the Shaw addition to the house. This image was used for a promotional brochure when the house was briefly the 'Ravenswood Private Hotel' during the mid-1920s
Bromley Borough Council. Ref: L26.8

such or not). An extremely convincing case has been made by a number of historians of architecture, design and gender, which explains and exposes the historical marginalisation of women within the processes of design and building.[67] However, in many senses, this chapter is concerned with the ways in which the manifestations of this process have led to the marginalisation and subjugation of the domestic sphere as a whole. Whether this arises as the refusal to hang 'old oak' for Emily Hall, or the refusal to 'allow' an ornamented ceiling for Mr Steuart, or the free and unquestioning supply of money from Mr Craik, this form of subjugation of the client's will seems to be an increasing factor in the practice of domestic architecture in the late nineteenth century and cannot simply be attributed to 'a more than usual scotch determination to be always in the right'.

Notes

1   Emily Hall. 6th November 1869, p. 76.
    When citing the Hall sisters' diaries this
    chapter will refer to the date of entry and
    page number. Because there is no
    systematic order regarding volumes and
    years this will avoid confusion.
    Throughout their diary writing Emily and
    Ellen Hall established conventions of
    grammar and punctuation, particularly
    using the characters –, and =. Although
    these initially appear somewhat
    idiosyncratic, in the period under study
    these are remarkably consistent and have
    been reproduced as faithfully as possible.

2   O.A. Sherrard, *Two Victorian Girls*,
    London: Frederick Muller Ltd, 1966, A.R.
    Mills, *The Halls of Ravenswood*, London:
    Frederick Muller Ltd, 1967, A.R. Mills,
    Two Victorian Ladies, London: Frederick
    Muller Ltd, 1969.

3   J. Walker. *Vanished West Wickham*, West
    Wickham, London: Hollies Publications,
    1994.

4   quoted in C. Cline, *Women's Diaries,
    Journals, and Letters: An Annotated
    Bibliography*, New York and London:
    Garland Publishing 1989, p. xi.

5   Sherrard, op. cit., p. vii.

6   L. Bloom, '"I Write for Myself and
    Strangers": Private Diaries as Public
    Documents,' in S.L. Bunkers and C.A.
    Huff (eds), *Inscribing the Daily: Critical
    Essays on Women's Diaries*, Amherst, MA:
    University of Massachusetts Press, 1996,
    p. 27.

7   S.L. Bunkers and C.A. Huff, op. cit.,
    pp.1–2

8   Quoted in S.L. Bunkers and C.A.Huff, op.
    cit., p 11.

9   G. Pollock, *Vision and Difference:
    Femininity, Feminism and Histories of Art*,
    London: Routledge, 1988, pp. 69–70.

10 A. Saint, *Richard Norman Shaw*, London:
    Yale University Press, 1976, p. 436.

11 The Corner House, 114 Shortlands Road,
    Beckenham, London was newly designed
    and built during the period 1868–69 with
    later additions in 1872 and West
    Wickham House, High Street, West
    Wickham, London, was remodelled
    during the period 1869–1871. See A.
    Saint, op. cit., pp. 406–7.

12 Emily Hall, *Diaries*, 6th May 1870, p. 94.

13 Emily Hall, *Diaries*, 7th May 1870, p. 96.

14 Ellen Hall, *Diaries*, 1st March 1870, pp.
    24–5.

15 Emily Hall, *Diaries*, 21st June 1870, p. 119.
16 Emily Hall, *Diaries*, 23rd June 1870, p. 121.
17 Emily Hall, *Diaries*, 2nd June 1870, p. 109.
18 Ibid.
19 Emily Hall, *Diaries*, 10th July 1870, pp. 135–6.
20 Emily Hall, *Diaries*, 11th July 1870, pp. 136–7.
21 Emily Hall, *Diaries*, 28th March 1870, p. 336.
22 Emily Hall, *Diaries*, 16th July 1871, p. 417.
23 Saint, op. cit., p. 116.
24 Ibid., p. 447.
25 Emily Hall, *Diaries*, 11th July 1870, pp. 136–7.
26 During May 1875 the *Furniture Gazette* published a series of suggestions for 'Mottos for Home Decoration and Furniture.' Published in three separate parts the articles made suggestions of mottos appropriate to particular rooms such as libraries or dining rooms. *Furniture Gazette*, vol. 3 Jan–Jun 1875 pp. 557, 591, 655.
27 Emily Hall, *Diaries*, 12th July 1870, p. 138.
28 Emily Hall, *Diaries*, 24th September 1870, p. 203.
29 Emily Hall, *Diaries*, 30th October 1870, pp. 226–7.
30 Ellen Hall, *Diaries*, 29th October 1870, p. 168.
31 Emily Hall, *Diaries*, 30th October 1870, pp. 226–7.
32 Ellen Hall, *Diaries*, 31st October 1870, p. 169.
33 Emily Hall, *Diaries*, 30th October 1870, pp. 226–7.
34 Emily Hall, *Diaries*, 26th November 1870, pp. 243–4.
35 Ibid, pp. 243–4.
36 Ibid, p. 244.
37 Emily Hall, *Diaries*, 6th December 1870 (unpaginated).
38 Emily Hall, *Diaries*, 7th December 1870, p. 254.
39 Ellen Hall, *Diaries*, 9th December 1870, p. 210.
40 Emily recorded that she discussed the design with her neighbour Mr Harrison who 'took great interest in the sketch & approved it highly' (Emily Hall, *Diaries*, 10th July 1870 pp. 135–6).
41 Emily Hall, *Diaries*, 10th December 1870, p. 255.
42 Emily Hall, *Diaries*, 12th December 1870, p. 256.
43 Mrs. H.R. Haweis, *The Art Of Decoration*, London: Chatto & Windus, 1881, p. 3.
44 Ibid., p. 20.
45 Ibid., p. 404.
46 R. Norman Shaw, 'The Fallacy that the Architect who Makes Design his First Consideration Must be Impractical,' in R. Norman Shaw and T.G. Jackson (eds), *Architecture: A Profession or an Art. Thirteen Short Essays on the Qualifications and Training of Architects*, London: John Murray, 1892, p. 4.
47 Ibid.
48 M. Crinson and J. Lubbock, *Architecture: Art or Profession. Three Hundred Years of Architectural Education in Britain*, Manchester: Manchester University Press, 1994, p. 62.
49 Ibid., p. 63.
50 Shaw, 'The Fallacy that the Architect.', p. 9.
51 Haweis, op. cit., p. 407.
52 Emily Hall, *Diaries*, 25th December 1870, pp. 267–8.
53 Emily Hall, *Diaries*, 7th March 1871, p. 322.
54 Ellen Hall, *Diaries*, 2nd April 1871, p. 273.
55 Emily Hall, *Diaries*, 23rd May 1871, p. 377.
56 Ellen Hall, *Diaries*, 27th January 1871, p. 232.
57 Emily Hall, *Diaries*, 13th March 1871, pp. 323–4.
58 Emily Hall, *Diaries*, 19th January 1871, pp. 284–5.
59 Emily Hall, *Diaries*, 18th July 1871, p. 420.
60 Emily Hall, *Diaries*, 27th July 1871, p. 432.
61 Emily Hall, *Diaries*, 5th July 1872, p. 770.

62 Emily Hall, *Diaries*, 29th January 1871, pp. 294–5.

63 Emily Hall, *Diaries*, 23rd May 1871, p. 377.

64 Emily Hall, *Diaries*, 16th February 1871, pp. 309–10.

65 L. Walker, 'Women Architects,' in J. Attfield and P. Kirkham (eds), *A View from the Interior: Women and Design*, London: The Women's Press, 1989, p. 96.

66 Ibid., p. 98.

67 J. Rendell, B. Penner, and I. Borden (eds) *Gender Space Architecture. An Interdisciplinary Introduction*, London: Routledge, 2000; Attfield and Kirkham, op. cit., P. Sparke, *As Long as It's Pink: The Sexual Politics of Taste*, London: Pandora, 1995.

Chapter 3

Elsie de Wolfe and her female clients, 1905–15

Gender, class and the professional interior decorator

Penny Sparke

> This American home is always a woman's home: a man may build
> and decorate a beautiful house, but it remains for a woman to
> make a home of it for him. It is the personality of the mistress
> that the house expresses. Men are forever guests in our homes,
> no matter how much happiness they may find there.
>
> Elsie de Wolfe[1]

The belief in the existence of a psychological link between women and the
domestic sphere contained in the above statement made by the interior
decorator, Elsie de Wolfe, in her 1913 home-decorating advice book, *The
House in Good Taste,* was rooted in the mid-nineteenth-century idea of the
'separate spheres'. It was clearly still alive and well in the early twentieth
century.[2] By that time, it had effected the emergence of a new female
professional, the interior decorator, an aesthetic practitioner who provided
decorative schemes for the homes of clients who were wealthy enough to
afford her services. That a number of women began to undertake this work
from the 1870s onwards in Britain and in the USA a couple of decades later,

was a result both of the growing custom of women taking on the responsibility for their domestic interior décor as part of their role as 'beautifiers of the home' and of the growing number of middle-class ladies seeking employment outside the home. Inevitably the latter turned to, and were encouraged to undertake, jobs which were extensions of their familiar domestic responsibilities; teaching and social work and a range of aesthetic practices among them.[3] This new imperative rendered ambiguous the much stricter division that had existed hitherto between the private and public spheres. Thus, the interior decorator began to occupy a middle ground, maintaining her commitment to the cultural links between domesticity and femininity but operating outside the home in the context of the 'masculine', public sphere of work defined as professional rather than amateur.

From the perspective of women's history the female interior decorator's occupation of a middle ground can be seen as a prelude to women's subsequent entrance into what had hitherto been considered masculine areas of work; their physical absorption into the public arena; their desire to align themselves with the rationalism associated with the world of work and industrial production; and their relinquishing of their sole responsibility for domestic work. As such, it provided an important moment within the dramatic changes in women's lives which were to occur through the twentieth century. From a design historical perspective, the work of the professional female interior decorators working at this time can be seen to represent the stylistic shift from nineteenth-century historicism to twentieth-century architectural and design modernism. Fully-fledged by the years following the First World War, that latter movement aligned itself more closely with stereotypically masculine cultural values – ones that were linked to the public sphere, to rationalism and to the technological metaphor – than with values associated with the world of domestic femininity.[4] Although, as a result of its perceived social elitism and its aesthetic historicism, it was rejected later by the proponents of modernism, the work of the pioneer American interior decorators of these years played, I wish to argue in this chapter, an important role in introducing women to modernity and in providing them with an active role, both as professionals and as amateurs, in the creation of the modern world. Interior decoration was restricted to the wealthy, but it both established and disseminated an aesthetic and cultural model which was more widely influential.[5] It also represented a key transitional moment without which fully-fledged modernism might not have emerged. Indeed, a number of leading female aesthetic practitioners, Charlotte Perriand and Eileen Gray among them, who by the 1920s had aligned themselves with 'masculine' avant-garde modernism, had backgrounds in interior decoration.

In this context the work of the American interior decorator, Elsie de Wolfe, undertaken in the early years of the twentieth century, provides a revealing case study. She came to the fore at a moment when women across a range of social classes were negotiating their entrance into modernity; at a time when the domestic interior had taken on a particular potency as a marker of class and gender identities; and, perhaps most significantly, before avant-garde modernism had come to define the hegemonic concept of 'good taste' which was to dominate design practice through the twentieth century. She entered the world of interior decoration in New York in the 1890s through unpaid work undertaken in the home she shared with her live-in partner, the theatrical agent, Elizabeth Marbury.[6] She went on, however, to work as a professional on her debut project of 1905 to 1907, the interior of New York's first all-women's club, the Colony Club on Madison Avenue, a building which was designed by the architect, Stanford White, a partner in the firm of McKim, Mead and White. De Wolfe's network of friends, supporters and clients was overwhelmingly female and her key preoccupations were with domestic and feminine values, although her business strategies were hard-headed, rational and highly successful financially. By the First World War she had become one of the USA's leading interior decorators. The work she undertook in the decade between 1905 and 1915 can be seen as the result of a female aesthetic practitioner operating on the boundary between the public and private spheres and for whom the world of feminine culture was paramount. Her contacts with women, her desire to express their needs and desires through an empathetic understanding of them, and her embrace of what was perceived as a stereotypically feminine visual language combined to make her a key player in the evolution of a feminine response to modernity. It was a response which was couched, not in a rational appeal to the future defined by technological progress, but in terms which referred to a past, characterised by emotional and proven aesthetic values of continuity and order but which nonetheless saw the need to respond to a world which was changing and which offered women a set of new opportunities.

This chapter will focus on the way in which de Wolfe's life and work were attuned to feminine values, to the effect this had upon her decorative schemes and, in turn, to the ethos of early twentieth-century interior decoration. Women played a key role in de Wolfe's life: She lived with them, wrote for them and, above all, designed interiors for them. She did so at a time when the meaning of the domestic interior had become particularly potent for women across a wide spectrum of American society. Following the Civil War, the idea of moving house every year on the 1st May in New York City had been replaced by the concept of domestic stability while, for the recently wealthy of the last years of the nineteenth century and early years of the twentieth who had made their money from the industrial boom of those years, their new level of social status was marked as much by their homes, and specifically by their interiors, as by anything else. The first generation of 'robber barons', who had made their money in the 1880s and 1890s, had tended to demonstrate their wealth through display and a level of ostentation in their interiors but the second generation, which had inherited money rather than made it, wished to distinguish itself from that earlier conspic-uousness through the acquisition of cultural, rather than pecuniary, capital, or 'taste'. Taste was de Wolfe's speciality and clients voraciously sought it as a marker of their having 'arrived' in society.

One of the ways in which de Wolfe introduced feminine culture into the world of interior decoration was through the mediation of the world of fashion and haute couture. Whereas male decorators tended to link interior work with the practices of architecture and upholstery, de Wolfe's philosophical approach to the interior derived less from the frame of the house or the furnishing items within it than from the identity of the female inhabitant.[7] 'You will express yourself in your house,' she wrote in *The House of Good Taste*, 'whether you want to or not.'[8] In her previous life as a professional actress, which she abandoned, in 1905, to become a decorator, she had been known as a fashion-conscious 'clothes horse' and she had revelled in wearing couture clothes created by Worth, Doucet, Paquin and others. It was this sensibility that she brought to interior decoration rather than that of the male architect. De Wolfe's close association with the world of fashion was reinforced by her close links with fashion-orientated magazines, such as *Harper's Bazaar*, *Vogue* and Theodor Dreiser's *The Delineator*, all of which reported on her interior work for their female audiences. For her fashionable dress was not only a marker of personal identity but also a decorative sign of social status and wealth. She transferred these ideas directly to the interior which provided, in her eyes, a second expressive container, after dress, for the body. The actress had also experimented with set design during her years on the stage and she incorporated a strong sense of theatricality in her later interior schemes. Central to her approach was the idea of the interior acting as a setting for the personality of its female inhabitant.

De Wolfe's overwhelming commitment to feminine culture was not theoretical but expressed in her daily life. While her homosexuality undoubtedly brought her into close contact and friendships with a number of women – Marbury, the Hewitt sisters and Anne Morgan, the daughter of the financier J.P. Morgan, among them – it was her 'homosociality' that was more significant in bringing her professional projects.[9] As members of the board of the Colony Club, for example, it was Marbury and Morgan, together with another friend, Daisy Harriman (Mrs J. Borden Harriman, née Florence

Jaffray Hurst, the President of the Club), who made it possible for de Wolfe to become a professional decorator in 1905. Through that ambitious project she became recognised for the first time as an innovative and professional decorator. The interior of the Club was well received by critics who highlighted, among other features, the trellised restaurant, the painted furniture in the private dining-room, the chintz in the bedrooms, and the use of pastel colours – soft grey, off-white, rose and cool green – throughout the project. The main impact of the club interior, as it had been of the Irving Place house, was de Wolfe's rejection of the heavy Victorian style of the previous generation and the blending of comfort and tradition with an overtly modern and restrained sensibility. In combination these aesthetic values appealed to the wealthy female clientèle of the Club who came from all over the USA to spend time in New York shopping, going to the theatre and socialising. It enabled them to keep a foot in the past while simultaneously defining themselves as modern, independent women. The role of the Colony Club commission was crucial in bringing de Wolfe future work, and allowing her to become a filter through which a generation of wealthy women of taste, most of them with wealthy husbands who sought to confirm their positions in society, could express themselves. As she explained some years later:

> The Colony Club started me on my way, in which I can think of my business only as a small snowball achieving the stature and shape of a giant snowman. From every part of the country I received letters asking for suggestions in interior decoration or containing orders. I had to enlarge my offices and staff.[10]

The Club made her work visible to this powerful network, the members of which shared a need to be fashionable and, above all, to be seen as possessing 'good taste', an attribution which could be bought for the price of an Elsie de Wolfe interior. It provided a model which could be replicated indefinitely in neo-Renaissance 'palaces' and neo-Colonial homes across the USA. Between 1907, the year in which the Club was completed, and 1912, that is exactly what happened. Most significantly it was women who facilitated it. Many of these projects were alluded to indirectly in de Wolfe's book, *The House in Good Taste*, of 1913 – photographs were used to illustrate general decorating themes and the clients' names were referred to in the captions – but de Wolfe's later autobiography, *After All* of 1935, was more explicit in listing a number of women with whom de Wolfe worked in 1907, among them Mrs William H. Crocker, a member of the Colony Club elected, along with Mrs Joseph G. Grant, to represent San Francisco, and Mrs Ogden Armour who had been elected as a Colony Club member, along with Mrs Potter Palmer, to represent Chicago.[11]

In *After All* de Wolfe told us that her first commission after the
Colony Club was for Ethel Crocker to work on her new house, 'New Place',
which was being built in Burlingame outside San Francisco (Figure 3.1).
The Crocker family had made its fortune through the building of the
Transcontinental Railroad, completed in 1869. William H. Crocker, Ethel's
husband, was a son of Charles, the railroad builder. Ethel Crocker, who was
clearly de Wolfe's link on the project, was described by the decorator as 'an

3.1
Miss Crocker's
Louis XVI bed,
illustrated in Elsie
de Wolfe, *The
House in Good
Taste*, New York,
The Century
Company, 1913

authority in matters of taste and decoration'.[12] She went on to explain that Mrs Crocker had a good colour sense and a fine collection of furniture and drawings including Fragonards, Bouchers and Watteaus. (There is evidence also that in 1902 Ethel Crocker had bought a pastel by Everett Shinn, a New York artist who went on to decorate the walls of the private dining-room in the Colony Club and who subsequently undertook a number of projects with de Wolfe.) By choosing to work with each other, both women were confirming each other's 'good taste'. Mrs. Crocker needed the 'seal of approval' guaranteed by being the proud owner of a de Wolfe interior and the decorator needed to maintain her own superior brand by being seen to be selective in her choice of clients, the main criterion being that they all had strong powers of aesthetic discrimination themselves, hence their choice of de Wolfe. This mutual admiration was a necessary strategy to show that this was not a simple case of status confirmation nor of routine commercial work but rather a highly creative project which was being undertaken by client and decorator together. Only by being considered a form of 'art' could interior decoration be made to function effectively as a form of cultural capital. *The House in Good Taste* contained an illustration of a Louis XVI canopied bed which was introduced into the bedroom of the Crocker's daughter and described it in the text as being of 'gray painted wood, and the hangings are of blue and cream chintz lined with blue taffetas'.[13] Although a strong sense of individualism was implied in every de Wolfe project this was not a one-off design. This was confirmed by the 1913 text which explained that the same idea had also been used in a New York bedroom.[14] Already, this early on in her career, it was apparent that the decorator was developing a personal repertoire of interior strategies which could be varied in different contexts in order to to make each individual project seem unique.

Mrs Ogden Armour, formerly Miss Lolita Sheldon of Connecticut, and one of the Colony Club's representative members for Chicago, was de Wolfe's next client and it appears that she gave the decorator a freer hand than Ethel Crocker. From de Wolfe's 1913 text we learn that she had a Chinese paper screen and that the decorator had a jardinière table with zinc-lined boxes to hold plants made for Mrs Ogden Armour's garden room[15] (Figures 3.2, 3.3). In *After All* de Wolfe described the room explaining that 'The winter garden, in the center of the house, is to my mind the perfection of beauty. I worked over it for three years, and have never repeated any of its individual features.'[16] The description of the garden room, which featured a trellis and long green and white sofas, made it sound like a cross between the Colony Club trellis restaurant and the roof garden. However individualised de Wolfe claimed the winter garden of the Ogden Armour's home, Mellody Farm in Lake Forest, to have been, there is little doubt that a trellised

 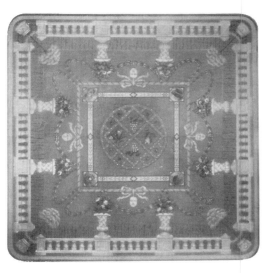

winter garden, complete with a fountain, was a distinctive hallmark of a de Wolfe interior in those years. A similar room was created for Mrs Ormond Smith's Long Island home, Shoremond, designed by Hoppin and Koen a few years later. The illustration of this large winter garden in the *The House of Good Taste* depicted tables with jardinières at their ends in the manner of those designed for Lolita Ogden Armour. In the text of the book the decorator explained that she created yet another trellis for Mrs Benjamin Guinness' New York home, located on Washington Square North, and that the craze for green and white lattice was becoming a feature of 'the smallest cottage' openly demonstrating the extensive influence of this popular feature.[17] In spite of her own work being executed for individual, wealthy clients, whose knowledge of art was such that the commissions were described as negotiations between the clients and the decorator, there was a strong sense that a formulaic de Wolfe interior language was being developed, albeit with variations, containing a number of identifiable features which could be applied both to the most expensive and to the most modest of interiors. The difference was, of course, that only the wealthy could afford the services of Miss de Wolfe herself.

The Ogden Armours were another second-generation wealthy family whose fortunes derived, this time, from meat-packing. J. Ogden Armour created a fantastic Renaissance palace, designed by the Chicago architect, Arthur Heun, for his wife and daughter in Lake Forest outside Chicago. A local newspaper from the 1950s described Mrs Ogden Armour as a great friend of Miss de Wolfe and as one of Chicago's great hostesses and a

3.2
Mrs Ogden Armour's Chinese-paper screen (left) and Mrs James Warren Lane's painted dining-table, illustrated in Elsie de Wolfe, *The House in Good Taste*, New York, The Century Company, 1913

3.3
Ogden Armour
dining-room,
illustrated in Elsie
de Wolfe, *After All*,
New York and
London, Harper &
Brothers, 1935

patron of the arts.[18] On her death in 1953 she donated her collection of historic shoes to the Chicago Art Institute. An article in *The Architectural Record* of 1916 was highly complimentary about de Wolfe's work undertaken in the interior of Mellody Farm, describing the lattice work in the winter garden as 'an intimation that we are approaching what far surpasses all that art may do'.[19] The images in the same article depicted much of the interior showing French furniture, Chinese ceramics, and painted screens in the main hallway, the music room with French furniture arranged in 'conversation groupings', sconces on either side of the marble fireplace, wood-panelled walls, and the winter garden described above. It had all the familiar hallmarks of a de Wolfe project and was clearly one of her most extensive domestic schemes of the early post-Colony Club years. Its execution in the grandiose setting of the Ogden Armour estate undoubtedly served to enhance her reputation and to encourage others to engage her services.

Little is known about de Wolfe's relationship with the other Colony Club representative member from Chicago, Mrs Potter Palmer, except for the fact that an article in *Good Housekeeping* of February 1913, entitled 'A Light, Gay Dining-Room' included an image of a little armchair which was captioned with the following words, 'This chair is known as the "Potter Palmer" chair because it was first made for that lady.'[20] It was described as a chintz-covered luxurious chair which would benefit from 'a little kidney table beside it to hold one's sewing or books or smoking things'.[21] Little else is known about de Wolfe's relationship with Mrs Potter Palmer although it is possible that she undertook more work for her. In 1910, at the age of 61, Mrs Potter Palmer moved to Sarasota in Florida where she had a house built for her called 'The Oaks'. There is no evidence to show that de Wolfe helped her decorate her new home – but Mrs. Potter Palmer's biography tells us that 'she used chintz with some of her Louis XVI furniture brought from Chicago' which suggests that the interior was in the style of de Wolfe if not created by her.[22]

In line with the other female clients described above, Mrs Potter Palmer – Bertha Honoré before her marriage to the wealthy Mr Potter Palmer the Second who had made his money in retailing – was involved with philanthropic work in the Arts. At Chicago's Columbian Exhibition of 1893, for example, she had been responsible for the Art and Handicraft display in the Women's Building, designed by Sophia Hayden. Potter Palmer's wedding gift to his wife had been a US$3.5 million house and the couple subsequently owned a hotel and, in the 1880s, a house on Lake Shore Drive in Chicago, the marble mosaic floor of which was laid by imported Italian craftsmen.[23] The drawing-room was in the French style while the music room had a Spanish flavour. Mrs Potter Palmer was known to be keen on women having a profession and would probably have warmed to Elsie de Wolfe when she met her in connection with the Colony Club after her husband's death in 1902. A middle-aged women by this time, Bertha Potter Palmer would have undoubtedly appreciated the comfort offered by the padded 'luxurious'

3.4
Mrs Frederick Havemeyer's chinoiserie chintz bed (left) and Mrs Payne Whitney's green feather chintz bed, illustrated in Elsie de Wolfe, *The House in Good Taste*, New York, The Century Company, 1913

armchair that de Wolfe created for her. A generation older than Ethel Crocker and Lolita Ogden Armour, Mrs Potter Palmer belonged to a social group which, along with the Vanderbilts, Astors and Belmonts, had frequented Newport in the 1890s, although she never fully penetrated that level of society. She was also a connoisseur of modern art and a fan of Monet and Pissarro whose work she helped introduce into the USA. It was rare at this time for women to buy art as collecting was an overtly masculine activity, the best-known protagonists of this activity in the USA at this time being Mellon and Joseph Duveen. While the men collected, their wives involved themselves with charity work and commissioned interior decorators. Bertha Palmer was a notable exception to this rule. Her association with de Wolfe, however slight, serves to reinforce the importance of this network of culturally sophisticated women to the emergence of the new interior decoration.

Mrs Frederick Havemeyer was also of de Wolfe's clients, as we learn from *The House of Good Taste* in which her chinoiserie chintz bed was illustrated.[24] A canopied bed in eighteenth-century French style, it was photographed in a room with wood-panelled walls adorned with framed prints and with little bedside tables and lights which betrayed all the familiar signs of a de Wolfe interior. Illustrated next to Mrs F. Havemeyer's bed was a similar piece of furniture, this time owned by Mrs Payne Whitney (née Helen Hay) the wife of the collector mentioned above and another client of de Wolfe (Figure 3.4). The Whitneys had a house built for them in 1905 in New York at 972 Fifth Avenue. It was a wedding present from the bridegroom's uncle, the financier Oliver Payne. His father was William C. Whitney, Secretary of the Navy and controller of most of New York's streetcar lines.[25] Helen Hay came from an equally prestigious family – her father was John Hay, Secretary of State under McKinley and Roosevelt – while her cultural *kudos* derived from the fact that she was a poet. The extravagant interior was created by the architect of the house – Stanford White. It is clear, however, that de Wolfe was also involved, more likely in her capacity as a dealer rather than as a decorator. Her early headed notepaper declared her to be a provider of 'objets d'art' as well as an interior decorator and she clearly worked with Stanford White in acquiring objects for his interiors. Documentation shows that she acquired objects for the Whitney house for White at the same time as she was working with him on the Colony Club. A 1906 letter from de Wolfe to White explained the level of her involvement,

> I am ordering the table for Mrs. Whitney. I have had it cut out at 3'10" on a piece of paper, and it seems to me absolutely right for the two, four and six. This will be cosy and just right for four. Of course, six would crowd it. It will have to be people who would

like to sit pretty near together. Let us hope they will all be friendly. I note that it is to be finished in pure white.[26]

De Wolfe's numerous female contacts and clients included, therefore, wealthy married women with an inclination towards the arts. They were all recipients of the same de Wolfe formula for the interior and its components which included the use of historical style, usually French eighteenth century, a mixture of old and new furnishings, simple patterned fabrics, usually chintz, and painted, pastel-coloured furniture items. These stylistic characteristics of the decorator's work were combined with a strong sense of practicality and comfort and a meticulous attention to detail which made her interiors easy places to live in. While they denoted tastefulness, social status and cultural awareness, her interiors were also liveable spaces adapted to the demands of modern life. Clients were undoubtedly attracted by the status confirmation they offered, the opportunity for self-identification that they proposed, their practicality, or, indeed, by all three.

The work that de Wolfe had undertaken for Ethel Crocker and Lolita Ogden Armour, both wives of sons of 'robber barons', established a pattern which was repeated several times over in the years leading up to 1914 and which undoubtedly provided the decorator with the significant wealth that she had acquired by that time. Several of the illustrations in *The House of Good Taste* revealed her collaborations with Mrs Ormond G. Smith, the wife of a dime novel publisher; Mrs James Warren Lane, whose husband's wealth came from his father's cotton merchandising firm; and Mrs C. W. Harkness, the wife of a director in the Standard Oil Company and son of Stephen Harkness who had amassed a fortune through the acquisition of Standard Oil and railroad company stocks in the 1870s (Figures 3.5, 3.6). All three women were most probably visitors to the Colony Club or acquaintances of women who were. Mrs. Harkness, whose living-room and cabinet for 'objets d'art' were depicted in *The House in Good Taste*, was the first of these three women to employ the fashionable decorator to work on the interior of her grand house, Mirador, in New Jersey. The house, which had fifty rooms, was built in the English Georgian style and the interior was created to match. The living room which de Wolfe created had panelled walls, a huge fireplace, a range of chairs in different styles grouped casually and a dramatic moulded ceiling in the English style. In her chapter on the 'Living Room' in *The House of Good Taste*, de Wolfe cited the reading room in the Colony Club as a model which undoubtedly inspired the grander room in Mirador. A comment in a local New Jersey paper of 1917, the year in which the estate was sold, twelve years after the house had been built, described the house's interior as being 'in good taste' and characterised by a tone which

3.5
The living-room in
the C.W. Harkness
House at
Morristown, New
Jersey, illustrated
in Elsie de Wolfe,
*The House in Good
Taste*, New York,
The Century
Company, 1913

3.6
Mrs Harkness's
cabinet for objets
d'art, illustrated
in Elsie de Wolfe
*The House in Good
Taste*, New York,
The Century
Company, 1913

3.7
Mrs Ormond
Smith's trellis
room at Center
Island, New York,
illustrated in Elsie
de Wolfe, *The
House in Good
Taste*, New York,
The Century
Company, 1913

'seems to have been created for rest, study and quiet enjoyment', a description which was completely in tune with de Wolfe's tone for the Colony Club reading room.[27]

Mrs Ormond G. Smith (née Grace Pellett) has already been mentioned in the context of winter gardens as de Wolfe created one for her which she subsequently illustrated in *The House in Good Taste*. It was an enormous room within a Georgian mansion, named Shoremond, designed by the architects, Hoppin and Koen of New York, for the Ormond Smiths in 1912 on Long Island (Figures 3.7, 3.8). This was a large project for de Wolfe who developed interior schemes for the music room, the library, two guest rooms, the breakfast room, the ladies' reception room, the boudoir, the men's reception room, the dining-room and the loggia of this enormous house. She included English, French and Chinese styles in her designs and developed individually themed schemes for each room. Once again the Colony Club, with its individualised rooms, undoubtedly provided both the model and the inspiration for this magnificent set of interiors. Nonetheless, the result was not excessive as a writer in *Architectural Record* explained:

3.8

Fountain in the trellis room of Mrs Ormond G. Smith and Mr James Deering's wall fountain, illustrated in Elsie de Wolfe, *The House in Good Taste*, New York, The Century Company, 1913

Owner, architect and decorator have proved themselves a trium-virate of good taste and able execution in the problem of conforming substantially to a 'period' design without being too liberal or too slavish. That they have done this and at the same time steered through the Scylla and Charybdis of interior decoration, in carefully avoiding the ostentatious and the commonplace, speaks well for the result.[28]

The other female client named in *The House of Good Taste*, Mrs James Warren Lane, was wealthy in her own right as the daughter of E.W. Bliss, a Brooklyn-based manufacturer of heavy machinery. The architect, Arthur Little, of Little and Browne, had already built two houses for Bliss and he moved the Warren Lane's home, Suffolk House, to a new location on Long Island in 1912. This provided the opportunity for Mrs Warren to commission de Wolfe to work on the interiors of this large house.[29]

At least two other women are known to have been clients of de Wolfe in the years just before and just after the outbreak of the First World

War, although they were not mentioned by the decorator in her autobiography. Nell Pruyn Cunningham commissioned her to decorate part of her Bigelow and Wadsworth-designed home in Glen Falls in the early 1920's. While there a strong suggestion Mai Coe (née Mai Huttleston Rogers, the daughter of one of the founders of Standard Oil) invited her to work with the artist Everett Shinn in the creation of a tea-house on her husband's (William Robertson Coe, an English immigrant) estate, Planting Fields, also on Long Island, in 1914 to 1915.[30] Like so many of de Wolfe's female clients, Mai Coe was a stylish, fashion-conscious figure and has been described as being interested in art and decoration. Evidence of her interest in all things artistic is provided by the fact that she also commissioned the artist Robert Chanler to execute murals for her in her bedroom and breakfast room.

De Wolfe also worked for a handful of other remarkable women who were known for a variety of personal achievements, not necessarily defined by marriage. The women in question included Isabella Stewart Gardner, Anne Morgan and Ethel Barrymore, all of them clients of de Wolfe, albeit to varying degrees. The only evidence to suggest that de Wolfe undertook any professional work for Mrs Gardner, the wife of Jack Gardner, a famous collector of European art (Renaissance furniture and paintings in particular) and creator of the remarkable Fenway Court in Boston, was the presence of a small, curved sofa table designed by de Wolfe in the room of early Italian paintings at Fenway Court. The two women had much in common and both met on frequent occasions and corresponded with each other.[31] The decorator did much more, however, for her close friend, Anne Morgan. The daughter of the wealthy banker, J. P. Morgan, Anne was introduced to de Wolfe through Elizabeth Marbury, who was a conduit for so many of the decorator's female contacts. She was an officer of the Colony Club and a frequent visitor to the Irving Place house at the turn of the century. Born in 1877, Anne Morgan had been a protected child and did not leave her secluded home until the age of 30. From around 1907 she became active in philanthropic work, however, and over the next two decades she became a forceful figure in social welfare and in the support of women, particularly from the lower ranks of society. In 1908 she worked with Marbury and Harriman to find funds for training poor southern whites and in the following year she opened a temperance restaurant in the Brooklyn Naval Yard.[32] She was an important force in de Wolfe's life and became very close to both Marbury and de Wolfe, joining them, for example, in their ownership of a house in Versailles in France and spending long summers with the two women in that country over a period of twenty years.

The House in Good Taste included three illustrations of a number of rooms created by de Wolfe for Anne's New York rooms, (Figure 3.9). They

**Miss Anne
Morgan's Louis
XVI boudoir,
illustrated in Elsie
de Wolfe,** *The
House in Good
Taste,* **New York,
The Century
Company, 1913**

depicted her Louis XVI boudoir, her 'lit de repos', and her Louis XVI dressing
room. The rooms in question were characteristic de Wolfe interiors with all
the usual familiar features – French painted eighteenth-century furniture,
panelled walls covered with framed prints, a painted screen and sconces on
either side of a marble fireplace which had a marble female bust on its
surface. The dressing room was lined with wardrobes with mirrored doors
to allow the inhabitant to see the back of her head. In contrast to the vast
spaces of Mellody Farm and other de Wolfe creations, however, Anne
Morgan's interiors conveyed a sense of privacy and intimacy which was not
present in the grander schemes. The boudoir had a personalised quality and
a lightness which were suggestive less of social status than of personal
identity. Combined with the practicality of the dressing room, these rooms
suggested an emphasis upon the individuality of the inhabitant rather than
making a statement about her wealth and social status. There was a strong
visual link between the interiors created for de Wolfe and Marbury's Irving
Place house and those created for Anne Morgan suggesting, perhaps, that the
latter was conceived of as more of a sanctuary than as a site for display, a
place for privacy rather than for publicity.

   The actress, Ethel Barrymore, was also on the receiving end of a de
Wolfe interior although no visual evidence of it remains. In this instance the

link between the two women had been established before the creation of
the Colony Club when de Wolfe was still an actress and Barrymore acted as
her understudy. In her autobiography Barrymore recalled the experience she
had had back in 1893 when she had had to go on stage in Miss de Wolfe's
Paquin clothes, remembering that:

> Miss de Wolfe was very indignant that her name was still on the
> program, with such an inadequate person taking her place on
> that matinée afternoon. It was not of sufficient importance, my
> appearance, for having the programs changed.[33]

As Miss Barrymore's career became increasingly successful, she moved into
a world in which it made more sense to commission an interior from de
Wolfe than to act as her understudy.

The women with whom de Wolfe worked in the years between
1907 and 1914 covered a wide range from wealthy socialites, wives
of second-generation wealthy industrialists, advocates of the arts,
philanthropists, social activists and cultural figures, both married and single.
For all of them she created domestic interiors which served their individual
purposes, whether private or public, and all of which were executed in a
language of the interior which had consistent and shared components. The
light, comfortable, feminine spaces she created were both fashionable and
functional at the same time and worked equally well on a grand and on an
intimate scale. While the vast majority of de Wolfe's work was undertaken
in private homes, the aesthetic arena, first and foremost, of the woman of the
house, she did not limit her application of this feminine domestic aesthetic
exclusively to the private sphere. A few projects involved her in working
with other kinds of institutions and spaces, still defined as female, among
them the residential building of a girls' college and a 'hotel' for a working
woman's charity. In 1907, for example, she was commissioned to design the
interior of Brooks Hall, a new building which provided bedrooms and a
common living area for the female students at Barnard College which had
been founded, across the road from Columbia University in New York, in
1889. In 1901 a new Dean, Miss Laura Drake Gill, instigated the construction
of a new student residence which opened in 1907. It consisted of ninety-
seven bedrooms, capable of being used singly or in various combinations as
suites, an extended parlour, a dining-room on the first floor, rooms for guests
and officers and an infirmary. De Wolfe was undoubtedly suggested for the
project by Stanford White, the architect of the Colony Club, as his firm was
used for the master plan of the area, although the firm of Lamb and Rich
actually designed Brooks Hall. However, de Wolfe's work for the Colony Club,
which was underway by the time she was commissioned by Miss Gill,

undoubtedly made her the right person for the task in hand. Indeed, the challenge was a very similar one, to create a 'home from home' not this time for wealthy wives but for well-to-do young ladies. The design approach adopted by de Wolfe was also a similar one, i.e., to decide upon a set of essential components for each bedroom – a bed, a bedside table, a student lamp, a desk, a couch, two easy chairs, a bookshelf, etc. – but to ensure that no two rooms looked alike. Fabrics, chintz in particular, were used to achieve variety and the floors were colour-coded to give a sense both of unity and diversity. The rooms on the eighth floor, for example, were decorated in blue, while those a floor below were pink. It was a similar strategy to the one the decorator had adopted at the Colony Club although the stylistic variation was more varied in that more exotic setting and the level of luxury inevitably higher.[34] As in all de Wolfe interiors, as much attention was paid to practicality as to aesthetics and the kitchen and storage areas were given a great deal of attention. However, she had clearly learnt from the Colony Club that she could not undertake everything and wrote in a letter of 25 May 1907, to Dean Gill,

> I have only seen Mrs. Osborne for a few moments, and merely know from her that I can have $3500 to cover all the furnishings, electric lights, Kitchen utensils, china, glass, linen &c. This does not include anything of the kitchen fitments, ranges, plumbing, tubs, &c., with which I prefer to have nothing to do.[35]

Although more austere, the parlour of Brooks Hall, with its groupings of easy chairs, tables with lamps, and piano, closely resembled the Colony Club reading room and the living room of Mirador which was to come later. Having achieved a workable formula, de Wolfe was able to adapt it to the project in hand, whatever the scale and whatever the budget.

Another project undertaken beyond the limits of the private house pushed the decorator's philosophical approach to its limits. In 1910, together with Anne Vanderbilt, Anne Morgan had established a charity to enable working girls in New York to have holidays outside the city. The idea was that they participated in a savings scheme which allowed them to take holidays in rural homes supported by the charity. The Vacation Committee, as it was first called, quickly became the Vacation Savings Association and in 1913 the idea of a working girls' clubhouse was mooted as an extension of the project. Three houses were acquired on West 38th and 39th Streets. The house on 39th Street became known as the Vacation Headquarters while the two 38th Street houses were divided into single and double bedrooms, the former renting for $5 a week and the latter for $9 a week. In 1914 it was reported that the cost of furniture and fixtures for the lodging houses has amounted to $3779.12.[36] De Wolfe was approached to design the interiors of both houses which comprised bedrooms, administration offices, a restaurant and lounging rooms. The houses were described as being 'charmingly furnished' and made an extensive use of oak (in contrast to the more 'upmarket' mahogany which had featured in the Colony Club).[37] The clubhouse was opened on 1 January 1914 and 700 people came to the house-warming. No visual evidence of the interior exists but the rooms would undoubtedly have been simplified versions of those created for the Colony Club and Brooks Hall.

In the years between 1905 and 1915 de Wolfe undertook a vast number of projects with a large number of women acting as her key clients. The most elaborate and influential schemes were undoubtedly those executed for the wives of wealthy men who would have employed de Wolfe for reasons of fashion and status, having come across her work at the Colony Club, or through word of mouth through networks of fashionable, status-conscious women. Alongside this prestigious and well paid work, however, de Wolfe also worked on her own homes, where she developed most of her decorating strategies, and for close friends for whom she created more intimate, personal spaces. A third category of substantial work involved her in a number of non-domestic, multi-residence projects in which she had to compromise between providing a level of standardisation for economic reasons and a sense of individualism for each resident. She undertook a range of such projects across a wide social spectrum, varying the schemes in terms of cost and elaboration but not in terms of her philosophical approach. In essence, even in these non-domestic settings de Wolfe was providing 'homes from homes' thereby still remaining true to her fundamental belief in a notion of 'domestic femininity'.

In order to succeed across such a range of projects in what was a relatively short period of time, de Wolfe developed a formulaic approach to the interior, a language of interior components which could be combined and recombined seemingly indefinitely. Such was the level of her skill that she managed to create interiors which exhibited a high level of individualism. Through their level of 'tastefulness', her design succeeded in providing the necessary evocation of status and cultural capital required by her new wealthy female clients. Simultaneously the same interior components could be used to provide a level of personal identity, intimacy, practicality and comfort for those female clients who were in need of those qualities in their homes or temporary residences.

Above all, although de Wolfe worked primarily in historicist styles, and made no attempt to conceal the essential stereotypical 'femininity' of her choice of furnishings and interior settings, she decorated, in terms of her understanding of the psychological and practical needs of her clients, in a modern way appealing to modern women. All the women she dealt with, from whichever class and however wealthy, were consciously inhabiting a modern world in which enhanced independence was a *sine qua non*, even if that independence was only made possible by their husband's wealth. As such, de Wolfe should be seen as a modern decorator who was supremely conscious of what it meant to be an active American woman in the early twentieth century, whether engaged in paid work, making independent taste decisions, being increasingly mobile or engaging in unpaid philanthropic and social work. Rejecting the dark interiors of the Victorians, she embraced a new world which was characterised by women living and working together and engaging with modernity but in which being in tune with one's domestic space, women's traditional sphere, was still a fundamental necessity.

Later avant-garde male modernists failed to understand the role that de Wolfe played within a primarily female community and the way in which her particular aesthetic decisions and interior decorating strategies were appropriate to that context. She was dismissed as elitist, historicist and absurd.[38] Now, however, that our gendered reading of the history of design and decoration is more finely tuned and sensitised, it is time to look back at women, such as Elsie de Wolfe, who catered almost exclusively for a female clientèle and, in so doing, developed a sophisticated, modern (albeit not modernist) approach to her discipline from which much can still be learnt today.

Notes

1   E. de Wolfe, *The House in Good Taste*, New York: The Century Company, 1913, p. 5.

2   See J. Wolff, 'The Culture of Separate Spheres: The Role of Culture in Nineteenth-Century Middle-Class Life,' in J. Wolff and J. Seed (eds), *The Culture of Capital: Art, Power and the Nineteenth-Century Middle-Class*, Manchester: Manchester University Press, 1988, for an extended discussion about the ideological separation of men and women at this time.

3   For a discussion about women taking on the responsibility of decorating the home see L. Davidoff and C. Hall, *Family Fortunes: Men and Women of the English Middle Class, 1780-1850*, Chicago: University of Chicago Press, 1987; for an account of the rise of the female decorating profession in England, see C. Gere and L. Hoskins, *The House Beautiful*, London: Lund Humphries, 2000; and for an account of its equivalent in the USA see, p. 11, Kirkham and P. Sparke, ' "A Woman's Place ..."?: Women Interior Designers', in P. Kirkham (ed.), *Women Designers in the USA 1900–2000: Diversity and Difference*, New York: The Bard Graduate Centre for Studies in the Decorative Arts, Design and Culture, 2000.

4   See P. Sparke, *As Long as It's Pink: The Sexual Politics of Taste*, London: Pandora, 1995, in which the author elaborates the idea that architectural and design modernism was rooted in stereotypical masculine values.

5   De Wolfe's *The House of Good Taste* of 1913 sold in vast numbers and went into a number of editions until 1920.

6   Elizabeth Marbury inherited the house on Irving Place which she inhabited with de

Wolfe on the death of her father in the early 1890s.

7   Architects such as Stanford White frequently created their own interiors while others were created by furnishing firms such as the New York-based Herter Brothers.

8   E. de Wolfe, *The House in Good Taste*, p. 5.

9   The term is used by Peter McNeil in his article 'Designing Women: Gender, Sexuality and the Interior Decorator, c.1890–1940', *Art History*, vol. 17, no. 4, Dec. 1994, pp. 631–57.

10   E. de Wolfe, *After All*, New York and London: Harper & Brothers, 1935, p. 67.

11   See E. de Wolfe, *After All*, p. 64.

12   De Wolfe, *After All* p. 68.

13   De Wolfe, *The House in Good Taste*, pp. 199 and 213.

14   De Wolfe, *The House in Good Taste*, p. 213.

15   De Wolfe, *The House in Good Taste*, pp. 184 and 280.

16   De Wolfe, *After All*, p. 68.

17   De Wolfe, *The House in Good Taste*, p. 279.

18   E. Page, 'Old J. Ogden Armour Home Now Lake Forest Academy', in the *Chicago Tribune*, 26 June, 1955, p. 7.

19   P. B. Wright, 'Mellody Farm, the Country House of J. Ogden Armour Esq.' *The Architectural Record*, vol. 33 no. 2., Feb. 1916, p. 102.

20   E. de Wolfe, 'A Light, Gay Dining-Room', *Good Housekeeping*, Feb. 1913, p. 357.

21   *Good Housekeeping*, Feb. 1913, p. 358.

22   I. Ross, *Silhouette in Diamonds: The Life of Mrs. Potter Palmer*, New York: Harper & Bros, 1960, p. 229.

23   Ibid., p. 17.

24   E. de Wolfe, *The House in Good Taste,* p. 212.

25   See S. G. White, *The Houses of McKim, Mead and White*, New York: Rizzoli, 1998, p. 224.

26   Letter from de Wolfe to Stanford White, Feb 3rd 1906, Payne Whitney file. Collections of the New York Historical Society.

27   'The Home of the Late Charles W. Harkness', *The Madison Eagle*, 15 June, 1917, p. 6.

28   D. W. Fessenden, 'The Country House of Ormond G. Smith Esq.', *The Architectural Record*, vol. 40. Aug. 1916, p. 117.

29   See R. B. Mackay, A. K. Baker and C. A. Traynor, *Long Island Country Houses and Their Architects*, 1860–1940, Long Island, New York: Long Island Historical Society, 1997, p. 258.

30   The three Pruyn sisters, Charlotte, Mary and Nell, built adjoining homes in Glen Falls, all designed by Bigelow and Wadsworth. The Hyde Collection Art Museum is located in the house created for Charlotte Pruyn and Louis Fiske Hyde in 1912.

31   See R. N. van Hadley, 'Elsie de Wolfe and Isabella Stewart Gardner', in *Fenway Court*, Boston: Isabella Stewart Gardner Museum, 1981. pp. 38–41.

32   See J. S. Smith, *Elsie de Wolfe: A Life in the High Style*, New York: Atheneum, 1982, p. 128 and 'Lady into Dynamo,' *New Yorker*, 22, Oct. 1927, p. 23.

33   E. Barrymore, *Memories: An Autobiography*, New York: Harper & Bros., 1955, p. 49.

34   Much of the information extracted from unpublished lecture, entitled 'Housing the Columbia Community' by A. S. Dolkart, lodged in the Barnard College Archive. Some of it is taken from an essay of 1995 by Jessica Dawson, entitled 'Residential Life at Barnard College', also lodged in the Barnard College Archive.

35   Letter from Elsie de Wolfe to Dean Gill, lodged in the Barnard College archive.

36   *Twelve Years and the Thirteenth*, an undated publication by the American Women's Association, lodged in the Barnard College Library, p.11.

37   *Fourth Annual Report of the Vacation Committee* 1914, lodged in the Barnard College Archive.

38   Both T. H. Robsjohn-Gibbings, in his book, *Goodbye, Mr Chippendale*, New York: Alfred A. Knopf, 1944, and R. Lynes, in his book, *The Tastemakers*, New York: Harper and Brothers, 1954, made disparaging remarks about Elsie de Wolfe and her work.

Chapter 4

Your Place or Mine?
The client's contribution
to domestic architecture

Alice T. Friedman

Over the past thirty years, the study of women and architecture has not only expanded our knowledge of the myriad contributions made by women – as architects, designers, clients and consumers – to the history of building and design, but it has also heightened our awareness of the complex mechanisms of culture and ideology which shape the environment in which design decisions are made and carried out. Whereas the earliest studies in the field focused mainly, and of necessity, on problems of attribution and revisionist history, bringing to light little-known works by women and assigning credit to women practitioners whose contributions had been neglected or actively suppressed, more recent interdisciplinary researches have emphasised the significance of gender (understood as a historically and culturally determined constellation of ideas and values that shape expectations about women's and men's roles in all aspects of society) and of other social factors within the design professions and in the making of built environments. In particular, feminist scholarship has called attention to the ways in which building types and programmes have been shaped not only by aesthetic criteria and formal conventions but also by cultural values and norms: social organisation and customs, etiquette, and gender ideology play as much of a role in the process as architectural style, consumer preferences and taste.

This chapter will consider the history of three twentieth-century houses which foreground the relationship between architecture and client identity, focusing in particular on codes of representation that relate to gender, sexuality, and race. My aims in analysing these cases are twofold: first, to call attention to the importance of gender as a category of analysis in the history of architecture and design, and to begin to explore the significance of other factors, such as sexuality and race, in design decisions; and second, to focus attention on works in which the role of the client as an 'outsider' in social and cultural terms contributed to the production of innovative or unconventional buildings and design solutions.

Some of these concepts are explored in greater detail in my book *Women and the Making of the Modern House*.[1] That study grew out of a question: why was it that so many of the most architecturally significant twentieth-century houses built in the United States and Europe were designed for women? In my earlier work on Elizabethan country houses, I had come across one outstanding example of a case in which an architect's thinking about design seems to have changed dramatically when he began working for a woman client: the architect, Robert Smythson, had been commissioned to build a large country house for Bess of Hardwick in 1591, and he used this as an opportunity to experiment with new designs drawn from his own sketchbooks and from pattern books devised by the most sophisticated architects of Europe.[2] Thus Smythson tried out ideas at Hardwick that were perhaps too radical and too new to suit the needs of his previous clients, all of whom, not surprisingly, were male. This discovery about Smythson and Hardwick motivated me to pay particular attention to the gender of clients and architects, particularly for buildings that are unconventional in design, programme or planning. What I found was that many of the most innovative houses – like the Schröder House, or Mies van der Rohe's Farnsworth House, or Frank Lloyd Wright's Dana and Barnsdall Houses – were designed and built for women who headed their own households – women who were single, divorced, or living in partnerships with other women – and I wondered what role gender and sexuality played in influencing design or in shaping the working relationships between architects and clients.

As it turned out, the fact that the clients were all women seems to have been less significant than something we might call 'gender relations' and their status as women whose lives and values placed them outside the norm. As single women, the clients I studied were all highly unconventional: they lived in ways that were viewed by themselves and their contemporaries as unusual, devoting their lives not to husbands and children but to other pursuits, to their careers, to charitable work or political activism or to whatever formed the passionate focus of their attention. When they commissioned houses, they turned to prominent architects to design the living environments which would accommodate the breadth and variety of their unusual activities and unconventional lives. In most cases, what these women clients asked for was so unusual that the architects they hired had to use their full creative energies to find design solutions; there was no point in going back to the stock designs from the office portfolio, because nowhere in any of their previous experience had they encountered such unusual programme requirements. When talented architects are confronted with difficult and unfamiliar challenges, the results are bound to be original and interesting.

Moreover, the women who commissioned these houses had very strong personalities and an unusually clear vision, expressed in exactly the sort of single-mindedness that one might imagine in a person who set out, alone, to build a building that would suit an entirely unconventional way of life. The stories of how the houses came to be designed and built revealed a great deal about the real challenges of collaborative relationships between architects and clients, and also suggested a complex historical picture that had been largely overlooked by architectural historians.

Briefly put, what these examples suggest is this: that since the conventions of planning and design in all periods respond not only to patterns of use (programme, circulation, siting, etc.) but are also markers of social values, gender identity and class status, it follows that buildings or interiors created to represent or accommodate unconventional ways of living and/or social values will deviate from the norm. Unconventionality in both social and architectural culture can take any number of forms, yet because the dominant architecture and visual culture of Europe and North America have been shaped by the needs and values of white men and by the imperatives of heterosexual culture and social relations, I am particularly interested in looking at examples of buildings made for clients whose identities lie, for one reason or another, outside this system.

Each of the three case studies in the present overview calls attention to a different set of conventions and to some of the ways in which they are mediated by architecture and design. The Rietveld–Schröder House in Utrecht was built in 1924 for a young widow and her children by an architect to whom she was linked in a passionate partnership that was both artistic and intimate. By choosing to live as a single parent (Gerrit Rietveld was married and had six children of his own) and as a mother who shared freely her life and her living space with her children, Truus Schröder set herself and her household apart. Moreover, by choosing to build in a radically modern style, she explicitly defined her differences with those around her, using architectural design to mark her avant-garde values, her feminism, and her embrace of unconventional ways of living.

My second case focuses on the houses, both built and unbuilt, of Josephine Baker, the African-American entertainer and social activist. From the 1920s to the 1970s, Baker used her work as a performer and patron in Europe and America to create a powerful yet mercurial image of herself as a black woman who was independent, unpredictable, and highly sexualised. At times, she could be flamboyant and outrageous, yet she could also be exaggeratedly respectable – for example, in her wartime service and in her work with orphaned children. In each of these modes, Baker used architecture and interior design intensively, setting the stage on which to enact the drama of her own life. Though she settled in France and lived there for many years, she never lost touch with her particularly American intuition concerning the importance of her image or of her audience for supporting and furthering her political and ideological goals. Though she had ample opportunity to choose a modernist style for her home, having been a friend of both Adolf Loos and Le Corbusier, she nevertheless remained a loyal partisan of historically resonant, aristocratic French architecture. Her châteaux and country estates on the outskirts of Paris and in the Dordogne were justly famous, becoming synonymous with Baker and the glamorous life she lived.[3]

The third case focuses on the New York City apartment of the American architect Paul Rudolph (1918–97), located on the top four floors of an elegant brownstone which he renovated as a home for himself and his male lover between 1967 and 1979. Through this brief analysis of a home for a gay man designed by himself, I want to emphasise a point that goes beyond gender as such: that the relationship between architecture and representation extends to conventions and values relating to sexual orientation as well as to more familiar (and less controversial) factors like family structure, household organisation and marital status. Thus, for our purposes as historians of design and culture, gay and lesbian clients and their domestic programmes represent a particularly significant group for further study.

The Schröder House

The Schröder House (Figure 4.1) was commissioned by a young widow with three children, a woman whose progressive ideas about child-rearing motivated her to commission an entirely new domestic environment in which to live.[4] Her husband, Frits Schröder, was a lawyer, somewhat older than herself, with whom she had little in common but who nonetheless indulged

4.1
**The Rietveld
Schröder House,
Utrecht, 1924**
Photo, courtesy of
Frank den Oudsten

her predilection for modern art and architecture. He died in 1923, leaving her a small inheritance. The couple had often quarrelled about how they would live – Truus found her lawyer husband's traditional notions about family life and social form completely suffocating – but as a young, independently wealthy widow she had considerable freedom over her own life and those of her children. Her intimate relationship with Rietveld, a local artist and furniture-maker whom she had met a few years earlier when he designed a small modern cabinet or study for her (at Frits's suggestion), caused her to turn her attention to an intensive investigation of modern design. Her interest in the style seems to have been inspired by her sister, a member of the avant-garde circle in Amsterdam, but it was her relationship with Rietveld that enable her to make her mark as a client and co-designer in her own right.

The house that she and Rietveld worked on together cuts an extraordinary figure in a very ordinary street on the outskirts of Utrecht where it is located. Even looking at it today, it comes as no surprise to learn that Schröder's children were teased at school and asked if they lived in the 'looney' house. The interior is extremely simple and open. The upper floor is essentially one large room (Figure 4.2) in which the family lived, worked and slept. Partitions could be pulled across to subdivide the space to create small bed-sitting rooms for the children. Truus's own bedroom at the back of the house had fixed walls and a door, but the goal of the project was to facilitate communal living, eliminating physical and social boundaries between children and adults.

4.2
Rietveld Schröder House, interior
Photo, courtesy Centraal Museum, Utrecht

Moreover, Schröder believed that a domestic environment free of old-fashioned furniture and heavy fabrics, and filled with colour, light and air, would allow her and her children to live in a healthier way and with a more profound awareness of themselves and of the world around them. For her, this consciousness was the essence of modernity, and her home was the key to that experience. A small library and artist's studio on the ground floor of the house would offer not only workspace for Rietveld – who lived in another part of Utrecht with his wife and their children until her death in the 1960s – but it would also create an opportunity to bring the day-to-day excitement and the comings and goings associated with an architectural office into the world of the home, providing both children and adults with a more stimulating intellectual environment than they would have had in a home planned and decorated along conventional lines.

Clearly the client's programme and her commitment to cultural reform within the home and family are central to the history of the house and to the work of its architect. The house, which understandably is given a full-colour illustration in almost every survey text of twentieth-century architecture, is not simply a beautiful work of De Stijl sculpture but a home shaped by two people's notion of artistic and social values as expressed through architectural language. While we might add here that, as a woman and mother, Schröder was particularly drawn to the domestic environment as an arena in which to experiment with social and artistic reforms, we should also recognise that the home and its design had a similar importance in the work of many male architects and social reformers of the twentieth-century, from Le Corbusier to Frank Lloyd Wright. This question of women's particular focus on the domestic realm calls out for further study.

Josephine Baker

In the almost contemporary case of Josephine Baker, the 19-year-old African-American singer and dancer who arrived in Paris in 1925 and joined up with a song and dance troupe called "La Revue Nègre," the architectural results are very different indeed.[5] Baker's patronage represents a particularly interesting case within the context of a discussion of culture and representation: like Marilyn Monroe and Jackie Kennedy, she was one of the most widely photographed women and also one of the most highly sophisticated manipulators of visual media in the history of twentieth-century culture. Perhaps it was as a result of the profusion of images that surrounded her from the earliest years of her career – from the famous 'banana skirt' (Figure 4.3) that created her reputation in France to the highly exaggerated, racially coded, posters by Paul Colin for the Folies Bergères – that she quickly became so adept at controlling and shaping her own public reputation and appearance. As the object of desire and curiosity, and as the subject of so much fantasy, Baker had a genuine purpose in knowing how visual codes worked and how she was portrayed by them. Like many women, she understood and took advantage of her ability to choreograph the spectacle of her public life and of her own beauty, enhanced by costumes and scripts of her own devising.

While her flamboyant manipulation of theatre, both public and private, and her status as a quixotic nightclub entertainer caused many to doubt her sincerity as either an advocate of civil rights reform or as the devoted mother of twelve children adopted from orphanages around the world – two roles that she took on with particular energy in the 1950s and 1960s – the evidence of her houses and estates suggests that her commitment to these goals was sincere. Cast by Europeans as a sex goddess and as a primitive, black-skinned, free spirit who had come to them from some exotic faraway place, Baker found that the heady cocktail of sexual and racial

4.3
Baker in the infamous 'banana skirt' c. 1925
Photo, courtesy of Visual Resources Department, Wellesley College

4.4
Model of Adolf Loos's 'House for Joséphine Baker' by Paul Groenendijk and Piet Vollard, Rotterdam
Photo, courtesy of Canadian Center for Architecture, Montreal

fantasy could make her a star, and she played it for all it was worth. She was the toast of Paris, performing to sold-out crowds at the Folie Bergères, when the architect Adolph Loos met her in a nightclub and became completely infatuated with her, reportedly, after Baker taught him to dance the Charleston. Loos's love letter to Baker, which took the form of a design for a boldly striped, modernist *maison de plaisance* designed in 1927 (Figure 4.4), is well known to scholars, thanks largely to Beatriz Colomina's excellent analysis of the role of spectatorship and voyeurism encoded in its bold interior planning.[6] With its black and white exterior and stripped down forms, the house represented Baker as glamorous, elemental and avant garde. It offered modest accommodations for eating, sleeping, and entertainment, but its centrepiece was the deep indoor swimming pool at its core which was intended as a sort of aquatic theatre for Baker's use. The below-water depths of this pool were surrounded by walkways on three sides so that visitors to the house could view Baker not only from above the surface of the pool but also as a shimmering dark figure seen through glazed portholes in the lower part of the walls.

Baker's reaction to this project is not known, but the house remained unbuilt. This is hardly surprising, based on its own merits or lack thereof, but it is especially understandable when we look at Beau Chêne, the house that Baker bought for herself in the late 1920s at Le Vesinet, a suburb of Paris. Here we can see clearly the image she herself was trying to project. Like the glamorous movie star poses that she learned to strike for photographers both on stage and off, this suburban chateau of the early twentieth century makes use of a combination of luxury, elegance, old-world sophistication and Baker's trademark star-power to construct a multi-faceted message. For Baker, Beau Chêne, with its French Renaissance Revival details, was appealing not only because it was conveniently located in an upmarket neighbourhood close to the city and had extensive grounds (she kept a large and varied menagerie), but also because the well-established bourgeois enclave of Le Vesinet, dotted with large houses and parks and criss-crossed by broad boulevards, helped to erase her former image as a lower-class showgirl. Whatever Loos's fantasies about Baker's private life might have been, her own architectural patronage emphasised her wealth and respectability.

In a publicity campaign crafted by Baker and her husband, she was transformed into a superstar and provided with the home she deserved for this role. The interior of her house was reportedly decorated in a wide variety of period and exotic styles, each room themed to create a different environment. The bathrooms were black and silver, and encrusted with mirrors. This particular combination of sexy spectacle, gracious living, and opulent decor had been a standby for nouveaux riches for almost a century by the time Baker arrived on the scene, and it was enjoying a heady revival in the Hollywood of the 1920s. Baker seized on Beau Chêne with her unfailing sense of how to make an impression on the public, and the house was an

4.5
Les Milandes
Photo, Author

indispensable part of her publicity campaign. Throughout the 1930s she was photographed and interviewed extensively, and while she was often the object of racism and snobbery in the capitals of Europe, she had her mansion and her stylish European way of life to point to when she was snubbed by the critics or treated as a vulgar American showgirl by the press.

In the 1940s, Baker acquired a chateau and estate in the Dordogne which would be her home and showplace for the remainder of her life. Les Milandes (Figure 4.5) went well beyond Beau Chêne as an expression of glamour, money and respectability, for it was a real fifteenth-century castle, with extensive grounds, a working farm, and a small village around it. First acquired by Baker as a refuge for herself and her entourage during the Second World War, Les Milandes later became her all-consuming project. It was to serve both as a home for herself and for her many adopted children – the so-called 'Rainbow Tribe' that she assembled as a gesture toward 'world brotherhood', as she put it – which would function as a conference centre devoted to the fight against racism, as a hotel and resort, complete with nightly entertainment provided by Baker herself accompanied by dancers, singers and musicians imported from Paris.

Here again, Baker and her then husband (her third, by this time) put their considerable skills to work to create a new post-war image for her: she was photographed in her military uniform (she did in fact play an important role as a spy and courier during the war, and she was cited for her bravery) and Les Milandes became a theme park devoted to promoting her career. Not only did she occupy its main stage nightly, she was also represented in a series of wax-work tableaux called the 'Jo Rama' which showed scenes from her life, beginning in the slums of East St Louis, Missouri, and highlighting more recent events, such as Baker being blessed by the Pope. Using photos of herself proudly posing like Marie Antoinette in her dairy on the model farm, which boasted of having the most advanced equipment and of sharing profits with farm labourers, or surrounded by children of all races, Baker created an image that counteracted the expectations of those for whom her race, class, and gender – to say nothing of her brash Americanness – were the dominant markers of her identity. Clearly, Baker did not thwart convention in the predictable way by creating an oppositional image either in her public activities or in her architectural patronage. Instead she embraced the conventions of glamour and pushed them to their extreme, turning away from modernism to foreground old-world respectability, and using her prominence and social status to push for change.

Stung by the racism she encountered when she toured the USA in the 1950s, she worked harder to make Les Milandes a haven for people of all races and nationalities, and particularly for children from around the world. Using the proceeds from her work as an entertainer to support the venture, Baker worked tirelessly to make her vision a reality. She gave speeches, appeared at public events, and wrote books about her life and work. Her emphasis on her home as a new sort of living environment for a mother and her children bears a great deal of similarity to Truus Schröder's vision of her role at Utrecht. For both women, the domestic realm was the locus of social and artistic change; even while Baker worked night after night on the stage (she died in 1975 after performing a come-back show at the Folies Bergères, celebrating her fifty years on the stage) she viewed her work for social and political change in and around her estate as her most significant contribution.

That Les Milandes was created in an image that was anything but modern is hardly surprising. As a black woman born in the ghetto and educated on the stage, she had to establish her class credentials, as many others before and since have done, by making use of the gilt swags and heavy ornament of a historicising, palatial style. In fact, this style reappears again and again in the socially mobile 1950s, from Hollywood and Las Vegas to the resort hotels of Miami Beach and the Riviera, and from suburban Paris to suburban New Jersey. At Les Milandes, Baker chose to cloak her political radicalism in architectural respectability, exploiting a design language that, in its apparent conservatism, would hardly strike us as revolutionary until we realise that for an audience more likely to see Baker as the maid than as the lady of the house, these trappings of royalty made a startling impression.

Paul Rudolph's apartment

In stylistic terms, nothing could be further from Les Milandes than Paul Rudolph's ultra-modern apartment on Beekman Place in New York City.[7] Rudolph, who died in 1997 at the age of 79, was a American Brutalist architect whose career flourished in the late 1950s and 1960s. Dean of the Yale School of Architecture from 1958 to 1965, he was the architect of a number of prominent buildings in the Northeast of the USA, including the Jewett Arts Center at Wellesley College of 1958, and the infamous concrete Yale Art and Architecture Building of 1962 which was set on fire by students in 1969 as a symbol of architectural oppression and faceless authority (it now has a significant cult following as a prime example of Mid-Century American Modernism).[8] While Rudolph's critical reputation has always been mixed, he is currently the subject of a revival of interest and study, not simply because he is another rediscovered 1950s' architect, but because he was a gifted

4.6
**Paul Rudolph's
Beekman Place
apartment,
interior, 1967-79**
Photographs ©
Peter Aaron Esto

designer who was capable of making both exquisitely rendered drawings and surprisingly complex and interesting spaces. On his death, an enormous archive of papers and models were sent to the Library of Congress in Washington, promising significant new opportunities for the study of his work.

The interest of the Rudolph apartment, for our purposes here, is similar to that of the Schröder House: it is a living environment in which the unconventional programme requirements and outsider status of the client acted as a catalyst for experimentation in modern design. Moreover, since Rudolph was a gay man as well as the architect and client for the house, it is also significant as an example of a home formed in response to what we might call a 'gay identity' as that was understood in the period from the late 1960s through the 1970s during which Rudolph was working on the building. Like Philip Johnson's Glass House/Guest House complex of 1949, Rudolph's apartment emphasises aspects of the domestic programme that are ordinarily suppressed: sexuality, theatricality, and the private functions of the body.[9] That this is all done within the language of a highly expressionist spatial composition makes it all the more significant as a work of architecture.

The most startling thing about the apartment is the extraordinary four-storey open space at its core (Figure 4.6), bounded by plexiglas parapets

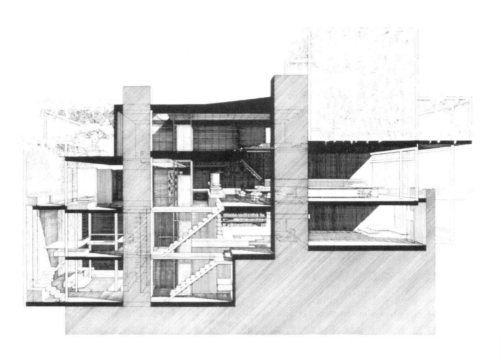

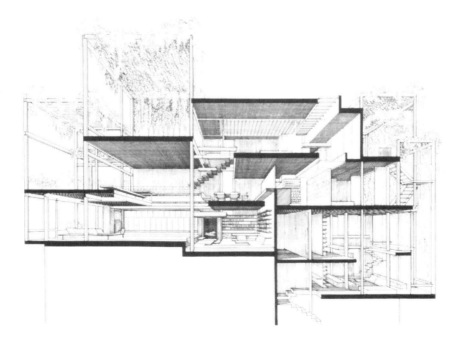

and shiny, reflective surfaces – a space which recalls the swimming pool in Loos's Baker House design. This deep, open atrium and the floating planes around it confuse and overwhelm the observer: cantilevered plexiglas platforms (one of which supports Rudolph's own drafting table) and narrow walkways connect the various parts of the room at unpredictable angles, disorienting and disarming the visitor while giving the house's occupant, who was familiar with these spaces and their physical boundaries, a considerable advantage. At once glamorous and disturbing, Rudolph's apartment uses architectural design as an expression of power, demonstrating the architect/inhabitant's ability to control both his own environment and the experiences of his guests.

In a recent article in *Casabella*, the architectural historian Tim Rohan analyses this project within the context of Rudolph's private life and sexuality (see note 7 above). For Rohan, the house's most significant feature is the fact that it conceals its occupant's secret life as a gay man behind a veil of architectural smoke and mirrors: although Rudolph's live-in lover also occupied this home for many years, his suite of rooms forms a sort of secret inner sanctum, a metaphorical closet that is largely hidden from view. From the interior of the main public rooms there is little intimation of the existence of this private world tucked away in a corner and only clearly visible in section drawings (Figure 4.7 a and b). This coded, ambivalent expression/suppression of the existence of the partner clearly marks a significant departure from the domestic norm in both social and architectural terms.

In the details of this hidden bedroom suite, Rudolph displays his considerable gifts as an architect as well as his sense of humour: here again he makes extensive use of transparent and reflective materials, demonstrating both his virtuoso handling of the section (stacking planes and spaces one above the other in unusual ways) and his talent for manipulating compact spaces. As in the main spaces of the apartment, the primary concern here is with revealing and concealing spatial and emotional linkages: while this suite represents a hyper-private area of the home in many respects, it is also quite disarmingly open to view, if one knows where to look. Not only can it be glimpsed from Rudolph's own master bedroom four floors and a long, oblique diagonal above it, but it also contains such odd devices as a transparent sink in the upstairs bathroom which enables viewers to watch the activities of other occupants unbeknownst to themselves. These architectural elements are clearly meant as private demonstrations of architectural virtuosity and of a perverse, campy sense of irony which highlight the difference between this home and other examples in which normative boundaries of social and physical space prevail. Moreover, they are undeniable demonstrations of Rudolph's magus-like power to dominate and deceive.

4.7a and b
**Paul Rudolph
apartment:
section drawings**
courtesy of Prints
and Photographs
Division, Library
of Congress,
Washington, DC

4.8
**Paul Rudolph
apartment,
bedroom.**
Ezra Stoller © Esto

Finally, in the master bedroom and bathroom (complete with a plexiglas bathtub fully visible from the guest room and kitchen below it), we again recognise Rudolph's architectural talent and his perverse theatricality. A white shag carpet, metal mesh curtains and an enormous billboard super graphic (Figure 4.8), showing a handsome, hairy-chested macho man surrounded by adoring women (reflected in the mirror-wall at the foot of the bed) not only sets the tone of the bedroom – no frilly Laura Ashley coverlets here – but does so with a hard-edged, ironic sense of humour. The overall result is an extremely original and creative essay on spatial relations as well as a radical – and to some people off-putting – representation of sexuality and domestic theatre. Indeed, Rudolph's approach in this project recalls the Pop experiments of the Independent Group, the Smithsons and Andy Warhol, placing his work in a wider context than the one in which he is usually viewed.

Conclusion

What, in the end, can we learn from these examples? Some possible findings include the following: first, that in architecture and design the unfamiliar and under-represented identity of the outsider (whether architect or client) is often a catalyst for change; second, that in those rare cases in which unmarried women, traditionally a disempowered group in the world of architectural patronage, are given a chance to build for themselves and their households, we often see original designs and creative responses to the domestic programme, emphasising hybrid types, blending of public and private spaces, and the establishment of new forms of community; third, that the conventions of gender representation are often exaggerated or foregrounded in significant ways by women clients, architects and designers, even in those cases in which these conventions are not subverted but apparently embraced; fourth, that although gender is one of the most significant categories of representation in architecture, and clearly occupies the core of the domestic programme, we must also attend carefully to questions of sexuality, taking particular care to recognise and interpret the role played by gay and lesbian identities; and fifth, that we must be careful not to generalise – each of these categories is historically and culturally constructed and deeply influenced by differences created by such factors as race, ethnicity, and class status.

As we confront the challenge of writing cultural history, the case of Josephine Baker serves as a compelling lesson about the importance of resisting stereotypes and going beyond predictable conclusions when dealing with the architecture of the past. In the making of place, those who stand outside the power structure or who do not conform to accepted norms – women, gay men and lesbians, people of colour – are frequently expert at navigating the treacherous waters of public imagery and representation, choosing when to reveal themselves and when to remain hidden. Our challenge as historians is to rediscover the multiple meanings of the buildings and spaces they left behind.

Notes

1 Alice T. Friedman, *Women and the Making of the Modern House: A Social and Architectural History*, New York: Harry N. Abrams, Inc., 1998.

2 Alice T. Friedman, *House and Household in Elizabethan England: Wollaton Hall and the Willoughby Family*, Chicago: University of Chicago Press, 1988.

3 For Le Corbusier's relationship with Baker see *Le Corbusier: une encyclopédie*, Paris: Centre Georges Pompidou, 1987, 'Baker, Joséphine'; and Jean Petit, (ed.), *Le Corbusier lui-même*, Geneva: Editions rousseau, 1970, pp.68–9.

4 For the Schröder House, see Paul Overy *et al.*, *The Rietveld Schröder House*, Cambridge, MA,: MIT Press, 1988, and Marijke Küper and Ida van Zijl, *Gerrit Th. Rietveld: The Complete Works*, Utrecht: Centraal Museum, 1992. My own research, published in Chapter 2 of *Women and the Making of the Modern House*, was conducted in collaboration with Maristella Casciato.

5 For Baker's life and fame, see Jean-Claude Baker and Christ Chase, *Joséphine: The Hungry Heart*, New York: Random House, 1993, and Phyllis Rose, *Jazz Cleopatra: Josephine Baker in Her Time*, New York: Doubleday, 1989.

6 Beatriz Colomina, 'The Split Wall: Domestic Voyeurism', in Beatriz Colomina (ed.), *Sexuality and Space*, New York: Princeton Architectural Press, 1982, pp.73–130.

7 The apartment is discussed by Tim Rohan,'Spettacoli pubblici e privati', *Casabella*, 673/674, LXIII, December 1999–January 2000, 138–150; see also Michael Sorkin, 'The Light House', *House and Garden*, 1, January 1988, 88-95, and Robert A. M. Stern *et al.*, *New York 1960: Architecture and Urbanism between the Second World War and the Bicentennial*, New York: Monacelli, 1995, p. 545.

8 For Rudolph's work at Wellesley College, see Timothy Rohan, 'The Dangers of Eclecticism: Paul Rudolph's Jewett Arts Center at Wellesley', in Sarah Goldhagen and Réjean Legault (eds), *Anxious Modernisms: Experimentation in Postwar Architectural Culture*, Montreal: Canadian Centre for Architecture and Cambridge, MA: MIT Press, 2000, pp.190–213, and Peter Fergusson, James F. O'Gorman and John Rhodes, *The Landscape and Architecture of Wellesley College*, Wellesley, MA: Wellesley College, 2000, Chapter 9. For an overview of Rudolph's career, see *The Architecture of Paul Rudolph*, Introduction by Sibyl Moholy-Nagy, New York: Praeger, 1970.

9 For the Glass House as a work of 'gay architecture', see Friedman, *Women and the Making of the Modern House*, Chapter 4; for Rudolph's gay sensibility see Rohan's 'The Dangers of Eclecticism'.

Chapter 5

Architecture and reputation
Eileen Gray, gender and Modernism

Lynne Walker

Quatre ans avant sa mort, Eileen Gray, devint célèbre[1]

Michael Raynaud

Issues of authorship, agency and authority have been central to critical writing and theory across a wide range of academic disciplines.[2] A major focus of the project of second wave feminism within the academy has laid claim to the authorial subject, to individual women as speaking subjects and subjects of history, which encompasses women as producers of architecture and the built environment. Since the early 1970s, the history of architecture has been investigated and rewritten from a feminist perspective, while lively, often fearless, debates have exposed the phallocentric stance of architectural culture, questioning how architecture is practised and the values of a male-dominated profession.[3] Conventionally, however, in architectural history and in architectural practice (as well as in the general public's perception), the idea of a female architect has been considered at best exceptional, but, more usually, a contradiction in terms, in spite of two decades of feminist research and writing. Meanwhile women's place in architecture remains generally on the lower and middle rungs of the professional ladder.

In this chapter, I want to consider the implications of gender on evaluations of architects and architecture and how gender operates to affect our understanding of history and historical importance. Extending the argument to how these series of judgements and their scale of merit are represented by the highly selected canonical works of architectural history, I want to focus on how this history is structured and organised by gender, mediated by disciplinary practices and valences both within architectural culture and appropriated from art history, through attribution and œuvre, quality and hierarchies, professionalism and visibility. Taking Eileen Gray as a case study, this chapter will examine the implications of gender for architectural history, assessing Eileen Gray's career, reputation and place in history as depicted by her contemporaries, by modernist historians and by feminist revisionists. Through re-reading a selection of historical and critical texts, this reassessment seeks to engage with sexual stereotypes and issues of difference, in positionality, age, class and race, as well as gender, to explain their cultural work and impact on critical reception and on the production of an authorial and historical subject. In this chapter there is also an awareness of our own position as latterday viewers of Gray's work, as readers and writers of history and I will attempt to tease out our investment in Eileen Gray's work – and in Gray herself. Why do we respond so strongly to to her and to her work? Has she become the feminists' heroine?

In many ways, Eileen Gray's status has never been higher: she has been the subject of numerous exhibitions, catalogues, books and articles – the recent work of Caroline Constant has been especially important in this process of research, analysis and interpretation.[4] Gray is listed in dictionaries of art, architecture and design and in the supreme accolade of subjecthood, the *Dictionary of National Biography*;[5] her work is illustrated in 'Banister Fletcher' among the self-proclaimed most important buildings of 'all times and all countries';[6] and her furniture is sold in smart design shops and on-line in reproductions, which compete with claims for its authenticity, while the originals go for astronomical prices. In addition to her furniture and other designs for the decorative arts, Eileen Gray's architectural drawings, models, photographs and related papers are held in the archives of national collections at the Victoria and Albert Museum, in the Royal Institute of British Architects, and have been most recently acquired by the National Museum of Ireland, Collins Barracks, Dublin.[7] Importantly, after years of neglect and vandalism, E.1027, Gray's major architectural work, has been declared a national monument of the highest importance by the French government and has been bought and is being restored, in partnership with Coastal Conservancy, by the local authority of Roquebrune Cap Martin which is raising funds for that purpose assisted by Friends of E.1027.[8]

Most significantly, Eileen Gray's buildings are now included as a matter of course in the curricula of academic architectural studies. In short, she has achieved canonical status in architectural history. She is, however, virtually alone. While a robust feminist perspective on the history of architecture has developed and feminist histories and theories of architecture have been written, the canon of architectural history is virtually unchanged. Have thirty years of feminist theorising and rewriting the history of architecture led only to Eileen Gray, the lone 'Exceptional Woman', the one outstanding woman, the exception that proves the rule that great architects are male? In this narrative of negativity, she has become either token woman or feminist icon. Feminist historians, such as Griselda Pollock, warn about the dangers of constructing 'great women' artists, of celebrating the mythic female along the lines of the male genius – substituting great women and their paintings for great men and theirs.[9] Is Eileen Gray in danger of becoming that mythic beast for architecture, the enigmatic, but great woman who designed canonical modernist buildings? Moreover, are we simply adding Eileen Gray to architectural history without challenging architectural histories' categories or changing the rules of the game? Modernist buildings and their architect 'masters', Le Corbusier, Mies van der Rohe, Walter Gropius and Frank Lloyd Wright, are still the most highly revered, most published and most widely taught subjects of twentieth-century architectural history, even after two generations of revisionist historians as diverse as Reyner Banham, David Watkin and Dolores Hayden. At worst are we, those readers and writers of Eileen Gray's work, merely providing the defining opposite of male creativity? Eileen Gray, as Sylvia Lavin points out, is most often set in opposition to Le Corbusier, a fact which highlights the need to disentangle Gray from Le Corbusier along with 'the concern for male agency and its desire to contain the feminine'.[10] Can we find a positive, more productive reading of 'Eileen Gray', the historical subject, in what Griselda Pollock has identified as 'a gap ... that space of possibility':[11] between gendered cultural prescriptions of femininity and difference which is outside 'dominant masculine meanings embodied'[12] in modernist history – a space for re-making history as its readers and writers, as well as for artistic production?

When Eileen Gray's architecture and decorative work were first exhibited in Britain thirty years ago (1972–3), the Women's Movement was reaching its peak and the challenge of second wave feminism was a galvanising context for the exhibition and its critical reception. However, gender issues arising from her work were scarcely addressed explicitly, as no feminist critique was in circulation in architectural discourse in Britain. Gray was merely inserted into an existing modernist history and her place in the hierarchy of the mainstream of modernist history was considered.

5.1
Installation of the Eileen Gray exhibition, RIBA Heinz Gallery, 1972–3
© Alan Irvine

Nevertheless, her work caused a sensation in an architectural culture which thought of 'history' as a knowable, finite proposition. What preoccupied many of the critics and historians who assessed her work in the building press in the early 1970s was the notion of Eileen Gray as a neglected pioneer of the Modern Movement[13] – a kind of female Mackintosh – and, as with Mackintosh, there was a grain of truth in it. Certainly, Eileen Gray's cutting edge modernist buildings and furniture were produced in the heady days of the 1920s and early 1930s and her work was virtually ignored for three decades, during which she continued working. Between 1938 until her 'rediscovery' in the late 1960s/early 1970s, she had neither clients nor recognition for previous work. Some architects, such as Wells Coates, admired her work, and her house at Roquebrune, E.1027, was known to French architects in the 1950s, as *L'Architecture d'Aujourd'hui* indicated when publishing Gray's Project for a Cultural Centre; 'Eileen Gray ... devoted a great part of her life to architecture and has carried out, with Jean Badovici, the house at Roquebrune that is known to all our readers.'[14] In spite of this flicker of recognition, Eileen Gray was outside the loop of history and unrecorded by modernist historians.

5.2
*L'Architecture
Vivante, Maison en
Bord de Mer*, 1929,
a special issue
devoted to E.1027
RIBA Library
Photographs
Collection

In an early reassessment of her work, Reyner Banham, the historian and critic, was the most powerful and influential voice to offer an explanation of Gray's work and reputation. In 'Nostalgia for Style', published in *New Society*, Banham reviewed the first exhibition of her work in London, held at the RIBA Heinz Gallery in 1972–3 (Figure 5.1). He too was interested in why Eileen Gray had been ignored by modernist historians and began by questioning the exhibition organisers about why Gray deserved an exhibition.[15] Their reply, based on the English tradition of connoisseurship, was 'that the quality of her work always justified it'. Although it was the one fact that most struck modernist critics and architects, Banham dismissed their reasoning as rather thin.

Although Banham was the most vital and effective questioner of the initial, narrow modernist history of architecture in his assessment of Eileen Gray's work, we can see the old rules of the game being applied and an appeal made to an unruffled vision of history as objective and rational, if occasionally remiss. Eileen Gray was depicted as marginal both to the litany of modernism – even expanded modernisms – and outside the select band of recognised 'masters' of modernism: Banham wrote:

> The case itself is really that Eileen Gray intersected the paths of conspicuous glory at only one point. She designed the seaside house at Cap Martin where Le Corbusier later did some famous murals. Her client/collaborator was Jean Badovici, publisher of the famous *Architecture Vivante* folders that made many a reputation in the twenties and thirties (Figure 5.2). Though he

duly did one on the *maison en bord de mer* [E.1027], with her name as large as his on the cover, it didn't make her reputation. She didn't even become a footnote, like the Futurists did.

Banham saw Eileen Gray as somewhat privileged in her friends (Edwin Lutyens' old, bad joke about women architects being as good as their collaborators seems to have been lurking in the back of his mind), owing any claim to fame to male connections. He implied a secondary role for her in the design of her best-known work – which was completely the reverse of what actually happened – and assumed generosity and even gallantry for her male collaborator. Gray's sub-footnote status in history seems deserved. Although she was in his analysis 'a genuine original and a mature talent by the mid-twenties', Banham declared: 'Part of the trouble, I suspect, was stylistic. Her work never quite aligned with either the International Modern style or the tolerated additions like Expressionism.' According to Banham, she was 'not a follower of the emerging steel-tube fashion. And where she does show tinges of fashion, it seems to be Art Deco.' He concludes: 'That, of course put it [Gray's work] beyond critical or historical attention for almost three decades.'[16]

The anxiety about fashion within modernism in relation to gendered notions of decoration is explained by Mark Wigley in his essay, 'White Out: Fashioning the Modern':

> Much of the discourse around modern architecture can therefore be understood as an on-going pre-emptive strike against the charge that it is itself fashion. Fashion is portrayed as an insidious phenomenon that will inevitably return to contaminate the pure logic of architecture unless it is held consciously in check ... [architecture] constantly monitors itself, publicly censoring certain architects, building types, compositions, materials and details as "decorative".[17]

Originality, which Banham mentions as counting against Gray's reputation was, however, one of the highest values of architectural modernism, and logically should have been a qualification for representation in history rather than cause for dismissal, but even this highly-prized quality was not sufficient to override the deviation from modernism in her early decorative work or reminders of Art Deco richness and elegance of materials and surfaces, the 'tinges of fashion', that could be detected in her modernist furniture designs. Although Wigley provided a well-supported case for 'the watchdog mentality'[18] of modernist historians, it is difficult to recreate today the climate of this obsessional categorising of modernist historians and the strict policing of the purity of modernism which Banham references, chides, but subtly reinforces. But the picture is vivid for those of us who learned about architecture in less pluralist times. There was an almost totalitarian strictness of criteria that required strict, untainted fulfilment, which Eileen Gray's work was thought to offend. Her 'deviant' early work outside modernism was held against her and even read into her later modernist designs which would have otherwise qualified for the modernist canon. Although Banham was one of the first voices to speak against the narrowness of modernism, his review of the Eileen Gray exhibition at the RIBA Heinz Gallery provides a salutory lesson about the rigid categories of modernism and the way in which they operated to exclude 'deviants' from modernist history. Banham commented:

> [Eileen Gray's work] was, also, in its day, part of a personal style and philosophy of interior design which was, by the look of things, too rich for the punditry to take. And if the punditry didn't publish you, particularly in the great canon-defining compendia of the thirties, forties and fifties you dropped out of the record, and ceased to be part of the universe of scholarly discourse.

Clearly, Banham was thinking here of modernist writers and texts, such as Hitchcock and Johnson's *The International Style* (1932); Nikolaus Pevsner's *Pioneers of the Modern Movement* (1936), and Sigfried Giedion's *Space, Time and Architecture* (1941), to say nothing of his own *Theory and Design in the First Machine Age* (1960). Although he admitted to finding Eileen Gray's design work 'fascinating' his musings on the rigidity of modernism could not mask his own lukewarm response to Gray's designs: 'It should be obvious by now that I don't consider her a major talent', he wrote. Although Banham said that it was useful to have a fuller 'view of the design world of the twenties and thirties' which did not 'divide into mutually incompatible schools (machinery v handicraft, Functionists v Expressionists)', ultimately, he saw Eileen Gray's work as a by-product of academic industry, a reinscription of narrow modernism.[19]

In spite of these vigorous comments about Gray's designs and their context, Banham did not analyse, or even describe, Gray's architecture, although it was in front of his eyes in the form of photographs and drawings in the exhibition. The socially constructed division between 'woman' and 'architect' as linguistic categories operated to make the work, not ignored or neglected, but invisible. Design for the applied arts and interior design were woman's place, not architecture; the sexual division of labour remained intact. His argument that to accept Eileen Gray's work into the most highly valued part of the canon of twentieth-century architecture was fashionable, politically

correct and careerist masked what Cheryl Buckley has identified as 'patriarchal assumptions [both conscious and unconscious] about women's roles and abilities as designers [which] have important consequences for historians',[20] in this case, for Banham's analysis of Eileen Gray as 'not a major talent'.[21]

In fact, at the peak of Eileen Gray's career in the 1920s and 1930s, her architecture and design for the applied arts were neither obscure, neglected, nor unsuccessful. In the 1920s, she was among the leading designers in France. Her designs for furniture received critical acclaim as early as 1913, and her shop in Paris, Jean Désert, sold her furniture, lacquer-work and carpets to a sophisticated and wealthy clientele. At the Salon d'Automne in 1922, she exhibited with other prominent designers, such as Mallet-Stevens and Le Corbusier, both of whom admired her work to the extent that Mallet-Stevens wanted her to work with him and Le Corbusier later displayed her design for a Vacation Centre (1936–7) as an exemplar of the best in French modernist architecture in his Pavillon des Temps Nouveaux at the International Exhibition in Paris in 1937[22] (Figure 5.4). After an exhibition of her work with French designers in Holland in 1924, a special issue of the prestigious avant-garde Dutch journal, *Wendingen*, was devoted to her furniture and interiors, and featured one of her earliest architectural projects, a design for a Small House with a Factory. The De Stijl architect, Jan Wils, wrote approvingly in the Introduction: 'Free from every tradition ... Eileen Gray is a very special, unique figure in the world of new form-finding.'[23] A special issue of *Architecture Vivante* was published in 1929 with her co-operation by her friend, admirer and collaborator, Jean Badovici, to celebrate the House by the Sea at Roquebrune (1926-9), known as E.1027 — a numerical representation of Gray's and Badovici's intertwined initials.[24]

While Gray's design work was well circulated in French journals of decorative art, stylish periodicals and newpapers on both sides of the Atlantic, her buildings and interiors were published in small, but landmark, issues of the architectural press.[25] She did not feature, however, in the established building press in France, England or the United States, which played a role in promoting the 'best' buildings of their day, or in standard texts on modernism, as Banham has rightly pointed out. Her early work was decorative, hand-made and often luxurious, even exotic, which placed it outside the mainstream and beyond the pale stylistically. It did not fit into modernism's rigid categories, or, from our contemporary perspective, it was not the right kind of modernism. To writers in the 1930s, 1940s and 1950s, it was thought to be Art Deco and as such not a candidate for inclusion in history which was about 'Modernism' and the 'International Style' exclusively. Decoration was identified traditionally with the 'feminine' in architectural theory, and from the mid-1920s, the severe limitation, concentration and

5.3
Eileen Gray
photographed at
her apartment in
Rue Bonaparte,
Paris 1974
© Alan Irvine

Lynne Walker

UN CENTRE DE VACANCES

5.4
Eileen Gray's
design for Un
Centre de
Vacances credited
to 'Eelen Gray –
France' by Le
Corbusier in
*Des Canons,
Des Munitions?
Merci! Des
Loges...S.V.P.*
(1938) monograph
of the Pavillon
des Temps
Nouveaux,
International
Exhibition of
Art and Technique,
Paris, 1937
RIBA Library
Photographs
Collection

ultimate rejection of applied decoration were cardinal principles of the new architecture. Even Gray's later modernist work was always seen through the unfavoured decorative feminine, as Banham's review indicates. Although the modern movement encouraged the connection between art, architecture and the applied arts, and promoted the idea of the architect as designer, modernist history nevertheless privileged the architect and architecture over the designer and design for the applied arts. Although there are exceptions, modernist historians generally did not study or write about designers in the decorative and applied arts, many of whom were women. Modernist writers did play the decorative card on occasion, most famously, when seeking causation for the decline of modernist genius (C.R. Mackintosh) in the decorative distractions of the female designer (Margaret Macdonald Mackintosh).[26]

Eileen Gray was a self-trained architect and not a card-carrying, fully paid-up member of the architectural profession. She was not educated formally alongside male architects in the rigorous, stratified programme of the École des Beaux-Arts, to which women had only been admitted in 1897, nor was she articled to an architect in the traditional manner. She did not set up on her own in an architectural office or work within an architectural practice, nor was she part of the professional networks of architectural culture. These social networks were, and are, a site for the production of architectural identity, profile and recognition, and they are crucial to getting commissions

5.5
Eileen Gray, Tempe a Pailla, street front, 1932-4, Castellar, France
Peter Adam

and having work published, the track which leads ultimately to incorporation in the canon of architectural history. Eileen Gray occupied the feminine space of the interior and design, doubly disqualified from being a professional architect, therefore, by lack of formal qualifications and by gender.

Analysing Eileen Gray's work in the narrow architectural context of the modern movement and seeing her as an 'exceptional pioneer' is problematic and counter-productive. Nor, indeed, is it useful to see her work only in its French setting. She was in spite of her long and fruitful association with France and with modernism, London-trained with strong connections of family and residence to Britain and to London.[27] The conditions of production of her early, formative period were indelibly marked by the Arts and Crafts Movement, which was embraced by thousands of women of her generation as well as by their male colleagues. As Esther McCoy noted after seeing the exhibition of Eileen Gray's work at the Women's Building in Los Angeles, 'in the 1890s [Gray] attended the Slade School and ... found craftsmanship and humaneness in the fading Morris movement'.[28] However, women's participation in the movement was not 'fading' in the 1890s but approaching its peak in Britain, and provided a framework for Gray's interest and a precedent for her craft activities in lacquerwork This beautiful, difficult craft had been admired, bought and collected in England in the late nineteenth century and was displayed at the Victoria and Albert Museum, which Gray often visited.[29]

The impact of the Arts and Crafts Movement on her architecture and on modernism was generally unexplored, but Tempe a Pailla, the house Eileen Gray designed and built for herself at Castellar, near Menton (1932–4), displays the close connection between her modernism and the Arts and Crafts approach, its tenets and attitudes to materials (Figures 5.5 and 5.6). In a similar practice to the Arts and Crafts ideal, Gray lived on the site and acted as builder and designer of all aspects of the architecture, including the furnishings and fittings. Both shared a commitment to craftsmanship and careful construction, as well as the practice of working closely with artisans. At Tempe a Pailla, truth to materials is not represented by the usual smooth white box of the modern movement, instead simple, local materials and concrete were used, which Gray combined in a flexible, experimental way, like Arts and Crafts architects, such as W.R. Lethaby and E.S. Prior.

It is significant that the Arts and Crafts Movement aimed to break down the hierarchy of the arts that favoured painting, sculpture and architecture over the applied arts and thus encouraged the collaboration of artists, designers and architects, which Gray explored throughout her career. Arts and Crafts approaches encouraged the crossing of artistic and professional boundaries with architects designing for the applied arts and sculptors and painters applying their work to architecture. Gray's move from painting to craft and design to architecture was undoubtedly facilitated by these ideas and needs to be considered in this context. Moreover, her architectural activities challenged and helped break down the repressive mechanism of the sexual division of labour, which limited women's design activities to areas associated with the applied or so-called lesser arts.

Gender not only circumscribed the choice of professional activities available to women around 1900, but determined access to architectural education. If Eileen Gray had stayed to study architecture at the University of London after her training at the Slade, she would have been offered only a very truncated, non-professional course which was all that was open to women at the Bartlett School of Architecture in those days.[30] The Architectural Association, the other school which would have undoubtedly been considered by her, had turned away women applicants in 1893 and did not take women until 1917. In Paris, at this time, Eileen Gray could probably not have gained entry into the architectural course at the École des Beaux-Arts, although, in 1902, it had accepted the American, Julia Morgan, in the architectural section. But Gray lacked Morgan's strong academic background and training in architecture and engineering which was then available to women at American universities (Morgan had a degree in engineering from the University of California, Berkeley).[31]

Eileen Gray was 51 years old when her first building was completed

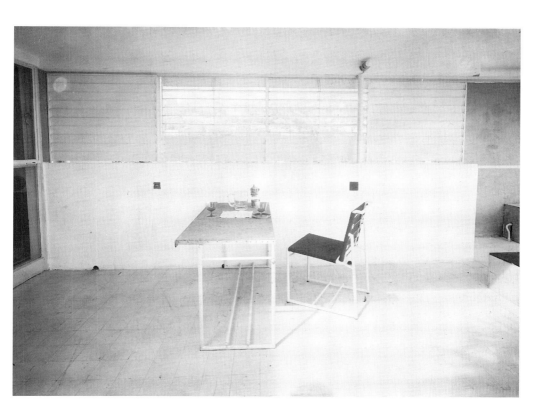

5.6
The living terrace at Tempe a Pailla
Archive of Art and Design, National Art Library, Victoria & Albert Museum and Peter Adam

(1927) and part of an older generation that had had fewer opportunities for architectural education and training. She taught herself architecture, approaching it in the same methodical way she had learned lacquer work, by travelling and carefully studying other work, by reading technical as well as theoretical books, by re-working earlier examples, by acquiring first-hand experience, and by associating herself with non-threatening, but knowledgeable professionals. In addition to Badovici, Gray learned from a young woman architect, Adrienne Gorska, who taught Gray the basics of architectural drawing and took her on to the building site (where Gorska was job architect) for first-hand experience of architectural construction.

Was Eileen Gray so exceptional? Or is she part of what Luce Irigaray has called 'maternal genealogy, a line of descent of women in creativity'?[32] Contrary perhaps to our retrospective assumptions, women's architectural production in the late 1920s and 1930s was substantial, well received and in Britain frequently illustrated in the building press. However, modernist history did not record the work of able modernist architects, such as Elisabeth Benjamin, a member of the MARS Group who, like Eileen Gray, built carefully conceived modernist houses[33] (Figure 5.7).

The landmark exhibition 'Modern Architecture: International Exhibition', held at the Museum of Modern Art in New York in 1932, and its assiduously researched catalogue, *The International Style: Since 1922*, which named and defined architecture's modernist principles and key buildings, did not feature Eileen Gray's E.1027, which was ignored by the distinguished exhibition curators, Henry-Russell Hitchcock and Philip Johnson. The sole illustration of a design by a woman in the catalogue was a room at the Berlin Building Exhibition of 1931, designed by Lilly Reich, which was captioned : 'Luxurious and feminine character achieved by combination of white materials of various textures'.[34] While other reproductions in the catalogue of *The International Style* consisted of exterior views of buildings by male architects, the single example of work by a woman at this defining moment of modern architecture depicted domestic space, the interior, the home, which was thought to be women's realm in architecture as in life. More specifically, Hitchcock and Johnson chose the bedroom, which, with the bathroom, is the most private space in the home, the most bodily room. In these influential modernist writings, a domestic interior represented the work of the only woman whose work was illustrated. Through the photograph and accompanying text, the gendered assumptions of the writers were inscribed in the fabric of both the text and the architecture, while the private spaces of the home were made emblematic of the architect's femininity.

Central to the writing out of women from history was the misattribution of work. Most importantly for Eileen Gray, she was deprived of the credit for her most prominent design, E.1027 (1926–9), a house by the sea at Roquebrune in the south of France. It was often assigned, by a string of historians and other writers, to her mentor, the architect and journalist, Jean Badovici[35] (Figure 5.8). This asset stripping is a familiar phenomenon. The attribution of an object or a building, and therefore the credit for it, is often given to the woman's male collaborator, partner or teacher. To be a part of history an architect, like an artist, has to have a body of work which can be seen and assessed, but when the exact role or contribution is unclear or in doubt, cultural assumptions about women's auxiliary role and subservient nature take over. For the Roquebrune house, Jean Badovici was at best a consultant architect and joint client with Eileen Gray. Caroline Constant, Gray's most scholarly biographer, attributes the house to Eileen Gray *with* Jean Badocivi.[36] His contribution was technical advice – the spiral staircase to the roof, and the inclusion of pilotis and the window system, which he patented. Badovici's depiction of himself as joint architect with Gray on the cover of the special issue of his magazine, *L'Architecture Vivante*, which was devoted to the house, stretched his contribution beyond what would normally justify such a credit. Gray is known for her generosity to Badovici, and he was known for self-promotion, sometimes adjusting the dates of his buildings to exaggerate their 'pioneering' status.[37]

Over the years, Eileen Gray's house was often credited to the well-connected Badovici without mention of her, its principal architect and designer. Most notably Badovici's obituary in *Techniques et Architecture* of November 1956 featured five illustrations of E.1027 and was claimed as the basis of Badovici's reputation; Eileen Gray was not mentioned. Not only E.1027 (1926–9) but Gray's design for Badovici's Paris apartment (1929/30–31) and Badovici House, Vézelay (1927), to which she contributed, were also omitted.[38] Panels, showing 'his work', and dated inaccurately, were prepared by Badovici just before his death, and displayed posthumously at the Pavillon de Marsan in the Louvre, as part of a tribute to 'the architect, publicist, and inventor'.[39] Eileen Gray, whose offer to assist in the preparation of the display was refused and who was known for her reticence, was sufficiently stung by the result that she immediately compiled folios preserving and documenting a record of her own work.

When Le Corbusier illustrated his now notorious murals for E.1027 in the architectural press, he neglected to name the architect of the house.[40] One of Eileen Gray's biographers has mused that 'it was almost as if Le Corbusier wanted the world to believe that the house was not built by her,'[41] but (to complete the thought) built by *him*. This act of public appropriation, in

5.7
St George and Dragon House, Gerrards Cross, Bucks., 1935-6
Courtesy of John Somerset Murray

fact, only set the seal on Le Corbusier's initial private territory marking – the painting of nine murals on the walls of the Roquebrune house. Executed without Eileen Gray's permission, the murals 'cover her clear and consciously low-key house with overtly sexual, garish paintings [which] she considered an act of vandalism'. Le Corbusier described his intervention provocatively in *L'Architecture d'Aujourd'hui*, May 1948: 'The walls chosen to receive nine large paintings were the most colorless and insignificant walls.'[42] Although he observed that the 'house ... was very pretty, and it could well have existed without my talents', Eileen Gray was not mentioned in either the text or captions of the illustrations.[43]

Beatriz Colomina, following Peter Adam's initial work, has documented the appropriation of Gray's work by misattribution. She has written that 'in subsequent publications [after Le Corbusier's article in *L'Architecture d'Aujourd'hui* of May 1948] the house is described as "Maison Badovici" or credited directly to Badovici.'[44] For example, the house and its furnishings were credited to Le Corbusier in *Interiors*, 1948, while assigned to Eileen Gray and Le Corbusier in the Milenese periodical, *Casa Vogue*, 1981, which also cited a sofa designed by Eileen Gray to Le Corbusier.[45]

For Eileen Gray, who, like Le Corbusier, believed that painting dissolved walls, his was a double refiguration of architecture and authorship and an unforgivable desecration. Lack of respect for another architects' work and, more fundamentally, 'the effacement of Gray as an architect',[46] which the murals represented and constituted, have become a focal point for broader feminist critiques of masculinist modernism. Beatriz Colomina has identified another level of effacement inflicted by Le Corbusier's murals as told by the woman who bought E.1027 from Badovici's estate:

> [Le Corbusier] explained to his friends that 'Badou' [Badovici] was depicted on the right, his friend Eileen Gray on the left; the outline of the head and the hairpiece of the sitting figure in the middle, he claimed, was 'the desired child, which was never born.' This extraordinary scene, a defacement of Gray's architecture, was perhaps even an effacement of her sexuality. For Gray was openly gay, her relationship with Badovici notwithstanding. And in so far as Badovici is here represented as one of three women, the mural may reveal as much as it conceals.[47]

Le Corbusier completed his attempted usurpation of E.1027 in a now well-known dominance gesture, building three structures, a two-storey hostel, cabanon and work hut behind E.1027, which formed, in Constant's phrase, 'a Corbusian frame' for surveillance and colonisation, imposed on the house.[48] In addition to this personal and artistic appropriation, these structures and their occupants' activities destroyed the sense of isolation, privacy and repose that the house enjoyed and Gray valued highly.

Although Jean Badovici could assert in 1924 that 'Eileen Gray occupies the centre of the modern movement', her critique of modernism specifically questioned the mechanistic analogies and formal preoccupations of modernism.[49] The Machine Age language of architectural discourse and practice represented male values and experience. As Adrian Forty has shown, 'the early twentieth-century machine aesthetic was characterised by repetition and rigidity – taken to be essentially masculine features,'[50] and part of a regime of gender distinctions that structure thought processes in modernism, in spite of its claims to gender neutrality.[51] In an argument for modernism but against the worship of the machine and excesses of machine culture, Eileen Grey opposed sterile functionalism with quality of life:

> The engineer's art is not enough, unless guided by human needs ... A house is not a machine to live-in. It is the shell of man, his extension, his release, his spiritual emanation. Not only its visual harmony but its organization as a whole, the whole work combined together make it human in the most profound sense.[52]

She asserted her priorities:

> The thing constructed has more importance than the way it is constructed, and the process is subordinate to the plan, *not the plan to the process*. It is not a matter of simply constructing beautiful ensembles of lines, but above all *dwellings for people*.[53]

In her critical writings, which were in the form of Platonic dialogues, Eileen Gray with Badovici argued for a more humane and richer architecture, guided by human needs and conditions, not formulae. Gray's theoretical position, which opposed the excesses of machine culture in architecture and focused on the requirements and comfort of the building's occupants, set her apart from the male elite of modernism.

Habitually, women's place in architectural history and their practice as professional architects and designers have been restricted by negative cultural assumptions and valuations. Eileen Gray's strong and systematic mind, which is apparent throughout her design work and in her writings, is normally overlooked or recast negatively and always gendered. Peter Adam argues that her design work was motivated primarily by instinct and emotion, terms that are highly gendered, and easily construed as pejorative. Contradictory to abundant evidence, Adam portrays her as a creature of instinct and emotion. 'Her instinct'[54] told her to move from painting to the decorative arts; this work, we are assured 'came effortlessly without much thinking'.[55] Gray's argument for emotion in architecture is taken at face value as the opposite of reason, which is a defining quality of the modernist architect and modern architecture itself. Attributes of femininity – instinct and emotion – are set against their binary opposites to produce hierarchical distinctions and meanings which favour the masculine term: reason over instinct and thought over emotion. This analysis, when applied to women and architecture, 'fulfil[s] a crucial structuring role in design history in that they [women] provide the negative to the male positive. They occupy the space left by men', as Cheryl Buckley has argued about women designers.[56] Gray's critical writings are discounted by even the most discerning writers, demoted from the most prestigious ground of architecture by arguing that Gray is atheoretical.[57] Women's designs are seen as a 'natural' expression of their femininity. Their approach to the design process is seen as instinctive and emotional. As Cheryl Buckley has pointed out:

> Women, as a result of their biology and their role in patriarchy as carers and nurturers of the family, are seen as being nearer to nature. Even when women transform nature into culture, as they do as designers in either a domestic or professional environment, they are still viewed in relation to biology and therefore nature.[58]

It was just such assumptions about women's nature and capacities that underpinned the arguments for women's exclusion from architectural practice in the nineteenth and early twentieth centuries. Socially prescribed attributes of femininity, like instinct and emotion, were thought to disqualify women from the higher order activity of architectural design and to limit them to a role in architecture as assistants to male architects who were thought to be intellectually and temperamentally better suited to the task.

What Eileen Gray actually argued for was instinct *and* reason, emotion *and* knowledge, guided by human needs and experience, 'an emotion purified by knowledge, enriched by ideas'.[59]

In most recently published works on Eileen Gray, her lesbianism and bisexuality have been recognised, but little analysed. It seems less important what her sexual activities were than to try to explain the role that sexuality played her creative life. More significantly, in a Freudian regime of feminist history, sexuality is important as a force involved in creativity. Gray had a wide circle of friends, acquaintances and colleagues which included lesbians leaders of the literary and artistic avant-garde in Paris, such as Gertrude Stein, Natalie Barney and Romaine Brooks. Her lifelong friendship and design collaboration with Evelyn Wyld was one of the most productive and sympathetic of her female friendships. Together Gray and Wyld travelled to North Africa to learn weaving and dyeing techniques from local women

5.8
E.1027, Gray's house, attributed to Jean Badovici in the journal, *Techniques et Architecture*, November 1956
RIBA Library Photographs Collection

1

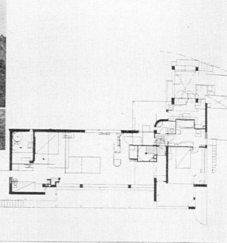

2

3

Jean Badovici 1893-1956

Le 7 novembre a eu lieu, au Pavillon de Marsan, Palais du Louvre, un hommage à l'architecte Jean Badovici, décédé dernièrement. René Herbst, André Lurçat et Paul Nelson ont rappelé les faits saillants de la vie de Badovici, vie consacrée au combat pour l'architecture moderne; le Colonel Maruelle a souligné l'intérêt de son invention faite en 1932, et ayant trait au sauvetage en mer. Une présentation sur panneaux, préparée par Badovici peu de temps avant sa mort, montrait en les commentant, ses principales œuvres; des exemplaires de l'*Architecture vivante*, revue d'avant-garde, fondée et dirigée par lui en 1922, des brevets, des croquis, des manuscrits et une maquette du paquebot équipé du dispositif de sauvetage breveté, maquette qui doit être transférée au Musée de la Marine, témoignaient de l'activité de l'architecte, du publiciste, de l'inventeur.

Jean Badovici, élève à l'atelier Gaudet et Paulin de l'École des Beaux-Arts à Paris, était sorti diplômé n° 1 de l'École Spéciale d'Architecture; il avait également obtenu les diplômes de l'Institut d'Urbanisme de Paris, de l'École des Hautes Études Sociales, et de l'École des Hautes Études Internationales de Paris.

En 1922, il fonda la revue *l'Architecture Vivante*, éditée par les Éditions Morancé, dans laquelle il allait lutter pendant de longues années pour l'avènement de l'architecture moderne et pour sa défense, en écrivant des manifestes, des professions de foi, des polémiques, des critiques, en publiant les réalisations les plus représentatives. Ce sont les 70 volumes de l'*Architecture Vivante* qui témoignent le mieux de l'effort constant de Badovici.

Après la dernière guerre, Jean Badovici avait été nommé Architecte en Chef adjoint de la Reconstruction. Il a édifié des îlots importants à Maubeuge et à Solesmes (Nord) comportant des immeubles à usage d'habitation et de commerce, et urbanisé les villes de Bavay et de Louvroil en 1949-1950. Cependant ses œuvres les plus marquantes resteront la maison à Vézelay (1924), la villa à Roquebrune-Cap Martin (1926) et son appartement à Paris (1934). C'est dans ces œuvres qu'apparaît avec la force d'un manifeste le souci de l'architecte de créer « avant tout des *habitations pour les hommes* ». « L'architecture doit être une symphonie où se trouvent exprimées toutes les formes de la vie intérieure. Le rêve et l'action trouvent en elle un soutien égal » ... « La théorie ne suffit pas à la vie et ne répond pas à tous les besoins... La chose construite a plus d'importance que la manière dont on la construit, et le procédé est subordonné au plan, *non le plan au procédé*... ».

Nous montrons sur cette page la villa à Roquebrune-Cap Martin et le tracé régulateur pour la façade de la maison à Vézelay. Pour les fenêtres de la villa à Roquebrune, Jean Badovici avait créé un système ingénieux qu'il a fait breveter en 1929. Cette « fenêtre mécanique type paravent » permet d'ouvrir complètement la baie, de la fermer hermétiquement; une boîte « différentielle » assure la ventilation, lorsque la fenêtre est fermée; des volets coulissants à lames protègent la baie contre le soleil, l'excès de lumière, tout en permettant une ventilation efficace. Les premières lignes du texte de ce brevet constituent un véritable manifeste : « Le mouvement architectural actuel est essentiellement une libération. Il rejette toutes les traditions, tous les partis-pris qui constituaient un obstacle au libre épanouissement des lignes, au libre jeu de la lumière. Son affranchissement se traduit non seulement dans l'ordonnance des lignes, dans l'agencement des détails, mais aussi dans une volonté systématique d'utiliser toutes les possibilités qu'apportent l'industrie et la mécanique modernes ».

M. Blumenthal.

4

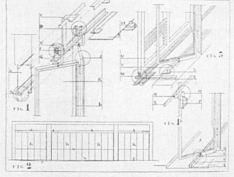

5

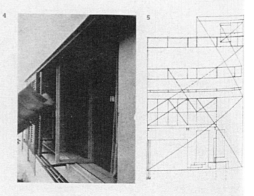

1 - Villa Roquebrune-Cap Martin (1926). 2 - Plan du rez-de-chaussée haut; les murs sont dessinés pour éviter que les points soient visibles. 3 - Détails de la fenêtre; ce dessin est extrait du brevet d'une « fenêtre mécanique type paravent » (1929).
4 - Une fenêtre de la Villa à Roquebrune.
5 - Élévation de la maison à Vézelay (1924).

and went on to establish a workshop in Paris in which Gray's designs were executed under Wyld's supervision. It was also with Wyld that Gray first travelled (as early as 1910) to the South of France, where she would later build.[60] Most importantly perhaps, her sexuality is related to her desire to escape from social and sexual convention, from England/Mother/Marriage in 1902. On her arrival in Paris, she cross-dressed to seek out urban pleasures and fell in love, not only with one of her best (female) friends, but with the life of the city and the idea of Paris – a symbol of personal freedom, modernity, and art – which became the creative matrix of her work and life. Here modernity, reconfigured as modernism, became a positive and central condition of her work.[61]

Like many other women of her generation and class, Eileen Gray went to art school,[62] where she studied drawing and painting, followed by periods of art training in Paris and more lessons in ateliers. Inspired by the Arts and Crafts Movement,[63] she moved from art into craft work, and then into architecture ameliorated by architecture's status as an art. Here modernism can be seen as facilitating Gray's architectural practice. As Alan Jackson has suggested, modernism too had artistic overtones with architects exploring form and space freely like non-objective painters and therefore appropriate to the class and position of the young women who entered its ranks from the middle and upper classes.[64] Within this context, her background as an artist and artistic designer can be seen to have facilitated her identity not only as an as an architect, but artistic-architect, a notion which was central to the selfimage of both the French and British architectural professions.

In Eileen Gray's work traces of colonial relations, imperialism and cultural appropriation must also be addressed in an assessment of her reputation. Racial and cultural difference is signified in Gray's work in the strong geometries, angularities and bold colours of 'African influence'. African art, especially the incised mask, were a central inspiration for Cubism, and in the 1920s, French West Africa provided cultural resources and objects which French designers freely appropriated. It is important to see Eileen Gray as a socially determined subject positioned in a culture and society deeply inflected by race, (as well as by gender difference) and related at many levels to French colonisation and imperialism.[65] At its most exotic and *luxe*, Eileen Gray's design work is replete with references to African culture – from the barque-like Pirogue sofa in the apartment of Madame Mathieu-Lévy in the rue de Lota, 1919–22, to the motif of large wooden snakes which Gray employed in a bedroom lamp of 1923. The later motif was originally associated with a particular village in West Africa where it was used for initiation rites, while some designers in the 1920s used Yoruba tribal thrones as foot stools in the living rooms of wealthy clients.[66] The dynamics of racial relations are understood to operate in and through material culture;[67] and Gray's snake lamp of 1923 needs to be seen not only as a product made in imperialism, but as producing imperialism at the intersection of metropolis and colony. At this point of intersection, luxury, designer interiors and their contents are complicit with the imperial project.[68] When interrogated, the snake lamp and other aspects of exoticism in Gray's design, such as animal skins and rare, tropical woods, can be understood as cultural objects replete with assumptions about race and sexuality, the primitive artist and the erotic. Whereas pre-industrial cultures were appropriated for the regeneration of an exhausted post-war society, material culture produced in Paris, such as the snake lamp, participated in the maintenance of colonial possessions as a source of fantasy, as well as power.

Like her status as an amateur, Gray's politics have been identified as limiting her architectural production. It has been suggested that her career in the 1930s was permanently sidetracked by her leftish social concern.[69] Reading Lenin and Trotsky and the literature of the Front Populaire (a movement of Socialists and other left of centre groups led by Léon Blum) and participating in the social climate of France led Gray to design for 'the masses': a prefabricated metal Tube House, the *Centre de Vacances*, a Project for a Workers' Club and a Cultural and Social Centre, which were all unexecuted. They are dismissed as distractions from her 'real' work of designing for individual clients.[70] Certainly this social awareness helps to explain the change in her work during the 1930s, but it does not deserve the sense of regret and failure associated with it. In fact, it was the social programme of modernism that, in many cases, attracted women's participation in architecture. The equation of architecture with social reform was, as a disapproving Sir Reginald Blomfield pointed out in the 1930s, 'a very modernist sentiment'.[71] Moreover, from a feminist perspective what has been overlooked in the debates about Gray's social architecture is that it represented a move out of domestic architecture and the private sphere – the least valued, least profitable area of architectural practice, which was regarded as suitable for women – into large-scale projects in the public sphere, which challenged exclusionary sexual divisions within architectural practice and by extension those of architectural history.

Today, modernism is understood in a more complicated way than the standard modernist histories portray, nuanced by readings of the highly permeable nature of discourse about modern design in France between the wars. Its catholic nature is understood as lacking the divisions imposed by historians on different ideologies representing modernity.[72] Eileen Gray was not excluded from that debate but contributed to it with words and buildings, ideas and objects, as this chapter has shown. From a feminist perspective, modernism can be read positively in terms of the conditions of production, as we have seen both in modernism's refiguring of the artistic architect and in the social programme of modernism, which facilitated the architectural practice of Gray and other women of her generation. However, with only occasional respite, for forty years between the defining historical moment of architectural modernism in 'The International Style' exhibition of 1932 and Eileen Gray's 'rediscovery' in the early 1970s, her uncertain and unstable pedigree – as a woman, pluralist, amateur, lesbian, foreigner – kept her and her work outside the charmed modernist circle which constituted not only the history of modernism but, as it was then perceived, the history of architecture in the twentieth century.

Examining critical reception and historical representation, 'woman' and 'architect' have been defined and investigated to account for how we view Eileen Gray today and what modernist history has made of her and her work. We have also been directed to 'that space of possibility' between cultural prescription and gendered subjectivities, where we have found 'not a "great woman", a heroine and idealised mother, but in Freud's phrase "a [woman] like ourselves to whom we might feel distantly related."'[73] Moreover, in order to reconceptualise 'Eileen Gray', the historical figure, and to explain the operations of gender relations in and through her work, it has been argued that her architecture and design and her critical writings must be read not only for dominant gendered meanings of the feminine but *in* the feminine.[74] While rejecting essentialist formulations, one can conclude that it is feminine difference which attracts both historians and architects alike to Eileen Gray's work. It is the core of her achievement as an architect, writer and designer, as much as it has disadvantaged her reputation. This difference is formed in the space between the culturally prescribed feminine and reading Eileen Gray's work according to modernism's masculine values. Difference reframes her architecture and confirms her reputation, as seen in her attention to the everyday, to use and to repose; the scope of her social and architectural concerns; the collaborative nature of her work, her intensely careful attention to detail and finish in user-centred designs, and perhaps most tellingly, if least predictably, the ability to think 'outside the box' which favours both feeling and reason in design and life.

Notes

1 M. Raynaud, *De l'eclectisme au doute, Eileen Gray et Jean Badovici, suivi de, La beauté du geste*, Paris: Altamira, 1994, p. 21.

2 For instance D. Cherry, *Painting Women: Victorian Women Artists*, London: Routledge, 1993; D. Cherry, *Beyond the Frame: Feminism and Visual Culture, Britain 1850–1900*, London: Routledge, 2000; G. Pollock, *Differencing the Canon: Feminist Desire and the Writing of Art's Histories*, London: Routledge, 1999. Key texts for the authorial subject are reprinted in S. Burke, *Authorship: From Plato to the Postmodern: A Reader*, Edinburgh: Edinburgh University Press, 1995.

3 Matrix, *Making Space: Women in the Man-Made Environment*, London: Pluto Press, 1984.

4 C. Constant, 'E.1027: The Nonheoroic Modernism of Eileen Gray', *Journal of the Society of Architectural Historians*, Sept. 1994, vol. 53, no. 3, 265–279; C. Constant, *Eileen Gray*, London: Phaidon, 2000; and C. Constant and W. Wang, (eds) *An Architecture for All Senses*, Tübingen: Wasmuth, 1996; exhibition catalogue, German Architecture Museum, Frankfurt.

5 F. Macarthy, 'Eileen Gray (1878–1976)', in *The Dictionary of National Biography 1986-1990*, Oxford: Oxford University Press, p. 1251.

6 B. Fletcher, *Sir Banister Fletcher's A History of Architecture* (1987), 19th edn, ed. J. Musgrove, London: Butterworths, p. 1329.

7 Archive of Art and Design, National Art Library, Victoria and Albert Museum, AAD 9–1980. Many items in Gray's private collection were purchased in 2000 by the Irish National Museum, Collins Barracks, Dublin, which has opened an Eileen Gray Gallery and is preparing a catalogue of the Eileen Gray archive.

8 See http://www.e1027.com.

9 G. Pollock, op. cit., esp. pp. xxiii–198.

10 S. Lavin, 'Colomina's Web: A reply to Beatriz Colomina', *The Sex of Architecture*, 1996, in D. Agrest, P. Conway and L. Kanes Weisman, (eds) NY: Harry N. Abrams, 1996, p. 184.

11 Pollock, op. cit., p.115.

12 Ibid.

13 Most notably, Rykwert, J. 'Eileen Gray: Pioneer of Design', *Architectural Review*, Dec. 1972, pp. 345–50 as well as Rykwert's earlier version in Italian with a summary in English 'Un Omaggio a Eileen Gray/Pioniera del Design', *Domus* Dec. 12 1968, vol. 469 pp. 19–34. The title of the Heinz Gallery exhibition in 1972–3 was 'Eileen Gray: Pioneer of Design'.

14 Anon., 'Project Pour Un Centre Culturel', *Architecture d'Aujourd'hui*, 1959, vol. 82, p.1:

15 R. Banham, 'Nostalgia for Style', *New Society*, Feb.1,1973, 248–9. All quotations attributed to Banham in this chapter come from this source.

16 Ibid, p. 249.

17 M. Wigley, 'White Out: Fashioning the Modern', in D. Fausch et al. (eds) *Architecture: In Fashion,* New York: Princeton Architectural Press, 1994, pp. 155–6; full text, pp. 148–268.

18 Ibid, p. 156. Wigley's phrase.

19 R. Banham, op. cit., p. 249.

20 C. Buckley, 'Designed by Women', *Art History*, Sept. 1986, vol. 9, no. 3, p. 401.

21 R. Banham, op. cit., p. 249.

22 Le Corbusier, *Des Canons, Des Munitions? Merci! Des Loges ... S.V.P.*, Paris: monograph from the International Exhibition of 1937, 1938, pp. 96–97.

23 Jan Wils, 'Eileen Gray: Furniture and Interiors', *Wendingen*, 1924, vol. 6, no. 6, p. 1; special issue devoted to Eileen Gray.

24 *Architecture Vivante*, special issue *Maison en Bord de Mer*, 1929; 'Eileen Gray/Jean Badovici' inscribed on cover.

25 See bibliography in Constant and Wang,

op. cit., pp. 199–206.

26 J. Helland, *The Studios of Frances and Margaret Macdonald*, Manchester: Manchester University Press, 1996, pp. 1–4.

27 Student register, 1900–2, Slade School of Fine Art, University College, London. In Paris Gray also trained at the Ecole Colarossi and at the Académie Julian. See also G.P. Weisberg and J.R. Becker, *Overcoming All Obstacles: Women of the Academy Julian*, New Brunswick, NJ: Rutgers University Press, 1999.

28 E. McCoy, 'Report from Los Angeles', *Progressive Architecture*, July 1975, vol. 56, p. 24.

29 S. Soros and C. Arbothnot, *Thomas Jeckyll 1827–1881*, London/New Haven: Yale University Press (forthcoming).

30 L. Walker, 'The Entry of Women into the Architectural Profession in England', in N. Bingham (ed.), *The Education of the Architect*, London: Society of Architectural Historians (GB), 1993, pp. 39–46.

31 S.M. Boutelle, *Julia Morgan Architect*, New York: Abbeville Press, 1988, p. 23.

32 Quoted in G. Pollock, op. cit., p. 231.

33 Modernist historians either ignored the work of women architects, as in the case of Factory Offices in Derby (1930–31) (designed by Norah Aiton and Betty Scott); misattributed their work (Mary Crowley); absorbed their names and reputations into their partners (Sadie Speight); had their work whispered about as 'ghosted' (Elisabeth Scott) or depicted as a representation of the designer's femininity (Lilly Reich). For a contemporary assessment, see, for instance, L. Walker, 'The Forgotten Architecture of Vision: Aiton & Scott's Factory Offices for Aiton & Co., Derby, 1930-1', special issue, *Industrial Architecture, Twentieth Century Architecture I*, 1994, pp.23–30; L. Walker, *Drawing on Diversity: Women, Architecture and Practice*, London: RIBA Heinz Gallery, 1997; also, L. Walker, *Women Architects: Their Work*, London: Sorella

Press, 1984.

34 H.-R. Hitchcock and P. Johnson, *The International Style: Since 1922*, New York: W.W. Norton, 1932, p. 204.

35 P. Adam, (1987), *Eileen Gray: Architect/designer: A Biography*, London: Thames and Hudson, 1987, p. 335.

36 Constant, op. cit., p. 5 and p. 94.

37 Constant's suggestion; see, for instance, dates on Badovici's exhibition panels cited in this chapter, p. 15 and note 38.

38 M. Blumenthal, 'Jean Badovici 1893–1956', *Architecture et Technique*, Nov. 1956, 16th series, p. 24. 'However, his most outstanding works will remain the house at Vézelay (1924), the villa at Roquebrune-Cap Martin (1926) [E.1027], and his apartment in Paris (1934)'; my translation.

39 Ibid, p.24.

40 Adam, op. cit., p. 335; and Le Corbusier, *L'Architecture d'Aujourd'hui*, May 1948, quoted and trans. in Adam, p. 334–5.

41 Ibid, Adam, p. 335.

42 Le Corbusier, *L'Architecture d'Aujourd'hui*, May 1948, quoted in Adam, ibid, p. 334.

43 Ibid, p. 111.

44 B. Colomina, 'Battle Lines: E.1027' in D Agrest *et al.* (eds) *The Sex of Architecture* New York: Princeton University Press, 1996, p.181, note 17.

45 Jean Paul Rayon and Brigitte Loye, 'Eileen Gray architetto 1879–1976', *Casabella*, May 1982, vol. 480, pp. 38–42, by Colomina, in 'Battle Lines', p. 181, note 18; and Adam, *Eileen Gray*, p.335.

46 B. Colomina, op. cit., p. 173.

47 Letter from M.L. Schelbert to S. von Moos, 14 Feb. 1969, quoted by Colomina, op. cit., p. 171.

48 Constant, op. cit., 2000, p. 124. 'Dominance gesture' is a term used by psychologists for non-verbal behaviour by which people and other animals assert their power and primacy over others.

49 J. Badovici, 'L'Art de Eileen Gray', *Wendingen*, 1924, vol. 6, no. 6, monograph on Eileen Gray.

50 A. Forty, *Words and Buildings: A Vocabulary of Modern Architecture*,

London: Thames & Hudson, 2000, p. 59; also pp. 43–61.

51 Ibid, p. 60.

52 E. Gray quoted and trans. in Adam, op. cit., p. 309.

53 E. Gray and J. Badovici, "Description", *Maison en Bord de Mer, L'Architecture Vivante*, 1929, quoted and trans. in Adam, op. cit., p. 233.

54 Ibid, p. 47.

55 Ibid, p. 53.

56 Buckley, op. cit., p. 402.

57 Constant, Eileen Gray, p.93.

58 Buckley, op. cit., p. 401.

59 Grey and Badovici, *L'Architecture Vivante*, 'From Eclecticism to Doubt', quoted and trans, in Adam, *Eileen Gray*, p. 233.

60 'Evelyn Wyld (1892–1974)', in Jill Lever (ed.) *Catalogue of the Drawings Collection of the Royal Institute of British Architects T–Z*, Amersham: Gregg International, 1984, p. 277.

61 See T. Gronberg, *Designs on Modernity: Exhibiting the City in 1920s Paris*, Manchester: Manchester University Press, 1998; and N. Troy, *Modernism and the Decorative Arts in France: Art Nouveau to Le Corbusier*, London/New Haven: Yale University Press, 1991.

62 Cherry, *Painting Women*, esp. pp. 27–9 and pp. 53–64.

63 A. Callen, *Women of the Arts and Crafts Movement*, London: Astragel, 1979.

64 A. Jackson, *The Politics of Architecture: A History of Modern Architecture in Britain*, London: Architectural Press, 1970, p. 55.

65 See, J. de Groot, '"Sex" and "race": The Construction of Language and Image in the Nineenth Century', in C. Hull (ed.) *Cultures of Empire, A Reader: Colonizers in Britain and the Empire in the Nineteenth and Twentieth Centuries*, Manchester: Manchester University Press, 2000, pp. 37–60.

66 M.R. Vendryes, quoted in J. Goldberg, 'Celebrating a Little-Known Influence on Art Deco', *New York Times*, 11 Jan. 1996.

67 P. Kirkham and J. Attfield, 'Introduction', P. Kikham, (ed.), *The Gendered Object* Manchester: Manchester University Press, 1996, pp. 1–2.

68 Cherry, *Beyond the Frame*, p. 5.

69 Adam, op. cit., p. 299.

70 Ibid, p. 299. Grey's work is contextualised in new legislation which opened up leisure to the working class through paid annual holidays, subsidised sports programmes and discounted railway tickets at week-ends (see Constant and Wang, pp. 154–67).

71 R. Blomfield, *Modernismus*, London: Macmillan, 1934, p. 79.

72 Troy, op. cit., p. 5.

73 Quoted in G. Pollock, op. cit., p. 164.

74 See H. Cixous, 'Castration or Decapitation?', *Signs*, 1981, vol. 7, reprinted in S. Burke, *Authorship*, Edinburgh: Edinburgh University Press, pp. 162–77).

Chapter 6

Marie Dormoy and the architectural conversation

Tanis Hinchcliffe

Architecture has been 'professionalised' more than the other arts, and we know from professions such as medicine and law, that part of the process of professionalism is to restrict entry. In the past this restriction has fallen heaviest on women since they come into so many of the barred categories. Rescuing from oblivion those pioneer women who, despite their sex, engaged directly with architectural design, has been, as Penny Sparke points out in the Introduction to this volume, a significant scholarly task. However, attention has shifted to women who have assumed gendered roles within the social practices of architecture and building, and it is now apparent that these roles have been crucial in the development of an architectural culture during the period under discussion. By social practices I mean those activities, which while not impinging directly on design, are nonetheless present to some extent where buildings are built, discussed, and visited. They then form the location for social interaction beyond the drawing board, where both men and women can participate. Such an activity is discussed by Lisa Koenigsberg who identifies a group of American women writing in an adjacent capacity between 1848 and 1913 about extant architecture.

They wrote, [she says], for a general public, in an occupation
made possible because architects needed allies and popularisers to
separate themselves from builders and to define themselves as
professionals. These writers… often served as intermediaries
between the general public of potential clients and the
professional establishment, translating many of the profession's
views for a lay audience.[1]

Marie Dormoy, a woman writing on architecture in France between
the wars, would seem to be an example of this type of female commentator.
What then can her career tell us about the social practice of architecture at
that time?

My first encounter with Marie Dormoy came when I was doing
some work on the architectural historian, Peter Collins, and I ran across the
dedication to her in Collins' book *Concrete, the Vision of a New Architecture*.[2]
Given that this is the most technical of all Collins' books, it seemed strange
that he would have dedicated it to a woman. Who could she be? While I
was working through the Collins' archives, I kept a look out for any reference
to Marie Dormoy and was rewarded by a brief note she had written to him
when asked if she would accept the dedication:

Dear friend, I am moved to tears by your proposition and I accept
with all my heart. I am very happy that your work is completed and
I wish it all the success that your perseverance and tenacity merits.[3]

And in a letter to Faber & Faber proposing his book, *Concrete*, Collins
mentioned as a qualification for writing on Auguste Perret, whose career was
to make up a large portion of the work, that he had met 'for the first time,
a number of his intimate acquaintances …'.[4] Could he have meant Marie
Dormoy among them? It soon emerged that she had been a friend of
Auguste Perret as well as a critic and writer on architecture and the arts, and
that she would have been a valuable source for anyone setting out in the
1950s to write about Perret.

Once I had become aware of Marie Dormoy, she began turning
up in different contexts, and everyone I encountered seemed to have a Marie
Dormoy story.[5] It occurred to me that her experience might illuminate the
social practices of architecture in the early twentieth century, something I
have been considering for some time in connection with other periods,
especially the eighteenth century.[6] Despite the fact that women in the past
have written about architecture, architectural criticism, which often forms the
basis of their work, determining which buildings are visited and which ideas
discussed, has been as much in the hands of the male profession as has the

6.1
Notre-Dame des Champs, blvd Montparnasse, Paris
Léon Ginain, 1876

design. Would this also be true for a woman writing in France at the period crucial for the development of modernism? And what other insights into gendered relations in architecture could her career provide?

Marie Dormoy's entry into the world of criticism came as she says, fortuitously, and depended on the persona she had developed for herself up to her mid-twenties.[7] Born in 1894, she grew up in Paris before and during the First World War in a comfortable, but pious bourgeois family.[8] Her expectations were circumscribed, since she was destined by her family to marry well, but she had other aspirations. Perhaps even unconsciously she set about fulfilling these by forming a friendship with an acquaintance of her father, the organist at the church of Notre Dame des Champs in Montparnasse, Lucien Michelot (Figure 6.1).[9] This was the first of many such friendships whereby she attached herself to a much older man as his acolyte. We can speculate on the psychological necessity which impelled Marie Dormoy to form these relationships with men old enough to be her father. On the other hand, they were a means by which she could acquire an education in the arts, without the advantage of formal instruction. In her *roman à clef, L'Initiation sentimentale*, 1929, she described the coming of age of a young girl, falling in love with a sculptor twenty-two years her senior, whom she then succeeds in marrying.[10] This may be how she would have wished these relationships to end, but none of Marie Dormoy's older men were to marry her.

During the First World War when, as she claimed, she became emancipated, she worked as a nurse, but her service was interrupted by illness, and during her convalescence she decided to set to work to translate all the texts of Michelangelo, study architecture, sculpture and painting.[11] Her undertakings were formidable and often seemed under the influence of whomever she had attached herself to at that moment. It was the futurist, Gino Severini, who suggested that since she knew about art she should become a critic.[12] After some preliminary articles on the decorative arts, she embarked on her course as critic by visiting the sculptor, Antoine Bourdelle, in his studio in the impasse du Maine in Montparnasse.[13] Her visits to the studio led her to follow Bourdelle's teaching at the famous Parisian art school, the Grande-Chaumière, and this resulted in an article in *Mercure de France*, entitled 'L'Enseignement du maître sculpteur, Antoine Bourdelle', in 1922.[14]

In the meantime, Marie Dormoy had discovered yet another tutor in the architect, Auguste Perret, whom she met in Bourdelle's studio when Perret came for a sitting.[15] In an undated typescript concerning Perret, she wrote that he had

> One passion only in his life: architecture. One amusement only, the automobile. After these dominating two, comes, in necessary harmony, a secret love of woman and of women which he disguises under a deliberate coldness, and a real taste for poetry and philosophy.[16]

Whatever personal story lies behind these words, Marie Dormoy soon became familiar with Perret's architectural ideas and a staunch supporter of his projects.

The 1920s proved a very fruitful time to be starting a career as a critic of architecture and the decorative arts. Marie Dormoy began writing for the newly founded journal *L'Amour de l'Art*, reviewing, for example, Dora Gordine's work in the 1927 Salon des Tuileries.[17] In March 1924 she made a trip to Czechoslovakia sponsored by the Institut Français with two lectures, 'L'architecture française contemporaine' and 'Trois sculpteurs français'. For these lectures she was billed as 'Mademoiselle Marie Dormoy critique d'art, membre du jury de l'Exposition des Arts Décoratifs en 1925'.[18] This trip was turned to good use the next year when back in Paris she gave a lecture in June at the Salle de Géographie in Boulevard St Germain entitled 'Les Arts appliqués en Tchécoslovaquie'.[19] But it was as an apologist for Perret's ideas that she is of most interest to us. In May 1925 she published an interview with Perret in *L'Amour de l'Art*, and in August that same year she sprang to his defence in the same journal when he was accused of plagiarising Henri van de Velde in his scheme for the theatre at the Decorative Arts Exhibition.[20] The division between Le Corbusier and the modernists, on the one hand, and Perret, on the other, had not become as great as it was to be a decade later, and existed more at this time between the modernists and the academy.

6.2
**Notre-Dame,
83 ave de la
République,
Le Raincy,
Seine-et-Oise**
Auguste Perret,
1923-4

The academy continued to be the problem during the 1930s, when Perret lost the rebuilding of the Trocadéro to Jacques Carlu, Louis-Hippolyte Boileau and Léon Azéma. *L'Architecture d'aujourd'hui* organised a petition to have Perret's scheme reinstated and Marie Dormoy was particularly active in obtaining signatures, for example, that of Picasso whom she had met by an 'incredible chance'.[21]

Marie Dormoy's most substantial service to architecture and to the ideas of Perret was her book *L'Architecture française* which was first published by *L'Architecture d'aujourd'hui* in 1938 and republished in 1951 with an introduction by the architectural historian, Louis Hautecoeur.[22] This was a slim volume but nonetheless covered a period from the fourth century to the middle of the twentieth, and the theme throughout the book was the continuity of the French spirit which had pervaded architecture during that long period. The text was flanked on both sides by pen sketches by Max Blumenthal and photographs of examples mentioned in the text (rather like the layout of Venturi's *Complexity and Contradiction in Architecture* twenty years later), and was clearly intended for a lay audience. What is most remarkable is the amount of space and number of illustrations dedicated to twentieth-century architecture.

At the beginning of the last chapter in the 1938 edition, Marie Dormoy claimed that 'The only architecture of the 20th century is the architecture of reinforced concrete.'[23] In France, however, three tendencies can be identified.[24] There is, first, traditionalist architecture, which renews the great periods of French architecture by employing new materials and by subordinating construction to use (Figure 6.2); second, academic architecture which while using new techniques, hides them under pastiche of old monuments; and, third, modernist architecture which employs new materials but which substitutes the influence of industrial buildings for that of works of art. Another tendency, hardly worth mentioning, is regionalism which arose with the rebuilding after the First World War. Although academic architecture was most prevalent, it was traditionalist architecture under the lead of Perret and modernist architecture under Le Corbusier which were the main contenders. For the author, Perret, of course, has the edge, for as Peter Collins noted '[the author] herself modestly asserts, [the book] was entirely inspired by Auguste Perret's ideas' (Figure 6.3).[25] That does not mean that she did not give a spirited account of Le Corbusier along with the inclusion of illustrations of his work, but the emphasis on structure as the guiding force in architectural design is derived directly from Perret.

The book was well received and complimented for its clear style, making architecture accessible to a wide readership. Perhaps this positive reception led to the republication after the Second World War, when some changes were made to reflect the additional buildings built since the last edition, but also changes in the architectural culture. There were still three tendencies identified, but now traditionalist architecture was described as 'classic' architecture.[26] And whereas academic architecture was placed second in 1938, it is relegated to third place behind modernist architecture which is now labelled as 'plastic more than constructive'. In the discussion of the tendencies it is claimed that Le Corbusier's works, few as they are, are almost

6.3
Garde Meuble, rue Croulebarbe, Paris
Auguste Perret,
1930

6.4
Musée des Travaux-Publics, ave du Président-Wilson, Paris
Auguste Perret, 1937

a declaration of war. As for Perret's classic architecture, 'After fifty years of effort, it is this school which predominates, and which perhaps, will conquer the world as crossed vaulting conquered Europe' (Figure 6.4).[27] In the reconstruction of France, the schools of Perret and Le Corbusier divided the country between them with Perret in Le Havre and Le Corbusier at the Unité in Marseilles. In conclusion Marie Dormoy says:

> French architecture has entered into a decisive phase where classic architecture and modernist architecture confront each other. The new impulse that was given by reinforced concrete is affirmed like the dawn of a great epoque. In order to continue what has been so courageously begun, it is necessary that technique and art be one, as it was in all the great epoques.[28]

At the end of the struggle the prize to be won is nothing less than the upholding of the living French tradition.

Short as this book is, it neither avoids controversy nor does it take the most conservative line, and although it does assume the position taken by Perret, the writing is assured and robust, not just a pale imitation. In 1952 Perret was persuaded to publish a book, *Contribution à une théorie de l'architecture*[29], a collection of his thoughts in gnomic form, appreciated by the profession, but not suitable for general consumption. The latter audience was catered for by Marie Dormoy, and she ensured to the best of her ability that it was Perret's version of contemporary architecture which engaged the public's interest. Here is a clear instance of a woman providing the necessary link between the architectural profession and the lay public, beyond the specialist debate.

Besides her writing and criticism, Marie Dormoy acted as librarian for the Bibliothèque Littéraire Jacques Doucet, thanks to her friendship with the elderly Monsieur Doucet. Doucet was a couturier and collector, first of eighteenth-century artefacts and then, after 1912, of modern decorative arts and literary manuscripts.[30] Marie Dormoy came to know Doucet through the critic and poet, André Suarès, and when in 1925 her father died suddenly leaving her and her mother with very little money, Doucet offered her the position of librarian which she retained for many years. This gave her the opportunity to meet many of the revered French authors in the quest for manuscripts to augment the existing collection, and it was while trying to acquire the *Journal Littéraire* of the diarist, Paul Léautaud, that she formed another relationship with an older man which was to last until his death in 1956.

Marie Dormoy liked to bring people together and frequently invited people to lunch or dinner who might not meet under ordinary circumstances. Léautaud, not only a misogynist but also a misanthrope, at first reacted badly to her invitations. On being invited to meet Perret he wrote in reply:

> lunches in the city, in society, are for me a trial. M. Perret is charming. But what has he to say to me, and I to him? Nothing? Well then? I have already come the other evening because you wanted Vollard to see me, he saw me. If it was only for that? . . . .[31]

Marie Dormoy persisted with Léautaud, ending up spending eighteen years typing a copy of the manuscript of his *Journal*, but in return she gained control over his work and published her own version of his life and his letters to her.[32] Her stated intention in publishing these letters was to reveal the many aspects of Léautaud's genius, but the result was a substantial book whose subject is herself. While we have only his side of the correspondence, the focus of the letters is Léautaud's relationship with Marie Dormoy, and her near unspoken presence is always there as a counter-balance to whatever is being expressed by Léautaud.

Léautaud wrote some cruelly perceptive remarks about Marie Dormoy, and in a *Journal* entry from the Second World War he notes that she has deposited his letters to her in the library: 'she will give them to the Bibliothèque Doucet like all the letters of Suarès, Perret and her "friends", so that posterity would know her to be loved and admired, and by such

6.5
Le Palais de Chaillot, Paris
Jacques Carlu,
Louis-Hippolyte
Boileau, Léon
Azéma, 1935-8

gentlemen'.[33] Certainly, her book *Souvenirs et portraits d'amis* contains the life stories almost exclusively of men, some of whom were hardly 'friends' at all. Nevertheless she usually is able to slip in some reference to herself somewhere. There is in these essays the hint of Simone de Beauvoir's description of the Narcissistic type in *The Second Sex*: 'We have to do here not with ambitious women using men for their own ends, but with women animated with a subjective desire for <u>importance</u>, which has no objective end, and intent on stealing the transcendence of another'.[34]

But again she has the control, since although the subjects of her memoirs are public figures, they fit into her memories. She gives a vivid account of Perret at the site of the Palais de Chaillot, the building he should have built to his designs, but lost to Carlu, Boileau and Azéma (Figure 6.5):

> One evening as I crossed the place du Trocadéro and when the work was already in progress, I saw, parked before the site, Auguste Perret's little car. It was empty. Casting about I noticed him standing against the hoarding around the future construction, trying to see, between the planks, what was happening behind them. After a long moment of observing, he left, along the hoarding, descending the steps of the rue Le Tasse, skirting the bassin below. Then he remounted by the Avenue Albert de Mun, stopped in order to look again at the site each time that it was

6.6
6 ave Paul Appel,
Paris, residence
of Marie Dormoy
from 1934

possible to scrutinise between the joints of the planks. I followed him at several metres. He was so absorbed that he did not even notice me. When he had returned to his point of departure, I advanced toward him. He had the same overwhelmed look, the same enflamed cheeks as the day when he had learned of the defeat of the Jeanne d'Arc project. He said to me only these words: 'It's a pity!' then got into his car and drove away.[35]

What this long extract reveals is Marie Dormoy as witness, surprising the architect at a hidden moment of defeat, and as a woman, her reaction is one of sympathy. It is certainly a haunting image of the small empty car and Perret peering into the site through the hoarding unaware he is being watched. Of course the scene described then gives us the opportunity to see Marie Dormoy observing Perret at this sensitive and secret moment, and instead of the great man alone, we have his experience modulated through her presence.

During her life Marie Dormoy brought together varied people along with her varied activities. She played the piano, wrote two novels, translated Michelangelo's poems, ran the Jacques Doucet library, lectured on architecture, wrote criticism while at the same time keeping up with a large circle of acquaintances. Léautaud said, 'She knows everyone.'[36] What we have not seen is her friendship with women, and that is an aspect of her life only glimpsed in Léautaud's *Journal*. She seemed to have many women friends and her relationship with them appears to have been less predictable than with her male friends.

So can Marie Dormoy's life tell us anything about the social practice of architecture? I think it can show us the significance of witness, and how the witness of the lay public can be as important as that of the professional architects and their buildings. By not being a specialist she could move easily among the arts, and she was as at home with music as she was with literature and the visual arts. Nevertheless, she was very professional and the notes for her lectures on architecture showed her well prepared to convince her audience with her arguments. From her book *L'Architecture française* we get a very direct feeling for the positions present in France at the time, perhaps more so than if we listened to the architects who were too involved with their reputations. But for all her professionalism, Marie Dormoy relied on personal contacts and operated in what must be regarded as a feminine manner.

Although it could be said that Marie Dormoy was a practitioner of the arts, her many activities suggest the old-fashioned amateur rather than the modern professional, and by education and social formation she was barred from this status. However, she did write about other women artists and she bore witness to contemporary controversy in the architectural debate. Her position in Parisian culture was as one who stands aside and comments on the players, but in doing that she controls the focus of her audience (Figure 6.6). Neither builder or architect herself, she is able to make meaningful for the general public the intricacies of the different approaches to architecture, but she can also afford to let the public into those private moments of the architect which would damage confidence if he were to expose them himself. However, in doing this she draws attention to herself as witness, and she is remembered, not for her own creative work, but the witness she bore to the work of others, even if that witness is not quite what they would have wanted for themselves.

Notes

1 Lisa Koenigsberg, 'Mariana van Rensselaer, An Architecture Critic in Context', in Ellen Perry Berkeley and Matilda McQuaid (eds), *Architecture: A Place for Women*, Washington and London: Smithsonian Press, 1989, p. 41.

2 Peter Collins, *Concrete, the Vision of a New Architecture: A Study of Auguste Perret and his Precursors*, London: Faber & Faber, 1959.

3 Letter from Marie Dormoy to Peter Collins (6 May 1957), Canadian Architecture Collection, McGill University, CAC 64 004 015.

4 Letter from Peter Collins to Richard de la Mare at Faber & Faber (13 August 1957), CAC 64 001 135.

5 For example, see Mavis Gallant, *Paris Notebooks*, London: Hamish Hamilton, 1986.

6 See Tanis Hinchcliffe, 'Gender and the Architect: Women Clients of French Architects During the Enlightenment', in Louise Durning and Richard Wrigley (eds), *Gender and Architecture*, Chichester: John Wiley, 2000, pp. 113–34.

7 Marie Dormoy's own account of her life is found in Marie Dormoy, *Souvenirs et portraits d'amis*, Paris: Mercure de France, 1963.

8 James Harding, *Lost Illusions: Paul Léautaud and His World*, London: George Allen and Unwin, 1974, p. 174.

9 Dormoy, *Souvenirs*, 1963, pp. 16–27.

10 Marie Dormoy, *L'Initiation sentimentale*, Paris: Flammarion, 1929.

11 Dormoy, *Souvenirs*, 1963, p. 71.

12 Ibid.

13 For example, Marie Dormoy, 'Un grand Artist d'hier: André Metthey', *La Grande Revue*, août 1920, p. 684; 'Mirroirs et Psychés', *Art et décoration*, 1921, 40, pp. 48–46; Dormoy, *Souvenirs*, 1963, p. 72.

14 Marie Dormoy, 'L'enseignement du maître sculpteur, Antoine Bourdelle', *Mercure de France*, 1 May 1922, pp. 684–702.

15 Dormoy, *Souvenirs*, 1963, p. 76.

16 Institut français d'Architecture, No. IFA Prov. 08.

17 Marie Dormoy, 'Dora Gordine, Sculpteur', *L'Amour de l'art*, May 1927, p. 166.

18 Institut français d'Architecture, 535 AP 319.

19 Ibid.

20 *L'Amour de l'art*, May, August 1925.

21 Dormoy, *Souvenirs*, 1963, p. 106.

22 Marie Dormoy, *L'Architecture française*, Paris: Architecture d'Aujourd'hui, 1938; 2nd ed. *L'Architecture française*, Paris: Vincent, Fréal Cie, 1951.

23 *L'Architecture française*, 1938, 'Vingtième siècle', unpaged.

24 Ibid.

25 Peter Collins, *Concrete*, 1959, p. 176.

26 *L'Architecture française*, 1951, p. 138.

27 Ibid., p. 140.

28 Ibid., p. 148.

29 Auguste Perret, *Contribution à une théorie de l'architecture*, Paris: A. Wahl, 1952.

30 Dormoy, *Souvenirs*, pp. 183–206.

31 Paul Léautaud, *Lettres à Marie Dormoy*, Paris: Editions Albin Michel, 1966, p. 31.

32 See the account of their relationship in Edith Silve, *Paul Léautaud et le Mercure de France*, Paris: Mercure de France, 1985.

33 Paul Léautaud, *Journal littéraire*, Paris: Mercure de France, vol 13, 1962, p. 177.

34 Simone de Beauvoir, *The Second Sex*, translated H.M. Parshley, New York: Bantam Books, 1961, p. 599.

35 Dormoy, *Souvenirs*, 1963, pp. 105–6.

36 Léautaud, *Journal*, 10, 1961, p. 194.

Chapter 7

A house of her own

Dora Gordine and
Dorich House (1936)

Brenda Martin

In 1936, as the newly-wed Hon. Mrs. Richard Hare, the sculptor Dora
Gordine (1898–1991) could claim international artistic recognition and
social status as the wife of the second son of the fourth Earl of Listowel, an
Irish peerage dating back to the 1790s (Figure 7.1) Her studio home, Dorich
House, on the southern side of Richmond Park near London was the
culmination of a dream for the Latvian-born sculptor (Figure 7.2) She
designed it at the pinnacle of her success and it embodied all her social and
professional aspirations.

     The actor, Trader Faulkner, a close family friend and constant
visitor to Dorich House until Gordine's death in 1991, described her in 1994
as follows:

> Dora was very stylish, with court shoes, dresses down to the ankle
> and hair like Carmen. She was a very charismatic person with
> enormous energy – overpowering if you could not match her. She
> was fascinated because I was doing flamenco with a Dutch girl
> from South Africa who was really like a Rubens. Dora was crazy
> about this girl and wanted to sculpt her – Dora liked big bodies
> and she much admired Maillol ... Dora had energy which people
> mistook for force. Dora had *duende* – the irrational demon of

inspiration which often presupposes the presence of death – and in that sense she was a true Russian.[1]

Gordine said to Trader, 'We have no children Richard and I, our children are the objets d'art. My children are my sculptures.'[2]

    The name *Dorich* – a conflation of their two names – reflects the symbiotic nature of the Hares' relationship and their passions for collecting and making art. Richard Hare was a brilliant scholar who graduated from Oxford with a first class degree in Politics, Philosophy and Economics in 1929. On the death of his father in 1932, his inheritance allowed him to became an avid collector and patron of the arts, an activity which later in life turned into an ambition to leave his, by then, impressive and rare collection of Imperial Russian art to the British nation. Hare's patronage extended to financing a new home and studio for his wife in 1935/36. They claimed to have designed it together, but it is Gordine's work as a sculptor which is represented more strongly in the two studios and gallery which form the heart of the house. Hare settled for a small study on the ground floor for his academic work as a translator of Russian Literature, and later, as a lecturer in Russian Literature and Culture at the School of Eastern European Studies at the University of London.

7.1
Dora Gordine, (right) in 1949 at her solo exhibition at the Leicester Galleries
Photo, Larkin Brothers

7.2
Dorich House
shortly after it
was built in 1936
Courtesy of English
Heritage, NMR

Dorich House was not reviewed in the architectural press when it was built, although the Hares were good friends with H. S. Goodhart-Rendal and other members of the architectural establishment of the time.[3] It was first photographed for *The Sketch* in January 1937 and described as 'The Hon. Mrs. Hare's Modern House; with Moon Doors and her Own Sculpture.' *Country Life* featured the house in 1938, describing it as

> Idiosyncratic and unique and designed by themselves, without professional architect or contractor, the brickwork, plumbing, flooring, plasterwork – all the hundred and one details of heating, lighting, and decoration – were chosen at the Building Centre and carried out by a number of sub-contractors.[4]

The article reported, 'As a sculptor [Dora Gordine] thinks naturally in terms of space and volume … She knew what she wanted in [her] house and studio, and … why she wanted it.' *Ideal Home* also featured the house in an article in 1946 entitled 'This is the House a Sculptor Built …' This publication reported that, 'after dispensing with the services of both architect and builder … [she] engaged craftsmen as she required them from the local labour exchange, and had enough personality to persuade the local authority to supervise the work'. It perceptively summarised the result as, 'A house built for a highly specialised set of requirements, completely successful in its own unusual way'. *Ideal Home* commented also that this was, 'One idea, not to be emulated by the less experienced', although it did not record what previous experience in designing houses Gordine might have had.[5] This was a pity since Gordine's experience of building and designing houses involved projects with two of the foremost architects of the European and English modern movement – August Perret and Godfrey Samuel. The first had built a studio residence for Gordine in Boulogne-Billancourt in Paris in 1928/9 and the second was commissioned to design a studio house on the edge of Hampstead Heath by Richard Hare in 1934, a project which remained unbuilt when planning permission was refused. The contentious issue of the ownership of the design of Dorich House, and the agencies which influenced its final form, are the subject of this chapter.

Dora Gordine's assertion to the press that the design and execution of the house were managed entirely by herself and Hare was not technically true. They had to employ Henry Ivor Cole, a builder and surveyor of Welling, Kent, to draw up suitable plans for the Council. Cole subsequently employed the necessary subcontractors and reported almost daily to Richard Hare on progress, orders and costs. In addition, the unusual conception of the spaces and the way the interiors worked within the house reflected both the rationalism of Perret, and the modernism of Samuel.

Dorich House is on three floors with the utility rooms, house-keeper's rooms, garage and plaster studio on the ground floor; the middle floor, a *piano nobile*, has an impressive gallery to the south and a modelling studio to the north. In contrast the top floor is low-ceilinged and intimate with living and dining room, kitchen, bathroom and two bedrooms. A small flight of stairs leads up to a roof terrace which is partially covered with a narrow loggia.

Gordine died in 1991 and, after protracted negotiations with the Executors who administered her estate, in 1993 Kingston University became custodians of Dorich House and its collections of Gordine's sculpture and Imperial Russian Art. During the renewed interest in the press, finding no listed architect for the building with its sheer façades, flat roof, metal window frames and reinforced concrete interiors, reporters and commentators assumed that Richard Hare was the architect and struggled to place it either within the canon of European modern architecture or the English vernacular.[6] Their difficulties arose because Dorich House represented a radical departure from both the architecture of the traditional homes of the English aristocracy and the studios of European modernism. It foregrounded an approach to design which demonstrated an awareness of both these traditions, but which represented a personal negotiation of them by Dora Gordine.

When compared with the studio built for Gordine by Perret in Paris, there is evidence of much reworking of his ideas at Dorich House, and one wonders if Gordine was trying to re-create her studio in Paris (the locus of so much success for her as a sculptor) in England. In the late 1920s she rented an apartment at 25 bis rue Franklin, above the office of the Perret Frères. A close friend and neighbour of Auguste Perret and his circle, in 1928/9 Gordine commissioned him to design a studio for her at 21 rue du Belvédère in the newly fashionable area for artists in Boulogne-sur-Seine, now known as Boulogne-Billancourt. Gordine's early years in Paris during the 1920s remain largely a mystery, but it seems likely that she arrived there in 1920 from a wealthy Jewish family home, then in Reval in Estonia, to study art, perhaps at the École des Beaux Arts. Her sculpture showed an affinity with the voluptuous bronzes of Maillol, whom she claimed encouraged her. Gordine also chose to take inspiration from ancient Khmer and Indian sculpture rather than break new ground with the Cubists and Surrealists. The bronze *Head of a Chinese Philosopher* which was shown at the Salon des Tuileries in 1926 received unanimous complimentary reviews, and led to her success, as did a number of solo exhibitions where her work sold for high prices. By 1928 Gordine was being referred to as a 'Girl Sculptor Genius', and she had acquired enough money to commission her own studio. [7]

Perret's design for Gordine at the rue du Belvédère had to fit a narrow terraced plot which measured nine and a quarter metres wide by fifteen and a quarter metres long. The façade was divided into three by two slender concrete columns, with an infill of five courses of decorative cast concrete bricks of a design used in other Perret studios. The first floor, double-height studio faced north onto the street, with the large square windows taking up the entire width of the façade. A double-height gallery extended towards the south end of the first floor. The space was divided by sliding doors. The living rooms were on the top floor and a garage, utility rooms, a further studio and a plaster store were on the ground floor. Neutral colours and wood flooring completed the classical aesthetic of a typical Perret studio. The few photographs taken in the rue du Belvédère either in the late 1920s or early 1930s show a spartan interior, containing little evidence of occupation, and, with Gordine leaving for a five-year sojourn in South East Asia in 1930, one wonders how long she lived there (Figure 7.3).

As Karla Britton has observed, Perret's studios were designed around the concept of work and usually had two studio spaces, one public and one for the sculptor to work in, with living accommodation being of secondary importance. [8] He raised the height of the ceilings and lowered the height of the floors in order to create large working spaces for the artists. In a studio for the Ukranian sculptor, Chana Orloff, whom Gordine also knew,

7.3
**21 rue du Belvédère
by August Perret
1928. Dora Gordine**
at work on Dyak
***c.*1933 in her studio**
Courtesy of English
Heritage, NMR

Perret recessed the living space on to different levels back from the street façade, thus creating more space for the studios. He followed the same rationale for the Gordine studio and one he created for the glass artist, Margaret Huré. Perret's prioritising of work space over living space would have appealed to Gordine, providing a perfect match for her own lifestyle, in which everything was subsumed to the act of creating sculpture. As Britton wrote, 'Perret's studio-residence is a space devoid of distraction, primarily

providing rooms for work with a simple but adequate living space.' [9]

Some details in Perret's studio were directly copied by Gordine in Dorich House. For example, in the ground floor studio the floor is one foot lower to create a larger room; fireplaces in the gallery and living room are copies of the Perret design (Figure 7.4); and window and balcony door arrangements for the bedrooms of Dorich House are very similar to those in rue du Belvédère. Above all, Perret's austere interiors, devoid of decoration and expressing the use of concrete in undisguised beams, were recreated in the airy rooms of Dorich House, although the sculptural forms of the window arches and doors softened the austerity of the bare rooms.

Gordine was clearly very pleased with Perret's studio as she based Dorich House on it. Perret's desire to please his clients has been noted by Pierre Vago, who wrote in his memoirs that Perret's aim was, 'To serve his client well, to construct well what was asked of him; he did not want to see anything else or look further, he believed that this was already enough – and a lot.'[10] For Gordine, an uncompromising woman, this willingness on the part of the architect to abide by the client's wishes was an important factor, demonstrated by the problems which beset her effort to build a studio home in 1934/5 on the edge of Hampstead Heath. The project was a collaboration with the architect Godfrey Samuel, which was not to be realised, as Gordine and Samuel struggled for ownership of the design and for their own personal visions of a modern studio home, a year prior to her move to Kingston upon Thames and the building of Dorich House.

In 1929, while Gordine was in Berlin for an exhibition of her work at the Galeries Alfred Flêchtheim, she was awarded a commission to make six heads of different racial types for the new Town Hall in British Colonial Singapore. It marked the beginning of a five-year sojourn in South East Asia, during which (probably in 1930) she married Dr. G. H. Garlick, physician to the Sultan of Jahore, thereby gaining entry into the highest society of British Colonial Singapore. She must have already known Richard Hare as he had bought one of her heads from the 1928 Leicester Galleries exhibition in London. He visited the couple in 1934 while touring South East Asia.[11] Even before Gordine left Garlick for Hare, he wrote from Singapore to the architect Godfrey Samuel, a fellow Peer from Oxford and an old school friend, on Gordine's behalf, asking him to find a plot and submit designs for a studio home within reach of London. The reason for the need to move to Britain rather than France is not clear, but possibly Gordine's marriage was not going well and she could not return to her Paris studio in the political climate of 1934 because of her Jewish origins. The choice of one of the foremost architects of the English modern movement suggests that Gordine wanted a modern building, using modern materials, such as reinforced concrete, cork insulation and metal windows. Folding and sliding doors and built-in storage space were also included in the design.

Reportedly, Godfrey Samuel was 'a philosopher, deliberate in all that he undertook, meticulous to the verge of pedantry, a careful planner, unwilling to compromise when it came to dealing with clients or planning authorities'.[12] Dora Gordine was also unwilling to compromise. Although the studio house was never built, the correspondence between client and

7.4
The Gallery at 21 rue du Belvédère, with the fireplace to August Perret's design
Courtesy of English Heritage, NMR

architect provides a valuable and reliable insight into the preferences and assumptions of both correspondents and is worthy of consideration here.[13]

The site selected was a plot being offered for sale in January 1934 from the estate of Highgate Lodge belonging to Sir Arthur Crosfield – about one and a half acres – on the corner of West Hill and Merton Lane overlooking Hampstead Heath.[14] It was deemed suitable because of its 'easy communication with the centre and general situation (high altitude and view on to Hampstead Heath), something which was important for Gordine since Hare wrote to Samuel early on in the project, 'Can you please let me know details about this and whether it will be possible to secure on this site a guaranteed open Heath aspect.'[15]

Correspondence continued across the continents through April 1934, while Hare appeared to be waiting for Dora to 'make up her mind about the Site'. It was not until January 1935 when Hare had returned to England and wrote from his family home at 10 Manchester Square that he offered the sum of £1,000 for the plot which had a frontage of about 40 feet.[16]

Samuel made various drawings and three different floor plans for the intended house. One, illustrated in Figure 7.5, consisted of two wings linked by a central glazed stairwell, similar perhaps to 'High and Over' at Amersham by Amyas Connell in 1929. An alternative design had a square, double-storey block perched on an egg-shaped ground floor, allowing cars to drive in and under the house, as in Le Corbusier's Villa Savoye at Poissy.

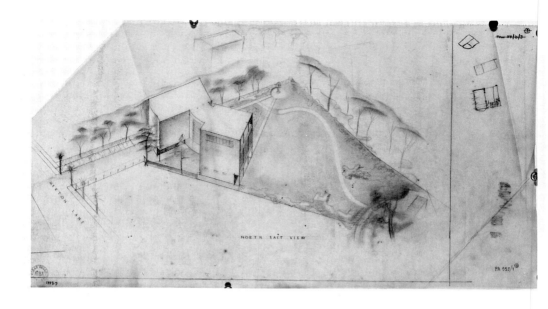

7.5
Merton Lane,
Highgate.
Perspective sketch
for a house and
studio for the Hon.
R. G. Hare by the
Hon. Godfrey
Samuel (1935)
Courtesy of British
Architectural
Library, RIBA
London

Another plan, which seems to have been the final one, was for a single square block, similar to what was later to become Dorich House. The project contained complete specifications and costings. An interesting letter to Gordine from Samuel exists answering a letter from her, in which she clearly criticised and modified his final design (unfortunately, the archive does not contain Gordine's original letter to him). Samuel's letter begins, 'Richard has shown me your letter criticising the various points in the scheme you saw. Some of these have now been answered by a revised scheme, which Richard will be sending you with this letter.' [17] The windows and natural lighting for the sculptures seemed to be a major source of difficulty between them. Samuel had designed two large windows at each end of the gallery but Gordine was not happy with them and proposed instead a set of three slender windows to light the sculptures from different angles. Samuel responded that they would end up 'looking like a Chelsea front drawing room'. The tone of animosity in the letter is unmistakable and Samuel clearly does not share Gordine's vision of her new studio home. (She was later to include two sets of three slender windows in the gallery of Dorich House.)

With regard to the top floor flat in Samuel's design, there was a dispute about the inclusion of two small wrought iron balconies and Samuel requested Gordine to consider the ' possibility of creating another balcony for the bedroom rather than to have a special and rather too small balcony elsewhere for the sake of the iron railings of Richard's'. However, a year later in Dorich House, Richard's 'iron railings' were made into features of the bedroom windows, and were noted as 'Spanish wrought iron architectural pieces' in a later article on the house.[18]

A circular doorway with two sliding doors, or 'Moon Door' , was also mentioned in Samuel's letter to Gordine. Samuel wrote that he liked Dora's idea of placing it in the partition between the living rooms, rather than as a door to a west terrace which he was proposing, where he feared it was 'liable to look too featuresque (*sic*) for its position'. But one feels he would rather have not included it at all, and that it had been foisted on him by his client. It is also evident that Gordine had suggested lower lintels to the top floor windows and the use of railings rather a parapet on the West terrace to make the most of the views from the top floor, a point which Samuel conceded, and which was obviously very important to Gordine since the windows and roof terrace of Dorich House are designed to make the most of the spectacular views over the surrounding countryside.

The letter also discussed the 'question of the circular headed openings from the staircase to gallery' which Dora had requested. Samuel and Richard Hare both disliked the idea. Hare in particular felt that 'that sort of thing should be reserved for the upper floor'.[19] Gordine must have pressed home a preference for arched doorways because Samuel responded that,

> A well proportioned square opening with a good curtain would look better to my mind, and would be more in the general spirit of the house; a round head here would be as out of style as the introduction of a patina on a piece of marble sculpture!

Perversely, and in contrast to Samuel's advice and Richard's opinions, arched doorways were to become the main architectural feature of the ground and first floors in Dorich House. Samuel's letter concluded, 'I hope you don't consider me too dogmatic. If I have not convinced you, I hope you will let me know – you may even convince me!' It is possible that Gordine did consider Samuel's version of English modernism too dogmatic, since she did not use him as the architect for Dorich House in Kingston upon Thames, which was begun only a month after the Samuel project was refused planning permission in Hampstead. The tension evident in the correspondence between Gordine as the client and Samuel as the architect suggests that Gordine had some skill as an architectural designer and an ability to visualise such an ambitious architectural project. This may have been derived from her experience with August Perret, from the modern houses which she saw around her in the high society of British Colonial Singapore, and possibly from her father, whom she claimed was also an architect.[20]

When Gordine designed Dorich House with Richard Hare for the new site in Kingston Vale, London SW15, a few months later, the result was

7.7
Dorich House.
Living Room
c. 1949, with
fireplace to August
Perret's designs
Photo, Larkin
Brothers

dramatically different. Progress from the front door and hall in the east façade was through a sequence of arches up wide, low stairs lit by a tall, round-topped window which opened into a square landing connecting the first floor gallery and studio. The sense of theatre and the drama of the arches opening into the lofty spaces of the gallery, flooded with daylight from two sets of three slender, round-topped windows, left the visitor in no doubt that they were in a house devoted to art (Figure 7.6). All this was of course appropriate for the diplomats, authors, actors, ballerinas and debutantes who came to model for their portraits by Gordine in the equally large, airy studio across the landing.[21] A small cloakroom tucked away behind the stairs on the middle floor enabled Gordine to keep her sitters within this professional environment with no need for them to go upstairs to the private area of the top floor flat, the stairs to which are steeper, and which turn away through a small archway from the first floor landing. Perhaps this was a deliberate strategy on the part of Gordine to keep her private life separate from her professional one. The small, south-facing living rooms of the flat are divided by the circular moon door, the shape of which is echoed in the favourite curved motif of the semi-circular windows with low sills used around the top floor. Two bedrooms were set at the north end of the house around a central hall, lit by a circular skylight. A small staircase from the hall led to the roof terrace. Throughout, the colour scheme featured matt white, pale grey or

7.6
Dorich House.
First floor landing
showing the
arched doorways
with a view
through to the
semicircular apse
at southern end of
the Gallery c. 1949
Photo, Larkin
Brothers

cream. Curtains which blended in with the neutral tones of the walls and oriental rugs on the highly polished wooden floors completed the spare modern interiors of the Dorich House of the mid-1930s.[22] *Ideal Home* reported that Gordine had returned from,

> several years in the Far East with a wonderful collection of Spanish tiles, Chinese pottery, Russian carving, Burmese sculpture, English glass, French china, Russian silver, light fittings designed by herself and beaten out of tin by Chinese coolies, and ancient furniture from the North of China which looks like the best modern Swedish work complete with Georg Jensen silver handles.[23]

The exotic mix of artefacts was displayed on the windowsills and low tables, amid square white chairs and modern seating units made in Paris in the late 1920s (Figure 7.7).

Moving on from architectural designs which may have influenced the design of Dorich House, Gordine's theatrical use of those influences to create a unique environment for herself and her husband can be interpreted in various ways. Recent texts by design historians, such as those of Alice T. Friedman, Pat Kirkham and Diana Agrest, have focused on the influence of gender in architectural design, providing new interpretations relating to the ownership of a particular design. In an essay on women as patrons of domestic architecture in early modern Europe (1550–1660), Friedman has written, 'Paying particular attention to changes in style, to historical context and audience … underscores the significance of gender as a factor in creating significant variations in the experience and interpretation of works of art.'[24] In this context, the difference in style and the meanings ascribed to those differences with regard to Dorich House can be seen to demonstrate both Gordine's personality and her individual interpretation of the contemporary ideas and styles of the European modern movement.

In her essay Friedman discusses the innovative design of Hardwick Hall in Derbyshire which was built in 1597 for Bess of Hardwick – a wealthy widow – by the architect Robert Smythson.[25] She argues that Smythson's building was possible because Bess was an anomaly. She did not come from a great family with a long lineage and had no need of an historical model on which to base a building which was customarily an affirmation of patriarchal power. Further, she writes that there existed 'no artistic codes and no fixed typology in place to express her particular female persona and program. Lacking conventions for representing female power, Smythson and Bess of Hardwick had to invent them'. In examining the difference between Bess's design and what would have been designed for a traditional male patron,

7.8
**Dorich House,
first floor gallery
c. 1949**
Photo, Larkin
Brothers

Friedman's analysis throws some light on why the plans by Godfrey Samuel were so unsuccessful. It would seem that, commissioned by Richard Hare, he had designed a studio home based on artistic codes and practices to suit his aristocratic and male client.

By the same argument, Gordine's own design for Dorich House related closely to her relationship with Hare within their marriage, as well as to her own gendered position. The gallery and modelling studio on the first floor signify a classical, traditionally formal area, where Gordine could meet her patrons and potential buyers and welcome them (Figure 7.8). The tall ceilings, arched doorways and grand proportions refer to the classical past, as well as to the houses of great collectors and art patrons in Russia, such as the Romanov family and the art collectors I.A. Morosov and P. I. Shchukin.[26] The mores of Richard Hare's own family, the Earls of Listowel, were also evoked as Richard Hare sustained his family's tradition of collecting art. Once the house was built, he continued to collect porcelain, paintings, icons and any other artefacts that appealed to him. After his death Dora continued to add to the collection through the network of antique dealers and other collectors they knew. As well as being a sculpture gallery the first floor was also designed to display the grandest items of the Hares' art collection. With its neutral tones and plain walls it is a significantly different arrangement from the usual statement of wealth and social standing which is

139

present in most reception rooms of large houses of aristocratic art connoisseurs. It makes particular reference to the Hares' unusual marriage, consummated through their passion for collecting and making art, and to the symbiotic relationship of Gordine as a sculptor with that of Richard Hare as her patron.

In the interior arrangement of the domestic accommodation of Dorich House, there is also a tension between the need for innovation and tradition. Alice T. Friedman has written:

> that one of the fundamental aspects of domestic architecture that transcends artistic, economic and class differences is that it should be a family orientated environment, separate from the place of work, and the locus of heterosexual reproduction. That it should provide a stage for ordered social and economic relations within the family group.[27]

The Goldfingers' house at Willow Road, where the whole of the top floor provided bedrooms for children and a nanny, is a good example. Here, Ernö Goldfinger's study was a separate room but Ursula Blackwell's studio was a conversion of part of the living room from a primarily domestic environment. This is in contrast to Dorich House, where most of the house provided a working environment for Gordine, with only a small area assigned for Hare's study. The arrangement of the top floor rooms in Gordine's design is a negation of most of Friedman's criteria for domestic architecture since the small dining room and exotic drawing room were intended to show off the more delicate and treasured items in the art collection and provide a setting for elegant dinner parties. The rooms were furnished with rare pieces of Chinese furniture and art, and there was no provision for children. Clearly, the Hares' private apartment was not designed to be 'the locus of heterosexual reproduction'. Friedman's argument continues that all the 'fundamental aspects' of a conventional house are defined by patriarchal gender relations, and, again, Ernö Goldfinger's house fits the model. The Hares' marriage was never a conventional one and it is the author's opinion and that of many of the Hares' friends, that Gordine's strong character completely overwhelmed Hare's quiet and reserved character. Dorich House was designed therefore according to matriarchal and unconventional criteria, (in this it has parallels with Hardwick Hall), in its unusual spaces which, although they convey modernity, relate quite differently to the prevalent model of male gendered European modernism.

Raymond Williams has highlighted the problems of a 'unified model' of European modernism.[28] There is no doubt that Dorich House is a 'modern' building in concept, and adheres to modernist principles of construction and space, but it is Gordine's own version of modernism. Williams has also discussed the notion of the 'modern' as arising from the influence of the émigré:

> The experience of visual and linguistic strangeness, the broken narrative of the journey and its inevitable accompaniment of transient encounters with characters whose self-presentation was bafflingly unfamiliar, raised to the level of universal myth this intense, singular narrative of unsettlement, homelessness, solitude and impoverished independence ... Modernism thus defined *divides* politically and simply – and not just between specific movements but even *within* them. In remaining anti-bourgeois, its representatives either choose the formerly aristocratic valuation of art as a sacred realm above money and commerce, or the revolutionary doctrines, promulgated since 1848, of art as the liberating vanguard of popular consciousness.[29]

Williams' deconstruction is helpful, since architectural modernism in England was often promoted through the work of male émigré architects, such as Walter Gropius, Berthold Lubetkin and Ernö Goldfinger who were committed to radical doctrines. Although Gordine was also an émigré and certainly subscribed to the narratives of unsettlement, solitude and independence, theirs was not a model of modernism with which Gordine can be connected.[30] Hare and Gordine, while actively interpreting the idea of modernism as anti-bourgeois chose the 'aristocratic valuation' of art over more 'revolutionary doctrines' for its expression. While Dorich House can be seen as a break with tradition, it can also seen as a negotiation of the modern through a series of complex and intersecting positionings, both social and cultural, and related to the geographies and histories of their past.

Penny Sparke has also written that modernism and modern architectural style have largely been represented through a dominant, masculine experience of modernity, the 'rational' and the 'good', which in turn was the product of an 'elite, middle-class movement, its aesthetic embedded within the high-minded moralising that characterised the public face of that particular social group'.[31] She has also said that little had been documented that was not, 'linked, in one way or another, to the "heroic" buildings, objects, ideas and people (mostly men) who made up the story of modernism'.[32] There is, therefore, a difficulty in using definitions of 'modern' or 'new architecture' to describe Dorich House, because they usually relate to a professional, specifically male, approach to architectural design. Gordine was an amateur and female. She designed her house from 'the inside out', considering the interior design first.[33] Her design was more a desire to produce a statement of her professional status as a sculptor, and to create an exotic stage for her private life, than the outcome of a scientific analysis of function. In terms of the canon of modern architecture, therefore, Dorich House is a unique, innovative creation, possessing a number of the defining architectural characteristics of a modern building – flat roof, minimal decoration, new construction methods, and cream or white interior decoration – but it remains outside the modernist canon. However, Gordine's wish to state her profession rather than her social position, may account for the external visual similarities of Dorich House to the industrial buildings of Peter Behrens, Hans Poelzig, Bruno Taut and the early Bauhaus (pre-Dessau) architects.

Cynthia Lawrence has written concerning female patronage that 'women needed wealth, significant freedom and influence' to commission architecture, something which Dora Gordine achieved by marrying Richard Hare and not having children. Lawrence continues that 'In many cases, however, commissions by female patrons subvert or reinvent traditional categories in order to achieve a more personal statement, one that reflected their own situations or convictions.'[34] She has also written that architectural patronage and design concern the 'promotion or defence of a dynasty or a family'.[35] Dora and Richard did not want to promote their dynasty through children: Instead they saw the sculpture, art and the house itself as their legacy. After a burglary in which some of the Russian artefacts were stolen from Dorich House in 1988, Dora Gordine told a newspaper reporter:

> I felt how unfair it was. Two people are working – Richard and me – working, not sparing ourselves, giving our hearts, our knowledge, our experience for posterity ... How can a stranger destroy fifty long years of creation, work, education? ... You have to be an idealist to work for it and not for yourselves.[36]

From the time of her arrival in Paris, Dora Gordine drew on the romantic idea of herself as a displaced aristocratic Russian to deliberately create an interesting identity. The collection of *Imperial* Russian art – not Soviet art – is also significant because it associates her with the power of the Russian aristocracy and its privileges. Taking this into account, Dorich House can perhaps be seen as an impressive architectural statement of a past Russian aristocratic heritage. As research progresses it is evident that this past was a partly invented one. Furthermore, in Singapore she acquired British citizenship as a colonial wife, and through marrying Richard Hare, she entered the British aristocracy at the highest levels. It seems credible that the house she designed for herself would reflect her rise in status.

Janet Wolff has written with regard to women writers that, 'There is something about women's social disengagement that has often worked against those constraints of gender which inhibit the discovery of self.' [37] This is equally true of women artists and, for Dora Gordine, social disengagement enabled her to create several different personae for herself during her life.

Both Wolff and Williams have put forward the idea that a stranger to a culture experiences and interprets that culture differently from those within it and Dorich House gave Dora Gordine the perfect opportunity to express her own interpretation of the rationalism of Perret and the English modernism of Godfrey Samuel. It was not only through her personal history that she reinvented herself, but also through the design of her house/studio, which became the conveyor of multiple meanings concerned with gender and background. Examined from this viewpoint, the elevations and façades of Dorich House can be seen to convey these meanings in various ways. First, they convey the impression that they are not traditional buildings. Second, they are partly influenced by Eastern European architecture and they can be seen as signifiers of Gordine's Jewish lineage and Baltic origins. The similarities are to the buildings of Riga and early French and German modernist architects and not to the English vernacular tradition expressed in the architecture of C.F. Voysey and Richard Norman Shaw. Third, they signify the fact that this is the home of a stranger to British culture. A building that may have had an influence on the design of Dorich House is the central synagogue in Libau, Latvia, the town where Gordine was born and lived until she was five years old. Dorich House replicates the central square towers of the façade, and the groupings of three slender windows either side of it with rounded tops. The little circular window of the synagogue (although of course this feature is not unique to the synagogue) is repeated somewhat idiosyncratically in the small bay on the south side of Dorich House. Perhaps, as an exile from the Baltic States and her family religion, there is also a touch of distant memories and nostalgia in the façades of Dorich House.

In discussing the philosophy of Walter Benjamin concerning memory, Esther Leslie has written:

> This arc between past and present, between past potentials unrealised and the present moment of cognisance frames Benjamin's topography of memory through his many writings. It is frequently hooked to the realisation of utopia in the future … Benjamin's arrow of memory, shooting back and forth between past and present and future, gains in political significance as through the 1930s Germany slips into a nightmare sleep that threatens, under the semblance of reanimating the past, to allot a present and a future to the few. [38]

As she was of Jewish descent, Gordine was probably unable to resume her life in Paris on her return to Europe from Singapore in 1935. If Dorich House was Gordine's 'Dream House' surely it contained some of the nostalgia for a lost childhood which she described in such glowing terms to Nancy Wise on Radio 4.[39] This was, however, quickly followed by a denial of the existence of the Soviet Union as a country.[40] Dorich House could thus be seen to represent a personal statement of the lost Latvia/Russia of Gordine's youth, but probably in an entirely subconscious way. As she lost contact with her childhood and her Jewishness, through her displacement and disconnection with her family, she may have felt the need to idealise the past and this need may have found subconscious expression in the appearance of Dorich House which became an expression of her association with Jewish Latvian nationality – in fact something with which she would have felt 'at home'.

Dorich House also conveys meaning about Gordine's status as an artist. With the favoured circles and curves, the elevations signify that this could be the house of a sculptor. Indeed, Gordine implied that she had treated the whole architectural project as one giant piece of sculpture.[41] Gordine's admiration for Chinese and Asian culture, expressed so strongly in her sculptures, is also expressed in the half-moon windows, which punctuate the top floor, their shape and placing derived from the architecture of the Straits Chinese in Singapore.

Inside the house, the design relates closely to different aspects of the Hare's life. The grand proportions of the first floor signify the importance that is given to Gordine's sculpture and the display of objets d'art. For Gordine this was the first aim of her design and she admits that she was trying to achieve a *sense de grandeur*. To clients, models and friends alike, the design presents the idea central to the Hares' existence – that art was the most important thing in life. The Hares' complex relationship to each other through art is encoded in the spaces allocated to each function in the house. Gordine places herself within a traditionally male role – that of a sculptor – rather than within the traditionally female role – the aristocratic wife – by creating a design in which her working environment takes precedence. In keeping with this interpretation, Richard's study is nearly the smallest room in the house, situated with the service rooms on the ground floor. There is no nice outlook and in fact the room is narrow and dark with a small doorway which was not wide enough for Hare's desk. Evidently Hare's work as a translator and author was not accorded the same importance as Dora's sculpting. His role as a collector was far more important to Gordine and his art collection is allocated space in the house accordingly.

Gordine celebrated her bohemian, artistic persona in the design of the private apartment on the top floor which is a stunning statement of her refusal to be a traditional aristocratic wife. The rooms contained 'the exotic' in the semi-circular windows which were placed in an even rhythm all round the top floor. In the bedrooms the function appears to have been subordinated to the design, as each bedroom has three semi-circular windows with low sills and a small balcony door, leaving little room for wardrobes and restricting the placing of the bed. With the exotic moon door and the addition of oriental rugs and the growing collection of porcelain and objets d'art, Gordine achieved an effect which was both bohemian and modern.

In conclusion, to return to the question of the many and complex agencies which influenced the design of Dorich House, it would seem that the unique design of Dorich House originated from the Continent, via the French classicism of August Perret, and via Gordine from Eastern Europe and South East Asia. The building reflected the lineage and passions of its designer, who, by 1936, had risen to the height of her artistic powers and social standing. Gordine's central belief in herself as a sculptor and her awareness of her social standing as Richard Hare's wife; her bohemian outlook; and her Eastern European origins produced the innovative design of Dorich House. She wished to create something which would signify the multiplicity of her positionings, both real and desired, as an aristocratic, bohemian, Russian sculptor.

Notes

1 Author's interview with Trader Faulkner, October, 1994, Dorich House Archives.
2 Ibid.
3 A bronze portrait head of H.S. Goodhart-Rendel by Gordine was exhibited at the Leicester Galleries in London in 1938.
4 M. Barron, 'Dorich House Kingston Vale', *Country Life*, 5 November 1938, pp. 456–7.
5 *Ideal Home*, October 1946, pp. 36–40.
6 N. Pevsner lists the house in *Surrey The Buildings of England*, Harmondsworth: Penguin 1983, suggesting it was slightly reminiscent of some German Expressionist buildings. Otherwise it was described as an 'idiosyncratic brick pile with a forbidding aspect', *Surrey Comet*, January 1992 and an 'electricity sub-station', *Kingston Informer*, 5 September 1996.

7 Art Critic, *Evening Standard*, 5 October 1928, Art Critic, *Daily Express*, 6 October 1928. Both articles report that she is introduced to London by the collector of oriental sculpture and pottery, Mr George Eumorfopoulos, which they see as a great compliment for a young sculptor.
8 For a fuller discussion of this idea, see K. Britton, *August Perret*, London, Phaidon 2001, Chapter 3.
9 Ibid., pp. 112–1.
10 P. Vago, *Une Vie Intense*, pp. 153–4, quoted from Britton, *August Perret*, p. 132.
11 Hare had come into his inheritance on the death of his father in 1932 and resigned from his job in the diplomatic service.
12 J. Bettley, 'Godfrey Samuel, 1904–1982', *RIBA Transactions* 7, 1984/5, p. 86.

13 The correspondence is part of the Godfrey Samuel archive. British Architectural Library ref: SaG/8/1.

14 In the 1920s and 1930s Sir Arthur Crosfield headed an active campaign to save the picturesque nature of Hampstead Heath and the surrounding areas. The Hares' house was refused planning permission because it was an ugly square block, in their opinion.

15 Hare to Samuel, 4 February 1934.

16 Folder 1, Private Letters, Dorich House Archives.

17 Samuel to Gordine, 29 March 1935.

18 'This is the House a Sculptor Built', *Ideal Home*, October 1946, pp. 36–40.

19 Noted in pencil by Samuel, after a conversation with Hare in preparation for the letter of 24 March 1935.

20 This is referred to in an early article on Gordine, by her friend Marie Dormoy, 'Dora Gordine, Sculpteur', *L'Amour de l'Art*, Paris, May 1927, p. 166.

21 Sitters included Dame Janet Vaughan and Lucien Pissaro (1928), Dame Edith Evans, Siân Phillips, Dorothy Tutin, Beryl Grey, H. S. E. Vanderpant, Lord and Lady Glenconner (1938), D. S. McColl (1939) Emlyn Williams, (1940), Sir Laurens van der Post (1955), G. I. Gurdjieff and Sir Kenneth Clark (1946),

22 Richard Hare imported the timber for the floors specially from Malaya, where it was called *Rengas*, and had it tested at laboratories in Princess Risborough for its suitability as flooring.

23 *Ideal Home*, October 1946.

24 A. T. Friedman, 'Wife in the English Country House, Gender and the Meaning of Style in Early Modern England' in C. Lawrence (ed.), *Women and Art in Early Modern Europe – Patrons, Collectors and Connoisseurs*, Philiedelphia: Pennsylvania State University, 1997.

25 The Smythson Collection at the RIBA was published by Mark Girouard in *Architectural History*, Vol. 5, 1962.

Friedman notes that Hardwick Hall did not contain the traditional great hall, a symbolic meeting place for men and for male hospitality which catered for the mass arrival of armoured knights on horseback and their attendant grooms and male servants.

26 I.A. Morosov and P. I. Shchukin were wealthy collectors of post-impressionist European art and Old Russia decorative arts respectively, who had impressive houses built in Moscow in the late nineteenth century which they used as art galleries as well as private homes.

27 A. T. Friedman, 'Not a Muse, the Client's Role at the Rietveld Schröder House', in D. Agrest, C. Conway and L. Weisman (eds), *The Sex of Architecture*, New York: Harry J. Abrams Inc., 1996.

28 Williams also said, 'Determining the process which fixed the moment of modernism is a matter, as so often, of identifying the machinery of selective tradition' and has noted that, 'this version of Modernism cannot be seen and grasped in a unified way, whatever the likeness of its imagery'. From a lecture delivered at Bristol University in 1987 and subsequently published in T. Pinkney (ed.) *The Politics of Modernism: Against the New Conformists*, London: 1989, pp. 32–5.

29 Ibid.

30 For her own accounts of her childhood and her early life, see the interviews with Nancy Wise, *A Second Home*, Radio 4, broadcast 5 September 1972, British Sound Archives; and Interview TAV 734A recorded 27 June 1990 for the Tate (Britain) Gallery archives.

31 P. Sparke, Preface, *As Long as It's Pink: the Sexual Politics of Taste*, London: Pandora 1995, p. ix.

32 Ibid., p. viii.

33 Gordine used this phrase when she discussed how she designed the house in a telephone interview with Michael Baws

in 1975 for an unpublished thesis
comparing Miramonte and Dorich House.
Baws has since donated his thesis to the
Dorich House Archives.

34 C. Lawrence (ed.), op. cit., Introduction,
p. 10.

35 Ibid., p. 15.

36 Tim Harrison, 'Sadness for Stolen Russian
Treasures but Dora Works on to Build a
Collection for the nation', *Surrey Comet*,
Friday, 5 February 1988.

37 J. Wolff, 'The Female Stranger:
Marginality and Modes of Writing', in
Resident Alien, Feminist Cultural Criticism,
Cambridge: Polity Press 1995, p. 3.

38 Esther Leslie, 'Souvenirs and Forgetting:
Walter Benjamin's Memory-work', in M.
Kwint (ed.) *Material Memories: Design
and Evocation*, Oxford: Berg, 1999, p.
107.

39 *Ideal Home*, 1946.

40 *A Second Home* interview with Nancy
Wise for Radio 4, 1972.

41 Gordine interview with Michael Baws,
Aug. 1975, Dorich House Archives.

Chapter 8

Elizabeth Denby or Maxwell Fry?

A matter of attribution

Elizabeth Darling

Twenty-five years ago, feminist architectural historians first started to examine the role played by women in the making of the built environment.[1] As is characteristic of the first phase of the feminist re-working of any branch of history, attention focused initially on the reclamation of formerly prominent but now obscured women. It quickly became apparent, however, that unlike the field of fine art and, to a lesser extent, design, there were comparatively few 'great women architects'.[2]

Rather than accepting this 'absence' as a natural occurrence, architectural historians used it as a starting point for a new approach to the discipline, one which was predicated on the notion that it was not necessarily architects alone who 'made' buildings. Gwendolyn Wright, writing in 1977, spoke of women's engagement with architecture as entailing 'a quandary of roles', and identified four areas of women's practice. Two of these were professional roles: the exceptional woman (such as Julia Morgan) and the anonymous designer. The other two, significantly, were figures from outside the profession, the adjunct (planner, critic, journalist) and the reformer.[3] In the same year, Suzanne Stephens developed this point further in her discussion of four women architecture critics, examples of Wright's 'adjuncts'. For the purposes of this chapter, she made a crucial observation:

Although none of these women was trained as an architect, each was able to postulate and communicate trenchant and prophetic issues both to the profession and to the general public. Their discourse was to influence the decisions that gave shape to the evolving physical landscape.[4]

By looking beyond the profession, historians such as Wright and Stephens, and subsequently Dolores Hayden and Alice Friedman, have been able to draw attention to a significant body of women who did, as Stephens argued, have influence. The patronage, reform work and critical writing of women such as Catherine Beecher Stowe, Charlotte Perkins Gilman, Catherine Bauer, Truus Schröder and Jane Jacobs have been shown to have informed the making of domestic architecture, new architectural ideologies and the design of cities.[5]

Such a conclusion correlates with, and arguably helped contribute to, current trends in the discipline of architectural history and criticism. A monographical and production-focused method has now been joined by an approach which posits architecture as a process rather than a discrete object whose meaning is locked into one historical moment. Hence the history of a building or environment is now viewed in terms of – *inter alia* – its production, its representation in words and image, and its use. Feminist approaches, meanwhile, have developed into a concern to read buildings as sites in which gender and gender relations are produced, reproduced and negotiated. These shifts in method, like those of the feminists of the late 1970s, are again predicated on the notion that the form and meaning of a building can only be understood as the work of many actors, not just the architect.

In this chapter, I want to bring together this 'older' concern with individual women 'outside' practice and newer ideas of architecture as process and consider how the expansion of those who are considered to 'design' a building affects what has been a traditional concern of architectural history and criticism: attribution.

Traditionally a building has always been seen as the work of an architect or architectural practice, usually the former. This paradigm conflates three procedures: the production of the ideas of what a building should be; the transformation of these ideas into drawing; and, finally, the conversion of these drawings into built form. This is usually labelled the 'act of design'. In their discussions of this act, architects and historians alike have conventionally emphasised not the ideas which have informed a building but the way these ideas have been transformed into plans and sections and the buildings which result from them. It is in this process of transformation that the creative ownership of a building is seen to be located and has always been associated with the figure of the architect. But if we accept, on the one hand, from the feminist route I have traced, the idea of discourse shaping the built landscape and, on the other, the contemporary notion of architecture as a process then such a position seems neither adequate nor accurate. Indeed, in my view, what makes this approach so useful is that it allows us to remove architects from their pivotal role in the architectural process and hence the 'problem' of no great women architects. We could reach a point where we say that the act of design does not necessarily mean the transformation of ideas into drawing and form, that creativity is not solely in the possession of the architect. For, if words and actions can shape buildings, who, then, is their creator?

For those interested in the nature of women's influence on the formation of the built environment, the downplaying of the role of the architect allows a raft of figures – Wright's quandary of roles – who were previously overlooked to be brought into the centre of discussion. For others, the re-positioning of the architect from director to bit player might be a reconfiguration too far. Again, we return to the figure of the architect, a member of a profession which has long used history and a mastery of contemporary media to assert its status and dominance, writing out the contributions of others to its work in order to privilege its own. Even now, practitioners who ostensibly acknowledge the notion that users, for example, might make meanings of their own from a designed space, assert their primary creative role through such phrases as 'can you design the condition without conditioning the design?'[6] Architects are unlikely to want to accede ground to 'adjuncts' – theorist, user, patron – either during the design process or in the act of writing about it.

The reluctance of a professional architect to allow that others might lay equal claim to the design of a building is the theme of this chapter. It will be explored through a series of events which took place in the London of the 1930s when a female 'non-professional', the housing consultant Elizabeth Denby, and a male 'professional', the architect Edwin Maxwell Fry (usually known as Max or Maxwell Fry), argued about who was primarily responsible and should gain most credit for the design of two buildings on which they had collaborated: R.E. Sassoon House, Peckham, south London (1934) and Kensal House, north Kensington, London (1937) (Figures 8.1 and 8.2). This debate, as will be shown, was really about what constituted the act of design and thus provides a useful historical example of what are usually seen as present-day concerns.

What is particularly interesting about Denby and Fry's argument is that its catalyst was the coverage both projects received in the architectural

8.1
R.E. Sassoon
House, south
London, 1934.
Designed by
Elizabeth Denby
and Maxwell Fry for
Mozelle Sassoon
Courtesy of the
Architectural Press

8.2
Kensal House,
west London,
1937. Designed by
Elizabeth Denby
and Maxwell Fry
for the Gas, Light
and Coke Company
Courtesy of the
Architectural Press

media in the course of 1937, by which time the pair had been working together for four years. During that period, each seems to have been working on the assumption that they shared the other's notion of what constituted the creative process. Then, in 1937, Denby's name was omitted from the credit list for both schemes in two major publications. Fry rallied to her defence but in so doing revealed precisely where he thought her contribution to the design of these projects lay. It became clear that, as far as he was concerned, he was their creator and Denby's role had, at most, been to refine some of his details. Denby, on the other hand, had assumed the opposite. In her mind, they were her creations because hers were the concepts for the designs. Fry was simply the conduit for her ideas; without them, he would have had nothing to draw.

The collaboration could not survive these differences and the partnership ended. Both recovered quickly and within a year had gone on to further success. Yet, today, Fry is the better-known figure and Denby is a perhaps familiar, but little-understood, name. Sassoon and Kensal Houses are still routinely attributed to Fry alone and Denby's role in the making of two projects which were central to the emergence of modernism into British architectural discourse has been overlooked.[7] This obfuscation reflects the production-focused paradigms of traditional architectural history and the architectural press, both of which privileged Fry's work over Denby's. Tellingly, it is almost entirely from Fry's accounts, which range from his autobiography and numerous articles to the obituaries he wrote for Denby, that I have reconstructed this debate. In these texts he constantly restated his pivotal role in the creation of the two schemes. His use of language and his account of the facts, however, when compared to the historical record, allow a different picture of events to emerge, one in which his primary role seems less certain.

'Elizabeth Denby or Maxwell Fry' is, then, an exemplary tale. It is one which allows an exploration, though not perhaps a resolution, of a number of themes. The first, and most obvious, is that Fry exemplifies the actors who 'lose' their primary position under the new approaches to architectural history. Denby, by virtue of her 'non-professional' status and her gender, exemplifies those who the new approaches have brought to light. Second, Denby's understanding of what constituted the design process offers an early model of the redefinition of the act of design. Finally, the mechanisms which each used to assert their primary authorship of these projects reveal much about the notion of architecture as process. Once designed, these buildings became objects to be absorbed into an armoury of techniques used by Denby and Fry to promote their individual activities, their theoretical positions and to create further work for themselves.

The collaboration

The collaboration between Denby and Fry came about by chance. In his autobiography, written in 1975, Fry described how, in the summer of 1933, he had attended a party in a studio in Hampstead, either Ben Nicholson's or Henry Moore's. He spent most of the evening perched in a window seat in conversation with 'a small dynamic woman with a lovely rich voice'.[8] This was Elizabeth Denby. The meeting was fortuitous, as both were at turning points in their careers. Each could make a valuable contribution to the other's progress.

Like most architects of his generation, Fry had trained as a classicist and since qualifying in 1924 had practised the neo-Georgian style of the day. He was a partner in the firm of Adams, Thompson and Fry which enjoyed considerable success throughout this period in both architectural design and town planning.[9] Membership of the Design and Industries

Association, however, introduced him to the development of modernism in continental Europe and by 1933 he had undergone a Damascene conversion to it, consigning his student work, so he recalled, to the dustbin.[10] In the same year he co-founded the Modern Architectural Research (MARS) Group as the central organisation and campaign body for the promotion of modernist architecture in Britain. Through his role in the MARS Group, and the events described here, he would go on to play a significant role in the process which led to the adoption of modernism as the accepted architectural expression of the British Welfare State. In 1933, however, he lacked the commissions which would allow him the chance to build on modernist lines. This had not prevented him, however, as he told Denby at their first meeting, from working on hypothetical plans for working-class flats based on the use of a portal truss frame manufactured from reinforced concrete.

In 1933, Denby was also undergoing a process of transformation from one career to another. She had attended the London School of Economics where she gained its Certificate in Social Science in 1917.[11] Most graduates of this course went onto a career in social work but Denby worked first as a civil servant at the Ministry of Labour. It was only in 1923 that she returned to the field of social welfare, when she began a decade's work in the voluntary sector. She was first employed by the Kensington Council of Social Service, an umbrella group for voluntary social work in the area, whose office was among the slums of north Kensington. From there she moved to one of its offshoots, the Kensington Housing Association – which campaigned for slum clearance and rebuilding in the area – and its building arm, the Kensington Housing Trust. Her job was as the Association's Organising Secretary, a post which ranged from carrying out case work on future Trust tenants to primary responsibility for what was then called propaganda and would now be called public relations and fundraising. She was outstanding at the job. A contemporary remembered how: 'her office fizzed with energy, new ideas and alarming outburst ... Elizabeth, always two jumps ahead of everyone else, impossible to catch up with, unpredictable, immensely stimulating'.[12]

By 1933, however, Denby described in a brief memoir how she had become 'intensely bored with the slums ... My life, my interest, my enjoyment and heart, lay with what was to take their place – with new building, with construction and everything that meant.'[13] This sentiment seems to have emerged as a result of Denby's involvement in housing debates outside her work in north Kensington. From the late 1920s onwards, she had played a central role in moves made by housing associations across London to promote the voluntary housing sector as an agency of the state in the provision of new accommodation to replace Britain's slums.

Her work included both the formulation of a scheme for some kind of collective housing organisation in London, and propaganda work whose goal was to persuade government and public opinion alike of the voluntary sector's suitability for a provisory role. In 1931 and 1932, for example, Denby was the chief organiser of what became a series of exhibitions called 'New Homes for Old'.[14] These were intended to draw attention to the slum problem and to show the model of housing which the voluntary sector had developed to answer it. Eschewing the profoundly material approach to social housing of central government, the voluntary sector viewed a new dwelling as only one part of the problem of rehousing. Most, including the Kensington Housing Trust, combined well-designed and equipped flats with extensive programmes of social amenities, differential rents and housing management.

The more public role which Denby had within the voluntary housing sector by the early 1930s seems to have fuelled an increasing dissatisfaction with her work in north Kensington. Although she did have some influence on the Trust's housing policy, she wanted to play a more active role in the production of new housing than seemed possible there. This desire was not helped by the housing legislation passed in mid-1933 which indicated that henceforth it would be public authorities rather than voluntary organisations which would be the main providers of social housing for slum clearance tenants.[15] Yet, the fact remained that a slum clearance programme was about to take place, one in which she might somehow play a part. Demands on her knowledge from outside the sector also seem to have convinced her that she might be able to pursue such a role.

At some point during 1932 or 1933, Denby became adviser to the Prince of Wales on housing. She led him on tours of London slums, outlining the main problems and solutions to the problem, as he sought to involve himself more directly in the country's political life.[16] She also began to write for the architectural press. In the spring of 1933 she contributed a number of articles on kitchen design and on town planning to the *Architectural Review* and *Design for Today* and discussed kitchen design in a wireless programme in the series 'Design in Modern Life' broadcast on the BBC.[17] She also applied for a Leverhulme Trust Fellowship in the summer of 1933 to study rehousing schemes across Europe in order to assess how the ideas developed there might be applied to British circumstances. She hoped that these endeavours and her experience in north Kensington would put her in a position to leave her job and start a new career as what she called a 'housing consultant'. This – a role entirely of Denby's invention – was someone who would advise on all aspects of the design and management of social housing: its form, its equipment, its furnishing and programme of social amenities.

Denby would not hear of the results of her application to the Leverhulme Trust until October 1933. Before then she had insufficient independent work to leave the security of Kensington. Then, another opportunity arose, one which would give physical expression to her ambitions but which she would need help to develop.

Fry gave his account of events in his autobiography. He described how, within a week of he and Denby meeting in Hampstead:

> My woman of the window seat ... came to me ... to say that Lady Sassoon would put up the money for my flats to be the first of a girdle of dwellings round the Peckham Health Centre ... And so I was launched.[18]

Mozelle Sassoon was an active philanthropist and well-known member of London society.[19] She had come to know Denby through their shared association with one of the strangest social experiments of the period, the Pioneer Health Centre.[20] Sassoon was among the Centre's financial backers, whilst Denby shared its founders' interest in an holistic approach to the improvement of workers' lives. In June 1933, Mrs Sassoon sought Denby's help in finding a site and architect for a block of model dwellings she wished to commission as a memorial to her son Reginald, who had been killed in a steeplechasing accident six months earlier.

Denby realised that the opportunity she had been awaiting had arrived. By helping Sassoon, she could become the de facto patron and designer of the block and see the ideas on social housing which she was exploring in her journalism and exhibition work translated into built form. In the studio in Hampstead she had found someone who could transform her ideas into drawings. Finding a site, however, took rather longer than Fry remembered. After initial attempts to persuade the Kensington Housing Trust to provide land failed, a plot of land in St Mary's Road, Peckham, was given by the Pioneer Health Centre in October 1933, not the week following the window-seat encounter as Fry had said.[21]

The outcome, R.E. Sassoon House, was then the means through which Denby and Fry could launch their new careers. To design a block of social housing was an archetypal modernist project: the commission would establish Fry's credentials as an adherent of this theory. For Denby, the scheme offered a three-dimensional representation of what a consultant could do and provided her with the security to leave north Kensington, which she duly did.[22]

The mutual partnership was to their equal benefit and, as it turned out, would not be confined to this one project. Within months of their first commission a further opportunity came for the pair to collaborate. In

November 1933 both were appointed to an Architects' Committee convened by the Gas, Light and Coke Company (GLCC), one of London's largest public utility companies, 'to advise … on architectural and kindred matters of common interest'.[23] Of the six members, Denby was both the only woman and only non-architect to be appointed. The Committee's task was to help the Company in its efforts to improve its public image and sales through the re-design of its product range and displays in order to compete with the new and flourishing electricity industry. While other members were assigned the redesign of gas showrooms, Denby and Fry were given the plum job of designing a block of model flats which would demonstrate the efficiency and cheapness of gas fuel and gas appliances. This would become Kensal House.

As they embarked on these two commissions, all seemed positive. Two people with complementary skills and knowledge would work to create two buildings which would exemplify the latest thinking – social, formal and spatial – on the design of social housing and be able to launch their careers in a very public fashion at the same time. Indeed, the two did not just benefit professionally from their collaboration. According to Fry, he and Denby formed an intense relationship in which they were able to combine a passion for one another with a passion for their work. He wrote: 'our temperaments interlocked …[and] we fell into no ordinary kind of loving'.[24]

How did this interlocking of temperaments translate into the process of designing the two schemes? The suggestion here is that we should envisage a scenario in which each contributed to the project in particular ways. To Sassoon House Denby brought the possibility to build in the first place and a vision of the ideal form of flats for working-class tenants. Hence her programme for the flats incorporated a labour-saving plan, a working kitchen, a large balcony to compensate for the lack of a garden and the inclusion of social amenities to be provided by the Pioneer Health Centre, whose new building was under construction on an adjacent site. Fry brought his ability to design both spatially and formally and to produce a strikingly modern, and hence highly visible, scheme for the London of the 1930s. It is not often remembered that this was the first modernist housing for workers in Britain. The process was similar at Kensal House. Fry was responsible for its form except for the kitchen which, evidence shows, was Denby's work.[25] Denby's was the architectural and social programme which, thanks to the free hand and finance she was given by the GLCC, was far more extensive than at Sassoon House and included a nursery school, playground, allotments and social clubs within the complex.

The sharing of mutual skills was a success. Each scheme was met with considerable approbation on completion; particularly Kensal House which received extensive coverage when it opened in March 1937. The Editor of the *Architect and Building News*, for example, declared, 'London can at last show to the world an up-to-date and original contribution to the housing question.'[26] In nearly all of the articles the blocks were credited to both Denby and Fry. In one instance Denby was called co-designer,[27] but she was most commonly cited under the title of Housing Consultant.[28]

So far, my account of the Denby–Fry partnership has presented a relationship in which there was give and take and not a little romance. The collaboration was to mutual advantage and all was well. As far as can be told, between 1933 and early 1937 it was, but the harmony could not be sustained. Two events, which took place after Kensal House was opened in March 1937, upset the balance of the alliance and suggested to each the illusions under which the other was operating. These misconceptions reveal much about the tensions between two definitions of design and were such that the partnership could not survive them.

The first event was that the reception of Sassoon House, and Kensal House, more particularly, seems to have led Denby to suggest a more formal professional partnership between the pair than had hitherto existed. As the originator of the ideas which informed both schemes, Denby identified herself with the creative process and as such saw no reason why she and Fry should not establish a practice equivalent to that of two architects in partnership. This was too much for Fry. He wrote later 'she would be my partner and I would not be managed', a revealing comment which suggests that Denby perhaps not only saw herself as a partner but as the leading member of the pair.[29]

If Denby's demands made Fry see her in a new light, actions on his part had the same revelatory impact for her. Fry outlined what he thought happened in a description of their relationship during and after their work on Kensal House:

> We hugged for the delight of achievement and fell apart reluctantly. I loved her for her compassion and for the widening of every sympathy I shared with her. We ascended together, nearly every care vanished. And then I broke the relationship in pieces. I failed publicly to acknowledge her and injured us both irreparably.[30]

It seems probable that this comment refers to the misattribution of Sassoon House and Kensal House in two major publications which came out in 1937: The Museum of Modern Art's catalogue of its exhibition, 'Modern Architecture in England', and Yorke and Gibberd's *The Modern Flat*. Both carried plates of Sassoon House and the former included a reference to

CORRECTION

Elizabeth Denby collaborated with E. Maxwell Fry in the design and construction of Sassoon House and her name should therefore have appeared together with that of E. Maxwell Fry at the head of this page.

Kensal House.[31] In all cases, the schemes were attributed only to Fry with no mention of Denby. Subsequently, *errata* slips naming her as a collaborator were inserted into the books (Figure 8.3).[32] Despite the fact that Denby's work on both schemes was widely known and acknowledged at this date, it was professionally damaging for her name not to have been cited in two of the major publications of the day, especially one which had an American audience. A slip of paper could not compensate for this oversight.

If this misattribution was not enough, Fry's subsequent actions seem to have sounded the death knell for their relationship. Clearly aware that he had snubbed his collaborator, Fry used an article about social housing for the *Architects' Journal* in December 1937 to acknowledge her contribution to Sassoon House.[33] In fact, this would be the first of the series of texts which he would produce well into the 1970s in which he sought simultaneously to justify his actions, attribute the scheme – in part – to Denby and assert his primary ownership of both projects.[34]

The theme of the 1937 article was, ostensibly, the lack of understanding among architects about the life of the working classes for whom they were designing low-cost flats. He argued that they needed not just to imagine what the lives of the poor were like but also to feel for them and noted 'it is my experience that this capacity is rare in architects'.[35] This observation allowed Fry to bring in to the discussion someone who could provide this ability to empathise, Elizabeth Denby and her role at Sassoon House. It was, he said:

> her intense feeling for those tenants, combined with a knowledge and insight into the needs of a working woman and her family that prompted innumerable suggestions, and turned a workable sort of plan into an intimately practical flat, suited to the real needs of the tenants ... a rough idea for a balcony only reached its final form ... through her knowledge of how poor people could live if they had a chance.[36]

This acknowledgement, of sorts, of Denby's contribution was immediately qualified in the next paragraph:

> Apart from my wish to establish Elizabeth Denby's contribution to this particular scheme, I make these points to underline the importance of a complete programme for housing, and to show how largely this is a matter of imagination, observation and true feeling.[37]

This equivocation is, to the author, extremely revealing. On the surface, this article appears to be an acknowledgement of Denby's role. Fry, even, as the final sentence quoted above implies, suggests that what she did was of significance. But this approbation was then subverted by his use of language. Terms such as 'innumerable suggestions' paint a scenario in which Denby contributed only once Fry had already conceptualised and drawn the plans for Sassoon House. The clear implication was that Denby tweaked and honed what was already there. At no point did Fry mention that had it not been for Denby, he would not have had the commission in the first place.

Fry's account of his work with Denby on Kensal House displays a similar re-writing of events. In his autobiography, Fry described how he won an internal competition for the scheme and that 'Elizabeth was allowed to join me in carrying it out'.[38] This suggests her addition to an existing committee, rather than her membership from its inception as shown by the evidence. It is clear from surviving plans and minutes of the GLCC Directors' Committee, as well as the press articles written when the flats were opened, that Denby and Fry were jointly responsible for the flats and were appointed at the same time.[39] Given that Fry's account of Kensal House was retrospective, rather than contemporary as in the case of Sassoon House discussed above, it may be the misrememberings of an elderly man. Nevertheless the implication again seems clear from his use of language. 'Elizabeth was *allowed* to join me' (my italics) is a statement which reinforces his belief in his primary role in events.

Why did Fry insist on his central role in the creation of these schemes? Because it was he who translated ideas into drawings and gave them formal expression, Fry assumed that the flats were his. His language is very much about ownership of the blocks. His 1975 description of the commission for Sassoon House was significant in this respect. He spoke of '*my* flats' and finished with the comment, 'and so *I* was launched' (my italics). He was the creator; his sole ownership of the schemes resided in the act of transformation of ideas into form. Denby was not able to do this therefore she could not assume responsibility for the schemes. The strength of his feeling on this matter is evident in his 1975 account where he insisted on what was 'in the midst of and at the end of all things received of her [Denby], my architecture (my italics).[40]

For Fry, Denby's demands and her definition of the creative process undermined his status as an architect; especially at a time when architecture had only recently become a legally-protected profession. He could not allow an unqualified person to be given credit for these schemes over him and he used his access to the media, both at the time and subsequently, to make sure his version of her role in the designs was well understood.

What was Denby's view of this? It is harder to reconstruct, for she left no written document of her response but Fry's protestations, and her subsequent practices, allow the inference that Denby conceptualised the creative process in completely the opposite manner. She owned the schemes because hers were the concepts underlying them. For her, creation lay in the formulation of the programme; Fry's role was akin to that of amanuensis. Because of this, she felt that she and Fry could enjoy some kind of professional, as well as personal, partnership, but as we have seen, this was something Fry could not concede.

For Denby the struggle between the two over their status within the partnership combined with what was, in effect, a complete dismissal of her contribution in two major books, could not have been assuaged by Fry's *Architects' Journal* article, especially since it fell short of citing her even as co-designer. It was time for the relationship to end and end it did. Henceforth she would work alone and make sure that she received sole credit for anything she produced.

A matter of attribution

Who, then, designed these schemes? Was it Denby with a little help from Fry? Or was it Fry with a little help from Denby? How could this be ascertained? Is it even important that we know? Clearly, for Denby and Fry, it was. To be the creative origin of each scheme bestowed a status and legitimacy which would further their careers, a concern which explains the tone of much architectural, and art, history and criticism.

For the purposes of this chapter, the point is not so much to prove that Denby was the designer of these schemes and that Fry was very fortunate to have met her, but to stress two points. First, that a discussion of the means through which she could assert her primary creative role allows us to see what kinds of evidence we might use to argue for the multiple ownership of the design process. And, the necessary corollary of this proposition, to use what I have identified as her definition of the creative process to note that there are other ideas beyond the formal which constitute the act of design.

In seeking to attribute a building, a traditional architectural historical approach would be to look at the drawings for the projects and to make stylistic comparisons with other work by our protagonists. There are few original drawings for Sassoon House but plenty for Kensal House. These, however, are signed by a member of Fry's office so can they be considered evidence of his involvement? Perhaps. Among Denby's papers there are various drawings for the kitchen of Kensal House which would suggest, at the very least, that she was responsible for both the programme and plan of this part of the flats.[41]

If we seek stylistic similarities, then the case is much stronger for attribution to Fry. Viewed together, Sassoon House and Kensal House share some common features, the balconies, for example. Compared with Fry's other early work in the modernist idiom, the flats also have formal, if not typological, resemblances to works such as the Sun House in Hampstead of 1934 and Miramonte, Kingston Hill, of 1937. Denby had no record of designing independently until after both blocks were completed. Her first solo design, a model house for the 1939 Ideal Home Exhibition, was in a modernist Georgian idiom and shows few similarities in plan or form to her and Fry's earlier work. To consider the act of design in these terms is, however, to define the importance of Sassoon House and Kensal House in terms of style and to equate the creative process with form. Perhaps this was the primary concern of Fry. It has certainly been a preoccupation of architectural historians but we should not allow their concerns to blind us to other definitions of what constitutes significance.

If, in contrast, we consider the ideas behind the projects, then Fry's role seems to have been minimal. He had written on slum housing but primarily in terms of the constructional aspect – his beloved concrete portal truss – and, in comparison with Denby, cannot be said to have a coherent theory of housing.[42] Both before and during their partnership, Denby wrote extensively on all aspects of housing design. In particular there are a series of articles, written between 1934 and 1935 for *Design for Today* and the *Architects' Journal* in which she articulated what we might call her theory of social housing.[43] This had three main concerns. First, she emphasised the need for research and planning before any programme of slum clearance; second, she argued that the latest advances in technology should be adopted in order to reduce costs. The savings produced in so doing would contribute to her final theme, the need to develop new types of housing and amenities for former slum dwellers. While these concerns, particularly the first, may be understood as having been informed by a concern to create work for the figure of the housing consultant, Denby's theory was, nevertheless, a sincere and coherent philosophy of housing, one which, she wrote:

required courage and enterprise, imagination and a determination to secure every new invention, every improvement, every beauty, and bring them within reach of the humblest family ... for it would not only create a civilized community, but [would] save on expenditure from the common rates on health services, on scavenging, on prisons. It's not a bad investment.[44]

A comparison between Denby's theory of housing and Sassoon House and Kensal House produces clear correlations. Both blocks featured labour-saving plans with kitchens designed on the latest continental lines with an exceptional level of equipment for social housing in Britain. They also represented a concerted attempt to avoid what Denby perceived as the failures of contemporary stateflatted dwellings which she described as 'Noah's arks towering above the surrounding properties ... cottages one above the other, but without the cottage garden or cottage privacy'.[45] The inclusion of large balconies was a deliberate attempt to provide the equivalent of a private open space to the flats and at Kensal House privacy was further enhanced by the use of staircase access to each flat rather than balcony access.

This desire to reinvent the tenement block was further developed in both schemes through the attention paid to the facilitation of a community life amongst the tenants. Denby had argued that it should be recognised that each new block of housing was analogous to a small village and as such should have the equivalent of a village hall built into each block. This was, she said, 'essential for communal life – somewhere to make and mend, to learn and play'.[46] The low budget for Sassoon House had, initially, seemed to limit the opportunity to include any such facility, but the donation of a site by the Pioneer Health Centre resolved this problem. The main reason the Centre had given the land was that it provided an instant clientele for its services. In return, Denby could offer her tenants a social life if not within, then at least next door to, the block.[47] At Kensal House, which had a great deal more funding, Denby was able to establish a complete and integral social programme. It included two social clubs, one for adults and one for children, a nursery school, allotments and a playground. Denby was appointed Housing Director to oversee, but not run, the estate. This was to be the responsibility of a tenants' committee. Denby believed that only by addressing both the material and the social aspects of housing could the slum problem be resolved rather than patched up.

Denby's emphasis on both the material and the social reiterates the central theme of this chapter, the difficulty of attributing the design of a building to someone other than the architect. This was a problem Denby had to address from the start of her career. Both schemes were tangible representations of Fry's skills as a modernist architect. They were also the means through which Denby could give a physical model of something otherwise intangible – her philosophy of housing. The problem for her, and us, is that since her ideas were adapted into architectural form, the assumption has always been – if we follow the tropes of traditional architectural history and criticism – that Fry was responsible for both. The conflation of ideas with form erased Denby's contribution.

How, then, could Denby, and historians who wish to challenge such a definition of design, ensure the acknowledgement of her work? The solution, then and now, was through a return to discourse. Just as Denby had established her theory of housing in the early 1930s through writing and exhibition work, she would continue to use the press and other media to keep her ideas in the public realm and reinforce the correlations between her theory and her practice. I have already shown how both Sassoon House and Kensal House incorporated many of the features she had advocated in her journalism. Once opened, it was important that her name was mentioned as co-designer, something she then reiterated wherever possible. For example, after Sassoon House was completed, she wrote a letter, in January 1935, to the *Architects' Journal* about the importance of sundecks for tenements.[48] Later that year, she drew on her work on the flats when she gave a paper at an international conference on scientific management in the home.[49] In 1938, after the break with Fry, the publication of her book *Europe Rehoused*, also served as an endorsement of her practice.[50] The suggestion here is that it was Denby's hope and expectation that her audience would make the correlation between the form taken by the projects with which she was involved and her writing and other practices and recognise her contribution. In the same way, we could reconstruct other contributors' roles today.

Denby and Fry went their separate ways after 1937. Fry turned his attention to his partnership with Walter Gropius and their work on a college for the Cambridge village of Impington. He also found a new love, Jane Drew. Significantly, she was an architect in the conventional sense, and Fry was to enter a lifelong partnership – personal and professional – with her. Denby was unbowed by her battle with Fry. Indeed, it seems to have galvanised her into a new phase of consultancy, even more interesting than the first. In 1938 she published *Europe Rehoused*, which, an enthusiastic critic in *The Listener* declared, 'every tax payer should read'.[51] It is still a standard text on European social housing. In 1939 she designed a complete urban regeneration scheme which was displayed, alongside a full-scale model house, the All-Europe House, at that year's Ideal Home Exhibition. This was well-received and was singled out as 'the one really worthwhile feature'.[52] All critics, no doubt to her delight, named Denby as the designer.[53]

By wartime Denby had become a well-known housing expert, respected by both the architectural and broader community. She was called as a witness to several government reconstruction committees and served on the Utility Furniture Advisory Committee. She also contributed an article on housing to the celebrated *Picture Post* issue of January 1941 which was devoted to a new plan for Britain,[54] and designed an exhibition, 'Homes to Live In' for the Council for the Encouragement of Music and the Arts, on the housing planned for Britain's post-war citizens.[55] She was recruited to the Housing Group formed by the Royal Institute of British Architects (RIBA) to promote its ideas for reconstruction and was also elected as an Honorary Associate of the Institute in June 1942. The *Architects' Journal* comment on this occasion offers a useful measure of her status by this date:

> the RIBA has conferred well-deserved recognition on one who occupies a unique position in the architecture world. Her experience in flat management and her researches abroad ... have enabled her to make important contributions to a number of housing schemes. Elizabeth Denby is the star in the profession she invented for herself: 'consultant on low-rental housing'.[56]

Conclusion

In the 1930s and 1940s, despite the misattributions of 1937, it is clear that Denby was a well-known figure and her contributions to Sassoon House and Kensal House, and other projects, were understood and respected. Yet, as was suggested at the start of this chapter, her role in these projects is now largely overlooked. My discussion was intended to address this discrepancy, one which, in this example is both an historical and contemporary one, and to use the debate between Denby and Fry about ownership of the projects to show how attribution is connected with struggles for status, legitimacy and work.

It was not a primary aim here to 'award' ownership of the projects to either one of the protagonists. Rather, the discussion was intended to suggest that Sassoon House and Kensal House should be attributed to Denby *and* Fry but, much more importantly, to a host of other actors as well: the inhabitants of the flats through their occupancy and appropriation of the spaces; the clients through their demands; and the historians of modernism who picture Kensal House on the cover of their books.[57] These, too, were and are designers of the schemes.

Finally, and of most significance, the intention of this chapter has to been stress that it has only been by viewing the act of design as constituted of something other than drawing that these new figures have been brought into light. The 'problem' for Denby, but not perhaps for Fry, was that conventions of what architecture constituted could not allow their work to be seen as a collaboration of equals and for Denby's *ideas* to be as important as Fry's *form*. The hope is that this chapter will contribute to the process of viewing architecture from all angles and seeing it as the work of many including, but not privileging, the architect.

Notes

1 See, for example, G.Wright, 'On the Fringe of the Profession: Women in American Architecture', in S. Kostof, *The Architect: Chapters in the History of a Profession*, Oxford: Oxford University Press, 1977, pp. 280–308; S. Torre (ed.), *Women in American Architecture: A Historic and Contemporary Perspective*, New York: Whitney Library of Design, 1977. This 'search' was initially undertaken by historians in North America and was subsequently pursued in Britain from the mid-1980s. For British exponents, see I. Anscombe, *A Woman's Touch: Women in Design from 1860 to the Present Day*, London: Virago, 1984 and J. Attfield and P. Kirkham (eds), *A View from the Interior: Feminism, Women and Design*, London: The Women's Press, 1989.

2 I paraphrase here from Linda Nochlin's seminal article of 1971. See L. Nochlin, 'Why Have There Been No Great Women Artists?' in L. Nochlin (ed.), *Women, Art and Power and Other Essays*, London: Thames and Hudson, 1989.

3 Wright, 'On the Fringe of the Profession', in Kostof, *The Architect*, pp. 283–4.

4 S. Stephens, 'Voices of Consequence: Four Architectural Critics', in S. Torre (ed.), op. cit., p. 136.

5 See, for example, the myriad of women brought to light in D. Hayden, *The Grand Domestic Revolution, A History of Feminist Designs for American Homes, Neighborhoods and Cities*, Cambridge, MA: MIT Press, 1981; Torre, op. cit., and more recently the contribution of women as patrons in A. Friedman, *Women and the Making of the Modern House: A Social and Architectural History*, New York: Harry N. Abrams, 1998.

6 B. Tschumi, *Architecture and Disjunction*, London: MIT Press, 1996, p. 6.

7 B. Cherry and N. Pevsner, *The Buildings of England: London 2: South*, Harmondsworth: Penguin, 1983, p. 630, for example refers to Max Fry as the sole designer of Sassoon House.

8 M. Fry, *Autobiographical Sketches*, London: Elek, 1975, p. 138.

9 Fry's employment at Adams, Thompson and Fry is discussed in M. Simpson, *Thomas Adams and the Modern Planning Movement in Britain, Canada and the United States*, London: Mansell, 1985, pp. 171–6.

10 Fry, *Autobiographical Sketches*, p.136.

11 I have explored Denby's work and life in detail in my doctoral thesis. See E. Darling, 'Elizabeth Denby, Housing Consultant: Social Reform and Cultural Politics in the Inter-war Period', unpublished PhD thesis, University of London, 2000.

12 E. Pepler, 'Elizabeth Denby, Obituary', *Housing Review*, 15, 1966, p. 9.

13 'Apprenticeship in North Kensington', undated autobiographical sketch amongst Denby's papers. Denby papers, Building Research Establishment (BRE) Library, box 11 67 75–11 68 20.

14 Five 'New Homes for Old' Exhibitions were held between December 1931 and September 1938. All except the first were held as part of the biennial Building Trades Exhibition held at London Olympia. Catalogues were produced for the exhibtions of 1932–38 and may be found within the general catalogue of the Building Trades show.

15 See P. Garside, 'Central Government, Local Authorities and the Voluntary Housing Sector 1919–1939', in A. O'Day (ed.), *Government and Institutions in the Post-1832 UK*, Lampeter: Edwin Meller Press, 1995, pp. 82–125, for a discussion of the context of voluntary sector housing in the 1930s.

16 Denby's work for the Prince of Wales is referred to in J.Woollcombe, 'The Rehousing Problem', *Daily Telegraph*, 14th November 1936, p. 6 and M. Fry, 'Harmony out of Discord', *RIBA Journal*, 86, 1979, p. 527.

17 See E. Denby, 'Overcrowded Kensington', *Architectural Review*, 74, 1933, pp. 115–8; E. Denby, 'Women and Kitchens', *Design for Today*, 1, 1933, pp. 113–5; E. Denby, 'In the Kitchen', *Architectural Review*, 74, 1933, pp. 199–200 and E. Denby, 'Design in the Kitchen', in J. Gloag (ed.), *Design in Modern Life*, London: George Allen and Unwin, 1934.

18 Fry, *Autobiographical Sketches*, p. 138.

19 Fry has made a mistake about Sassoon's title. She was not titled and was usually referred to as Mrs Meyer Sassoon. See C. Roth, *The Sassoon Dynasty*, London: Robert Hale Ltd, 1941.

20 See I. Pearse and G. Scott Williamson, *The Peckham Experiment*, London: Faber & Faber, 1943, for the founders' account of their work at the Pioneer Health Centre.

21 Minutes of the Executive Committee of the Pioneer Health Centre, 26 October 1933. Papers held at the Wellcome Institute for the History of Medicine, Contemporary Medical Archives Centre, SA/PHC.

22 Denby resigned from the Kensington Housing Association and Trust on 2 October 1933, see Kensington Housing Trust Management Committee minutes for 2 October 1933 held at the Royal Borough of Kensington and Chelsea Central Library. Denby was awarded a scholarship by the Leverhulme Trust on 6 October 1933, source: author's correspondence with the Trust, May 1998.

23 Minutes of the Directors' Court of the Gas, Light and Coke Company, meeting held 3 November 1933. GLCC papers held at the London Metropolitan Archive, B/GLCC/54.

24 Fry, *Autobiographical Sketches*, p. 144.

25 Blueprints and drawings of Kensal House kitchens amongst Denby papers at the BRE Library, reference 11 66 99.

26 Anon, 'Events and Comments', *Architect and Building News*, 149, 1937, p. 347.

27 See Anon, 'Five Hundred apply for Model Flats', *South London Press*, 20 November 1934, p.1 for a description of Denby as the designer of Sassoon House.

28 See, for example, Anon, 'Kensal House', *Journal of the Royal Institute of British Architects*, 44, 1937, p. 500.

29 Fry, *Autobiographical Sketches*, p. 144.

30 Ibid.

31 Museum of Modern Art, *Modern Architecture in England*, New York: Museum of Modern Art, 1937, see plate 19 and pp. 96–7 for the attribution of R.E. Sassoon House and Kensal House to Fry alone. See F.R.S. Yorke and F. Gibberd, *The Modern Flat*, London: The Architectural Press, 1937, pp. 102–3 for Fry's sole credit for R.E. Sassoon House.

32 The MOMA catalogue placed the errata slip on p. 5, *The Modern Flat* placed it on the spread which featured Sassoon House.

33 M. Fry, 'Housing', *Architects' Journal*, 86, 1937, pp. 947–948.

34 See, for example, Fry, *Autobiographical Sketches*; M. Fry, 'Miss Elizabeth Denby', *The Times*, 9 November 1965; How Modern Architecture came to England (audio-visual set c.1975) and M. Fry, 'Harmony out of Discord'.

35 Fry, 'Housing', p. 947.

36 Ibid., pp. 947–8.

37 Ibid., p. 948.

38 Fry, *Autobiographical Sketches*, p. 143.

39 Minutes of the Directors' Court of the Gas, Light and Coke Company, meeting held 3 November 1933. GLCC papers held at the London Metropolitan Archive, B/GLCC/54.

40 Fry, *Autobiographical Sketches*, p.144.

41 Blueprints and drawings of Kensal House kitchens among Denby papers at the BRE Library, reference 11 66 99.

42 See M. Fry, 'The Architect's Problem', *Architects' Journal*, 77, 1933, pp. 844–846.

43 See E. Denby, 'Planning Future Cities, Slum Clearance is no Policy', *Design for Today*, 2, 1934, pp. 122–7; E. Denby, 'First Report of the Council for Research into Housing Construction', *Architects' Journal*, 80, 1934, pp. 937–43; E. Denby, 'Review of a Council for Research into Housing Construction Report', *Design for Today*, 2, 1934, 270–1 and E. Denby, 'The Designs Reviewed', *Architects' Journal*, 81, 1935, pp. 438–40.

44 E. Denby, 'Planning Future Cities', p. 126.

45 Ibid.

46 E. Denby, 'Review of a Council for Research into Housing Construction Report', p. 270.

47 Sassoon formed the Pioneer Housing Trust in November 1933 to own and manage R.E. Sassoon House. Jack Donaldson, a member of the Pioneer Health Centre's Management Committee, became a member of the Trust and Denby, in turn, became a member of the Centre's Executive Committee. See Pioneer Housing Trust Ltd, *Articles of Association*, 1934.

48 E. Denby, 'Sundecks for Tenements', *Architects' Journal*, 81, 1935, p. 104.

49 E. Denby, 'The Role of Organised Services outside the Home in relation to Scientific Management in the Home', in Sixth International Congress for Scientific Management in the Home, *Papers*, London: P.S. King Ltd, 1935.

50 E. Denby, *Europe Rehoused*, London: George Allen and Unwin, 1938.

51 Anon, 'Europe Rehoused', *The Listener*, 19, 1938, p. 1140.

52 Anon, 'Homes and Ideals', *Architect and Building News*, 158, 1939, pp. 25–26.

53 Astragal in the *Architects' Journal*, observed that the house was 'the best exhibit ... designed by Miss Elizabeth Denby ... a really beautiful and well-equipped job'. See Astragal, 'Farewell to Ideal Homes, *Architects' Journal*, 84, 1939, p. 718.

54 E. Denby, 'Plan the Home', *Picture Post*, 10, 1941, pp. 21–3.

55 'Homes to Live In' is discussed by Denby's collaborator on the project in N. Carrington, *Industrial Design in Britain*, London: Allen and Unwin, 1976.

56 Anon, 'Miss Elizabeth Denby', *Architects' Journal*, 95, 1942, p. 400.

57 See the cover of J.M. Richards, *An Introduction to Modern Architecture*, Harmondsworth: Pelican, 1940 and J. Gold, *The Experience of Modernism: Modern Architects and the Future City, 1928-53*, London: E. and FN Spon, 1997.

Bibliography

Adam, P. *Eileen Gray: Architect/designer: A Biography*, London: Thames & Hudson, 1987 (2nd edn London, Phaidon, 2000).

Agrest, D., Conway, P. and L. Kanes Weisman (eds) *The Sex of Architecture*, New York: Harry N. Abrams Inc., 1996.

Anon 'Projet pour un Centre Culturel: Conception architecturale: Eileen Gray', *Architecture d'Aujourd'hui*, no. 82, 1959.

Aslin, E. *The Aesthetic Movement: Prelude to Art Nouveau*, London: Ferndale, 1981.

Attfield, J. and Kirkham, P. (eds) *A View from the Interior: Women and Design*, London: The Women's Press, 1989.

Banham, R. *Theory and Design in the First Machine Age*, London: Architectural Press, 1960.

Banham, R. 'Nostalgia for Style' *New Society*,
1 Feb 1973.

Barringer, T. and Flynn, T., *Colonalism and the Object: Empire, Material Culture and the Museum*, London/NY: Routledge, 1998.

Barrymore, E. *Memories*, New York: Harper & Brothers, 1955.

Baudot, F. *Eileen Gray*, London: Thames & Hudson, 1998.

Bloom, L. '"I Write For Myself and Strangers": Private Diaries as Public Documents', in S. L. Bunkers and C. A. Huff, (eds) *Inscribing the Daily: Critical Essays on Women's Diaries*, Amherst, MA: University of Massachusetts Press, 1996.

Blumenthal, M. 'Jean Badovici 1893–1956' [obit], *Techniques et Architecture*, November 1956, 16th series.

Britten, K. *Auguste Perret*, London: Phaidon, 2001.

Buckley, C. 'Designed by Women', *Art History*, 9, Sept. 1986.

Bunkers, S. L. and Huff, C. A. (eds) 'Issues in Studying Women's Diaries: A Theoretical and Critical Introduction' in S. L. Bunkers and C. A. Huff (eds) *Inscribing the Daily*, Amhurst, MA: University of Massachusetts Press, 1996.

Burke, S. *Authorship: From Plato to the Postmodern*, Edinburgh: Edinburgh University Press, 1995.

Callen, A. *Women in the Arts and Crafts Movement 1870–1914*, London: Astragal, 1977.

Campbell, N. and Seebohm, C. *Elsie de Wolfe: A Decorative Life*, New York: Panache Press, 1992.

Cherry, D. *Painting Women: Victorian Women Artists*, London: Routledge, 1993.

Cherry, D. *Beyond the Frame: Feminism and Visual Culture, Britain 1850–1900*, London: Routledge, 2000.

Cline, C. *Women's Diaries, Journals, and Letters: An Annotated Bibliography*, New York and London: Garland Publishing, 1989.

Coleman, D., Danze E. and Henderson, C. (eds) *Architecture and Feminism*, New York: Princeton Architectural Press, 1996.

Colomina, B. 'The Split Wall: Domestic Voyeurism', in B. Colomina (ed.) *Sexuality and Space*, New York: Princeton Architectural Press, 1982.

Colomina, B. 'Battle Lines: E.1027' in D. Agrest, P. Conway, and L. Kanes Weisman (eds), *The Sex of Architecture*, NY: Princeton University Press, 1996.

Constant, C. 'E.1027: The Nonheroic Modernism of Eileen Gray', *Journal of the Society of Architectural Historians*, 53, 3, Sept 1994.

Constant, C. *Eileen Gray*, London: Phaidon, 2000.

Constant, C. and Wang, W. (eds) *An Architecture for All Senses*, Tübingen/Berlin: Wasmuth, 1996.

Crinson, M. and Lubbock, J. *Architecture. Art or Profession: Three Hundred Years of Architectural Education in Britain*, Manchester: Manchester University Press, 1994.

Darling, E. ' "What the Tenants think of Kensal House": Experts' Assumptions versus Tenants' Realities in the Modern Home', *Journal of Architectural Education*, 53, 2, 2000.

De Wolfe, E. *The House in Good Taste*, New York: The Century Company, 1913.

De Wolfe, E. *After All*, New York: Harper & Brothers, 1935.

Dormoy, M. *L'Initiation sentimentale*, Paris: Flammarion, 1929.

Dormoy, M. 'L'Architecture française', *Architecture d'Aujourd'hui*, Paris 1938.

Dormoy, M. *Souvenirs et portraits d'amis*, Paris: Mercure de France, 1963.

Engen, R. *Kate Greenaway: A Biography*, London: Macdonald Futura, 1981.

Forty, A. *Words and Buildings: A Vocabulary of Modern Architecture*, London: Thames & Hudson, 2000.

Friedman, Alice T. *Women and the Making of the Modern House: A Social and Architectural History*, New York: Harry N. Abrams, Inc., 1998.

Furniture Gazette, Vol. 3, London 1875.

Gargiani, R. Auguste Perret, *La théorie et l'oeuvre*, Paris: Gallimard/Electa, 1994.

Garner, P. *Eileen Gray: Design and Architecture, 1878-1976*, London: Thames & Hudson, 1993.

Gillett, P. *The Victorian Painter's World*, Gloucester: Alan Sutton, 1990.

Girouard, M. *Sweetness and Light: the 'Queen Anne' Movement, 1860–1900*, Oxford: Oxford University Press, 1977.

Goldberg, J. 'Celebrating a Little-Known Influence on Art Deco', New York Times, 11, Jan. 1996.

Goldhagen, S. and Réjean L. (eds) *Anxious Modernisms: Experimentation in Postwar Architectural Culture*, Montreal: Canadian Center for Architecture and Cambridge, MA, MIT Press, 2000.

Hall, E. A. *Diaries*, 22 vols, unpublished manuscripts, ref. 855/F3/1–22. Bromley Borough Council 1838–1901.

Hall, E. M. Diaries, 23 vols, unpublished manuscripts, ref. 855/F2/1–23. Bromley Borough Council 1838–1901.

Hampton, M. *Legendary Decorators of the Twentieth Century*, New York: Doubleday, 1992.

Harding, J. *Lost Illusions Paul Léautaud and his World*, London: George Allen and Unwin, 1974.

Haweis, H. R. *The Art of Decoration*, London: Chatto & Windus, 1881.

Hayden, D. *The Grand Domestic Revolution: A History of Feminist Designs for American Neighborhoods and Cities*, Cambridge, MA: MIT Press, 1981.

Jackson, A. *The Politics of Architecture: A History of Modern Architecture in Britain*, London: Architectural Press, 1970.

Jackson Lears, T. J. *No Place of Grace: Antimodernism and the Transformation of American Culture, 1880–1920*, Chicago and London: University of Chicago Press, 1994.

Koenigsberg, L. 'Mariana van Rensselaer: An Architecture Critic in Context', in E. P. Berkeley and M. McQuaid (eds) *Architecture: A Place for Women*, Washington, DC, and London:

Smithsonian Institution Press, 1989.
Kwint, M. (ed.) *Material Memories: Design and Evocation*, Oxford: Berg, 1999.

Lawrence, C. (ed.) *Women and Art in Early Modern Europe: Patrons, Collectors and Connoisseurs*, Philadelphia, USA: Pennsylvania State University Press, 1997.
Léautaud, P., *Journal littéraire*, 19 vols, Paris: Mercure de France, 1954–66.
Léautaud, P. *Correspondence: Lettres à Marie Dormoy*, Paris: Editions Albin Michel, 1966.
Le Corbusier, *Des Canons, Des Munitions? Merci! Des Loges … S.V.P* [monograph of the International Exhibition, 1937, Pavillon des Temps Nouveaux] Paris, 1938.
Lever, J. (ed.) 'Evelyn Wyld (1892–1974)', *Catalogue of the Drawings Collection of the Royal Institute of British Architects T–Z*, Amersham: Gregg International, 1984.
Loupiac, C. and Mengin, C. *L'Architecture moderne en France, 1889–1940*, vol. 1, Paris: Picard, 1997.

Macarthy, F. 'Eileen Gray (1878–1976)', *The Dictionary of National Biography 1986–1990*, Oxford: Oxford University Press.
McCoy, E. 'Report from Los Angeles', *Progressive Architecture*, 56, July 1975, 24.
Mills, A. R. *The Halls of Ravenswood*, London: Frederick Muller Ltd, 1967.
Mills, A. R. *Two Victorian Ladies*, London: Frederick Muller Ltd, 1969.

Nevins, D. F. 'Gray, Eileen', in *Macmillan Encyclopedia of Architects*, vol. 2, ed. A.K. Placzek, London: 1982.

Pollock, G. *Differencing the Canon: Feminist Desire and the Writing of Art's Histories*, London: Routledge, 1999.
Raynaud, M. *De l'eclectisme au doute, Eileen Gray et Jean Badovici, suivi de, La beauté du geste*, Paris: Altamira, 1994.
Rendell, J., Penner, B. and Borden, I. *Gender Space Architecture: An Interdisciplinary Introduction*, London: Routledge, 2000.
Rothschild, J. (ed.) *Design and Feminism: Re-visioning Spaces, Places, and Everyday Things*, New Brunswick, NJ: Rutgers University Press, 1999.
Rowan, T. 'Spettacoli pubblici e privati', *Casabella*, 673/674, LXIII, Dec 1999–Jan 2000.
Rykwert, J. 'Un Omaggio a Eileen Gray/Pionera del Design', *Domus*, Dec. 12, 1968.
Rykwert, J. 'Eileen Gray: Pioneer of Design' *Architectural Review*, Dec. 1972.

Saint, A. *Richard Norman Shaw*, New Haven, CT: Yale University Press, 1976.
Scanlon, J. *Inarticulate Longings: The Ladies' Home Journal, Gender and the Promises of Consumer Culture*, New York and London: Routledge, 1995.
Seddon, J. and Worden, S. (eds) *Women Designing: Redefining Design in Britain between the Wars*, Brighton: University of Brighton Press, 1994.
Shaw, R. N. 'The Fallacy that the Architect who Makes Design his First Consideration, Must be Unpractical', in R. Norman Shaw and T. G. Jackson, (eds) *Architecture. A Profession or an Art: Thirteen Short Essays on the Qualifications and Training of Architects*, London: John Murray, 1892.
Sherrard, O. A. *Two Victorian Girls*, London: Frederick Muller Ltd, 1966.
Silve, E. *Paul Léautaud et le Mercure de France*, Paris: Mercure de France, 1985.
Smith, J. S. *Elsie de Wolfe, A Life in the High Style: The Elegant Life and Remarkable Career of Elsie de Wolfe, Lady Mendl*, New York: Atheneum, 1982.
Soros, S. Weber *E.W. Godwin: Aesthetic Movement Architect and Designer*, New York: Yale University Press, 2000.
Sparke, P. *As Long As It's Pink: The Sexual Politics of Taste*. London and California: Pandora, 1995.

Select Bibliography

Spencer, R. *The Aesthetic Movement:*
   Theory and Practice, London: Studio Vista, 1972.
Stein, R. (ed.) *In Pursuit of Beauty: Americans and the Aesthetic Movement*, New York:
   Metropolitan Museum of Art/Rizzoli, 1987.
Stern, Robert A. M. et al. *New York 1960: Architecture and Urbanism between the Second World
   War and the Bicentennial*, New York: Monacelli, 1995.

Wake, J. *Princess Louise: Queen Victoria's Unconventional Daughter*, London: Collins, 1988.
Walker, J. *Vanished West Wickham*, West Wickham: Hollies Publications, 1994.
Walker, L. (ed.) *Women Architects: Their Work*, London: Sorella Press, 1984.
Walker, L. 'The Arts and Crafts Alternative', in J. Attfield and P. Kirkham, (eds) *A View From the
   Interior*, London: The Women's Press, 1989.
Walker, L. *Drawing on Diversity: Women, Architecture and Practice*, London: RIBA Drawings
   Collection, 1997.
Walkley, G. *Artists' Houses in London 1764–1914*, London: Scolar Press, 1994.
Warner Blanchard, M. *Oscar Wilde's America*, New Haven. CT: Yale University Press, 1998.
Watkin, D. *Morality and Architecture: The Development of a Theme in Architectural History and
   Theory from the Gothic Revival to the Modern Movement*, Oxford: Clarendon Press, 1977.
Wendingen, 1924, vol.6, no.6, Amsterdam; monograph on Eileen Gray, includes J. Badorici, L'Art
   d'Eileen Gray par Jean Badorici Architecte, and J. Wils, 'Meubelen en interiors'.
White, M. C. *A History of Barnard College*, New York: Columbia University Press, 1954.
Whiteley, N. *Reyner Banham: Historian of the Immediate Future*, Cambridge, MA: MIT Press, 2002.
Wigley, M. 'White Out: Fashioning the Modern', in D. Fausch, P. Singley, and R. El-Khoury (eds)
   Architecture: In Fashion, New York: Princeton Architectural Press, 1994.
Wolff, J. *Feminine Sentences. Essays on Women and Culture*, Cambridge: Polity Press, 1990.
Wolff, J. *Resident Alien: Feminist Cultural Criticism*, Cambridge: Polity Press, 1995.

Index

References to the illustrations are in *italics*

Index

Index